Anne Maree Jensen was born in 1954 in Toowoomba. At the age of nineteen, she entered the Presentation Sisters of Queensland Congregation and trained as a primary school teacher. In 1989 she obtained her unrestricted pilot's licence and became the first female pilot to serve the outer reaches of the Rockhampton and Toowoomba Dioceses. In 1995 she was named Australian Achiever of the year in recognition of the service and support she provides outback communities. She currently lives in Longreach, Queensland.

Jeanne Ryckmans was born in 1966. After graduating from the Australian National University with a Bachelor of Arts in 1988, she studied Comparative Literature at the Sorbonne in Paris. She has worked as a reporter, presenter and producer for both French and Australian television networks; she is also a freelance journalist. In 1995 she produced and directed a documentary, *The Flying Nun*, for SBS Television which provided the inspiration for this book. She currently lives in Sydney.

Also by Jeanne Ryckmans
Les Deux Acrobates (with Simon Leys)
The Two Acrobats (with Simon Leys)

The flying Nun

AND THE WOMEN OF THE WEST

SISTER ANNE MAREE JENSEN
with JEANNE RYCKMANS

RANDOM HOUSE PTY LTD

Published by
Random House Australia Pty Ltd
20 Alfred Street, Milsons Point, NSW 2061
http://www.randomhouse.com.au

Sydney   New York   Toronto
London   Auckland   Johannesburg
and agencies throughout the world

First published in 1998

National Library of Australia
Cataloguing-in-Publication Data

Ryckmans, Jeanne.
 The flying nun : and the women of the west.

ISBN 0 091 83509 7.

1. Jensen, Anne Maree. 2. Rural women – Queensland. 3.
Nuns – Queensland. 4. Women air pilots – Queensland. 5.
Visitations (Church work) – Queensland. I. Jensen,
Anne-Maree. II. Title.

629.13092

Design by Yolande Gray, Sydney
Photography by Gerald Jenkins
Typeset by Midland Typesetters, Victoria
Printed by Griffin Paperbacks, Adelaide

10 9 8 7 6 5 4 3 2

The poem appearing in Liz Debney's chapter has been previously published in *You Can't Make it Rain: The Story of the North Australian Pastoral Company 1877–1991* by Margaret Kowald and W Ross Johnston; 1992.

Sister Anne Maree Jensen
I dedicate this book to the many courageous people who have touched
my life; my parents, my family and friends, the people of the outback,
my congregation, our foundress Nano Nagle and the early pioneers
of Australia.

Jeanne Ryckmans
To my mother

Acknowledgements

Sister Anne Maree

It is with sincere thanks that I acknowledge the following people for their contributions to this book:

The thirteen women who took up the challenge to share their stories.

The families of the outback who have opened their hearts and homes to me over the years.

My parents, family and friends for their support and encouragement.

My congregation and those who have been directly involved with the Aerial Ministry: Bishops Bernard Wallace, Brian Heenan and William Morris; Fathers Tom Martin, Justin Clare and Terry Loth; Sisters Joan Shannon and Marie Carroll MSS; the priests of the Rockhampton and Toowoomba dioceses.

My thanks also to Jeanne Ryckmans who recognised the story within each of us, and our editor Belinda Gibbon for her professional and sensitive approach.

Jeanne Ryckmans

With all my gratitude to:

The women of the west for their hospitality and the time they generously gave in telling me their life stories.

Mark Allan and Eli Theeboom from Jackaroo Aviation for keeping me safely in the air.

Sisters Rosa MacGinley and Agatha Freeman.

The Jensen family.

David Garling—Polaroid Australia.

Andy Lloyd James.

Margie Sullivan, Deb Callaghan and Roberta Ivers at Random House Australia.

I am particularly indebted to the following people:

Jean-Marie, Etienne, Marc and Louis, for their moral support.

Belinda Gibbon, my editor, who has the 'patience of Job'!

And finally, my father Pierre.

CONTENTS

FOREWORD

If Sister Anne Maree Jensen had stayed in town where she used to belong, no-one would be writing a book about her. But she decided to spread her wings in the service of some of the most isolated people on earth. Her parish became the families on stations of Western Queensland, whatever their religion or none. She learnt to fly and became a lifeline and bush telegraph for many people on properties where everyone does it hard. The drone of her single engine Cessna is a call to put on the kettle and catch up on the thrills and spills which mark the stories of any outback community.

Anne Maree is a methodical nun and a careful pilot. She is very thorough with all those pre-flight checks which occur in the small cockpit of a Cessna. But there is always one more routine task before take off—a prayer for the passenger and the flight. She is proud of her 'flying nun' cap. But she does not push religion in anyone's face. On landing, she settles into a gentle routine. Often the heat is sweltering and the dust gets into everything. With women, she talks women's business, and with some of the toughest men of the west, she is the one gentle contact whose difference evokes deeper reflection about the demands of the bush.

During the *Wik* debate which divided the outback, I spent a week with Sister Anne Maree flying vast distances, landing on ready made dirt strips, and meeting with people who were hurting. They felt so isolated from the cities where decisions about their future were made. Some were angry; others just confused. Some hated the church; others saw the Christian community as a hopeful way of belonging beyond the horizon of the station's barbed wire fences. Anne Maree was the ever listening ear and the link that brought them together. On no one visit does she work any magic. By regular visitation, she brings refreshment and opens hearts.

She is no public speaker. If she has any politics, I have no idea what they are. She is a faithful listener. Being a pilot ever watchful for the rough air pockets, she has an uncanny sense of where the turbulence in human relations might be. In small, dust ridden wooden churches, she calls the community to worship. At their kitchen tables she hears their woes and celebrates their joys. She does not come with any cargo load of answers. She evokes answers and ways of coping from the people on the ground and then flies above the clouds again, thanking God for the grace in ordinary things and for the intimacies possible only in such distances and isolation.

This pilot is never in a hurry; she is never out to impress. This nun has covered more miles in a year than most readers will cover in a lifetime. Her story is the story of the people she sees, the ones to whom she listens. And that is true service. She will be embarrassed about the book in so far as it is about her. She will enjoy the stories about others. She flies so others may remain grounded. An ordinary person has made a difference across vast areas simply by faithfully returning and listening. The sound of that engine is always good news whatever the weather, whatever the wool price, and whatever of *Wik*. This book places you alongside her in the cockpit and over a cuppa, the length and breadth of outback Queensland. Fasten your seat belt, sit back and enjoy the read.

Fr Frank Brennan SJ AO

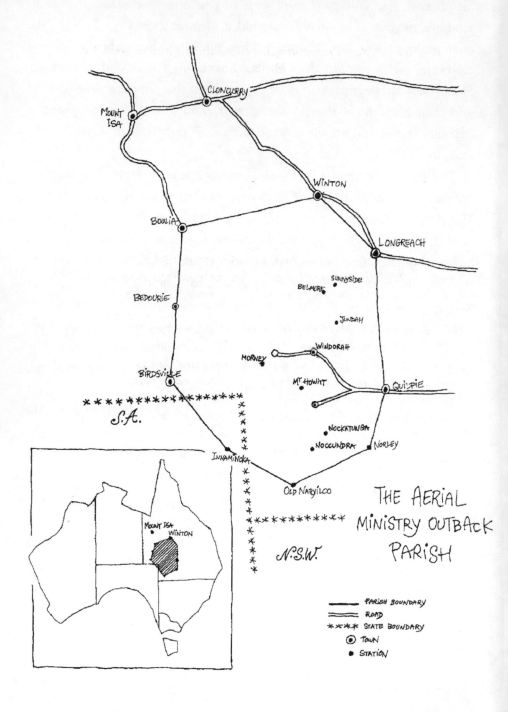

THE AERIAL
MINISTRY OUTBACK
PARISH

CLONCURRY
MOUNT ISA
WINTON
BOULIA
LONGREACH
SUNNYSIDE
BELMORE
BEDOURIE
JUNDAH
WINDORAH
MORNEY
Mt HOWITT
BIRDSVILLE
QUILPIE
S.A.
NOCKATUNGA
NOCCUNDRA
NORLEY
INNAMINCKA
OLD NARYILCO
N.S.W.

MOUNT ISA
WINTON

———— PARISH BOUNDARY
════════ ROAD
* * * * STATE BOUNDARY
◉ TOWN
● STATION

We can do no great things, only small things with great love.
Mother Teresa

The red sun robs their beauty, and, in weariness and pain,
The slow years steal the nameless grace that never comes again;
And there are hours men cannot soothe, and words men cannot
   say—
The nearest woman's face may be a hundred miles away.

The wide Bush holds the secrets of their longings and desires,
When the white stars in reverence light their holy altar-fires,
And silence, like the touch of God, sinks deep into the breast—
Perchance He hears and understands the Women of the West.

from *The Women of the West*, George Essex Evans

INTRODUCTION

I'll never forget the day when the veil of Sister Eugenie, my third grade teacher, lifted off in a sudden gust of wind while she was on tuckshop duty. We all froze as the rather ungainly sister—the most ferocious nun at the school—scrambled to retrieve her runaway headdress. Even the tuckshop mums stopped in mid-service to gape.

What a nun hid underneath her black veil had always been the subject of much speculation at my small Catholic primary school. No-one had ever seen a nun without her veil. Naturally we were all very disappointed to discover that instead of horns or a shaved scalp, Sister Eugenie sported a full head of hair. For me, this startling revelation was the first indication that nuns were perhaps human beings—real women—and not mysterious creatures who, under their long robes, hovered inches above ground.

Twenty years later, on my way to Longreach to meet the woman affectionately nicknamed the 'Flying Nun', a new surprise awaited me. Intrigued by the idea of a Catholic sister piloting a plane around the bush, I'd made the long trip from Sydney to outback Queensland to persuade Sister Anne Maree Jensen to be the subject of a documentary for SBS Television.

From the little I had already gleaned about her work—flying out to the far reaches of south-west Queensland to visit the women of her bush parish—it was evident that this sister did not bear much resemblance to any of the nuns I'd known. Naively, I expected to see a sister dressed in a traditional habit and veil. Instead, the small, fit woman who warmly greeted me on the tarmac

Sister Anne Maree Jensen

was wearing bermuda shorts and a baseball cap. Apart from a silver Presentation Sisters badge discreetly pinned to her T-shirt, I saw no other visible sign to identify Sister Anne Maree as a Catholic nun. Religious life had obviously evolved by leaps and bounds since my primary school days. As she tossed my backpack into the boot of her Falcon, Sister Anne Maree must have sensed my disappointment at finding her not dressed for the part because she suddenly leaned across and confided, *'Don't worry, the habit's at the cleaners!'*

The locals of Longreach who see Sister Anne Maree driving up the main street of town are quick to point out that their Catholic sister is the bona fide Flying Nun and not the aerodynamic 1967 television character played by actress Sally Field.

A quiet outback town lying on the Tropic of Capricorn some seven hundred kilometres west of Rockhampton, Longreach may have earned its place on the map as the birthplace of Qantas Airways and for its Stockman's Hall of Fame, but since 1985 it has also boasted a Catholic sister who has traded in her veil and habit for an Akubra and jeans, and a Cessna plane.

Step into any of Longreach's watering holes on Eagle Street, whether it be the Royal, the Central or the Lyceum, and the locals will raise their schooners to the Flying Nun. From Barcaldine to Birdsville, Winton to Windorah, the sound of Sister Anne Maree's plane coming in to land on a dirt airstrip or tussocky paddock is perhaps the sweetest sound for many women living in isolation. Her aerial exploits have won her the respect and admiration of even the hardiest and most experienced bush pilots. Air traffic controllers in Brisbane all know her call signal: Foxtrot Bravo Delta, and although some purists may not approve of the various unorthodox short cuts she has devised to manoeuvre her green-striped Cessna in and out of its hangar, everyone agrees that this sister is a real professional in the air.

Across the road from the Longreach Line Dancing Federation in Duck Street is a modest four-bedroom fibro bungalow which serves as the Presentation Sisters' convent and Sister Anne Maree's home base. But on the rare occasions when she is in town and not airborne, she is far more likely to be found at the hangar down the road tinkering with her Cessna 172 or talking bush mechanics with fellow pilots.

Almost a century after the first Presentation Sisters set foot in Long-reach, only two sisters remain: Sister Anne Maree and Sister Marie-Therese Dwyer, a retired sister who helps out in the parish.

The congregation originated in County Cork, Ireland, and was founded in the mid-eighteenth century by a former Ursuline Sister, Nano Nagle, to provide education and help for the Irish poor. At the turn of the century, anxious to spread their missionary work in Catholic education, five Presentation Sisters were dispatched from the Wagga Wagga convent to the far-off frontier of Longreach. Gazetted in November 1887, by 1892 the tiny township in central western Queensland had become the terminus of the Central Railway and the chief supply and business centre for the vast station properties in the outlying districts. Father Michael Slattery, a parish priest from Wagga, accompanied

The Presentation Sisters of Longreach with three of the five pioneering sisters: Sister Agatha (back row, sixth from left), Mother Patrick (front row, second from left) and Mother Ursula (front row, third from left).

the sisters on the long trip north. On 1 February 1900, the feast day of Saint Brigid, tearful farewells saw the party off by train to Sydney. A few days later, they boarded a coastal steamer, the *Arawatta*, for Keppel Bay where they anchored on 11 February. A smaller boat took the passengers up the Fitzroy River to Rockhampton, and after a brief stay with the Sisters of Mercy, the volunteer sisters boarded the Western Mail to Longreach. The Bishop of Rockhampton, Bishop Joseph Higgins, who had never visited the western outpost, joined them on their journey. On Tuesday, 13 February, they finally reached their destination.

Severely attired in heavy serge habits, the exhausted sisters, coated in dirt and coal dust, must have presented a curious sight for the crowd of well-wishers who had turned out to greet them at the railway station. The sisters were driven solemnly through the main street of Longreach in a buggy, preceded by the town marching band in all its pomp and glory. It was one of the hottest days on record with the thermometer reaching forty-six degrees Celsius. The sisters were ushered into a small, poorly ventilated church for the official presentation and listened for nearly two hours to speeches delivered by the welcoming committee. When the ordeal was over, the tired travellers were taken to the local presbytery to recover from the sweltering February heat.

In the weeks that followed, the sisters found the isolation, flies and intense heat almost impossible to bear. Longreach was in the grip of a severe drought, and the landscape had turned bare and desolate. One of the sisters, Mother Alphonsus Burke, was so overwhelmed by the extreme conditions that she became deranged. Found wandering in the streets in a state of shock, she was sent home to Wagga. The remaining sisters bravely struggled on, sustained no doubt by their strong Christian faith. They opened their first primary school on 19 February in the church, with six desks, a blackboard, and an impressive eighty-nine pupils in attendance. The following week there were over a hundred children and by the end of that year, almost two hundred children had been enrolled. The sisters certainly caught the imagination of their pupils, at least with their religious classes, as one brave lad memorably remarked, *'There was no hell in Longreach until the sisters came.'*

Conditions have improved dramatically since then and Longreach—named after the 'long reach' of the Thomson River which borders the town—is, of course, no longer a primitive bush settlement notorious for cattle rustling. However, for Sister Anne Maree, the transfer from the Presentation Convent in Brisbane in 1985, to a teaching position in the outback, proved as rude a shock as the one experienced by the original pioneering sisters. At the time of our first meeting in December 1994, she evoked the fate of the unfortunate Mother Alphonsus Burke and added with a wry smile, *'At least back in those days, the sisters didn't have to put up with road trains thundering past their bedroom windows.'*

The documentary crew

In May 1995, I chartered a twin-engine Baron aeroplane and with a cameraman and sound recordist in tow, began filming an hour-length documentary on Sister Anne Maree and her aerial ministry.

For three weeks, the crew and I braved dust storms and overcame our fear of flying in light aircraft as we followed Sister Anne Maree on one of her regular circuits. Occasionally I would fly with her in the Cessna. It was her usual practice before each take-off to run through the routine safety and instrument checks out aloud. Once I remember yelling out to her as the plane noisily hurtled down the runway, *'Thanks for doing that. It makes me feel a whole lot safer.'*

'Don't be silly,' she shouted back. *'I'm not doing this for your benefit, I'm doing it for mine!'*

As one stockman wisely pointed out to me later, *'You've got nothing to worry about. She has the "Big Fella" on her side you know.'*

Wherever we landed, Sister Anne Maree was welcomed by everyone, but it was the women who particularly looked forward to her flying visits. Often, she was the only female they would see from one month to the next. I admired these women who lived miles away—hundreds of miles in some cases—from their closest neighbour or town.

The Flying Nun documentary screened on SBS Television in October 1995. Sister Anne Maree flew to a property near Longreach, where there was a satellite dish, to watch it go to air.

In the weeks that followed, interest generated by the documentary led to the commissioning of this book. Once again, I found myself back on a plane headed for Longreach.

'Holy heck!' said Sister Anne Maree, *'Don't you ever give up?'*

Eight of the thirteen women who agreed to contribute their stories to this book appeared in the documentary. The other five were introduced to me by Sister Anne Maree on my second visit to the west. I am indebted to each of them for taking the time out of their hectic lives to share their experiences and entrust their stories to me. Like them, Sister Anne Maree gave up so many precious hours to work on the book. Her enthusiasm was such at the start that she would scribble pages from the cockpit at 4,500 feet in the air. Finally, at the end of several years of working on *The Flying Nun* I am convinced that Sister Anne Maree certainly does have the 'Big Fella' on her side!

Jeanne Ryckmans,
September 1998

THE AERIAL MINISTRY

Thank goodness for Pope John Paul XXIII and the Second Vatican Council. If not for them, I'd have to struggle with a long, mediaeval-style habit every time I climbed in and out of my small Cessna plane. And that's three or four times a day. If I had to wear a veil and stockings too, like the Catholic sisters of old, I'd also find it hard to cope with the forty degree heat of outback Queensland.

Fortunately, times have changed and with them the clothing considered suitable for a Presentation Sister. Shorts and a T-shirt are far more fitting for my pastoral work, which, along with religious instruction, includes pulling sheep out of bogs, attending the Birdsville Races, helping a publican's wife pull beers in an outback pub and, even joining in the odd bit of line dancing!

Refuelling the Cessna.

My pastoral work is similar to that of the other sisters of my congregation who visit people living within their parish. I suppose what makes my work different is simply the way I travel—whereas all our other sisters drive, I have to get into my single engine aeroplane and fly. Flying is the only way for me to overcome the long distances between each small town, station and property in my 280,000 square kilometre outback parish. I don't see it as anything unusual or out of the ordinary, it's just the way I get around.

My full-time ministry involves flying out to the far reaches of southwest Queensland to be with the women who have become my close friends and my extended family. On most occasions I have been the only female these women have seen in the past month, and it's often around a 'cuppa' that I hear of their hopes and dreams, joys and sorrows, and feel their pain.

Is it really such an unusual vocation? Perhaps. Certainly it's an exhausting and demanding ministry but I thrive on it. With almost three thousand flying hours under my belt and averaging forty dirt strip landings a month, I suppose I'm not doing too badly for a bush pilot. In these parts I have two nicknames, the 'Flying Nun' and the 'Sundowner'. Appropriate, I think, as I always seem to land just as the sun is setting.

Never in my wildest dreams would I have thought, ten years ago, that I would be sharing so intimately the significant moments of other people's lives. My parishioners, living in the isolation of the outback, impress me with their spirit, their way of accepting remoteness and hardships, and their love of life. The richness of their lives, particularly the women's, has touched my own life. It is their courage, their tenacity, their 'stick-at-it-ness' that most inspires me. We can enrich each other by our own stories—hence this book.

The Aerial Ministry for which I work is based in Longreach. When I was first appointed its pilot in 1989, after my predecessor, Father Terry Loth, stopped flying, I decided to follow his schedule closely—three weekly circuits over a one-month period—and not stray too far from his original route. (I was not plucky or adventurous enough then.) Since this time, I have extended the territory covered by the Aerial Ministry from 250,000 square kilometres to 280,000 square kilometres.

This entire area, with a population of roughly 1,500, is larger than the State of Victoria. The United Kingdom is slightly bigger—384,000 square kilometres—but has a population of 57 million. One property I land at, Davenport Downs, is almost the same size as Sydney and Newcastle combined, but there are only fourteen people living there. That's how vast my territory is. And, instead of shrinking each year, it keeps growing.

My outback parish consists of mainly sheep and cattle stations dotted around the Cooper and Diamantina rivers, taking in Naryilco station on the New South Wales border and Innamincka station in South Australia. It extends westward as far as the Northern Territory border, encompassing the towns of Birdsville and Bedourie. Although the area I cover could be carved into 400 million suburban blocks, there are only nine small communities and a little over 130 families living here.

It was in Longreach in the mid-1980s that I first met Father Terry Loth and became aware of the Aerial Ministry. I was teaching at the local Catholic primary school while he worked as a 'pilot priest'.

Terry played a great game of squash. He was a strong and able opponent who always gave me a tough workout on the court. Who won usually depended on who had the harder week.

'I only play to win, Anne Maree,' he would shout, as he smashed the rubber ball expertly into the corner, making it impossible for me to return the shot. Every Friday night after several strenuous sets at the Longreach squash club, Terry and I walked back to the Presentation Convent in Duck Street, sat down to tea, and played a round of cards with the other sisters.

Father Terry Loth

Terry was a keen gardener and sporty man, a person after my own heart. When I was introduced to him in early 1985, I knew he was a priest and that he went bush every week, but he never talked much about what he did when he returned. Over many games of cards, I eventually learnt more about his ministry.

He described his work as visiting people living in isolation, ministering to their spiritual and human needs. He flew a small Cessna around the south-west outback for three, weekly circuits every month. With a Missionary Sister of Service in tow, either Sister Joan Shannon or Sister Marie Carroll, he visited families on properties extending from Longreach to Birdsville. I was already aware that the Rockhampton Diocese covered quite a bit of territory, but I had no idea that there were over a hundred families scattered within its 250,000 square kilometre parish. Flying, as Terry explained, was the only means of overcoming the long distances. The more I heard about Terry's ministry, the more impressed I became with his dedication to such an unusual vocation. To me, he was responding in a very real way to the needs of the people in the outback.

I soon discovered from Sister Joan Shannon that Terry had invited the two Missionary Sisters to accompany him on his flying circuits because he realised that the particular problems of the women living in the bush could only be addressed by women. Most of the women he visited were comfortable and relaxed in the presence of a priest, but it was becoming obvious to him that what they lacked, and longed for most, was the opportunity of opening their hearts to another female. On most occasions when Terry came calling, the women were at home alone on the property. Their husbands were out working stock in the yards or at mustering camp. The women were always grateful to see a new face and visitors were welcomed because they brought news from the 'outside world'. But there were times when only talking with another woman could have brought them real support and comfort.

Listening to Terry's stories, I got a first inkling of these women's daily experiences—how they coped on their own, how they struggled to survive in times of drought. I began to realise how admirable they were—without complaint or fuss, they led lives which, in the eyes of a city person such as myself, appeared nothing short of heroic.

The Aerial Ministry was a new concept for me, but it was certainly nothing unusual for the people of the bush. Australia's first 'flying parson', Reverend Len Daniels, took to the air in 1928, the very year when the Australian Inland Mission began its Flying Doctor Service. Reverend Daniels ministered to some five thousand people scattered over 66,000 square kilometres in outback western New South Wales. In an article he wrote for the *Melbourne Herald* in 1928 titled 'Chasing Sin on the Wing', he brought the importance of an aerial ministry in Australia to national attention:

Now that I have my Moth it will be possible for me to hold church services in one day at my three main centres, where previously I was only able to travel once a month. Every one of my 5,000 parishioners will be within a couple of hours as a result of the new aeroplane. To these people it will be a great boon to see my Moth growing plainer in the sky, to hear the hum of my engine, and to realise that in a few minutes they will be in touch with the outer world. It is veritable exile to these people to live at the back o' Beyant as they do. They sacrifice much that their fellows enjoy. It is a wonderful thing to me that no longer will they have to sacrifice what is the right of all men—the right to worship God together in a properly constituted Church. Believe me, the coming of the aeroplane means much to these people.

The problem of ministering to the spiritual needs of people living in remote or relatively inaccessible areas of the outback has always preoccupied the various Churches and religious organisations in Australia. Determined to break the tyranny of distance, societies such as the Bush Brotherhoods and the Bush Church Aid Society were established in the early 1900s. Ministers would travel long distances to visit outlying settlers on horseback, or later, by motor car. These travelling priests and preachers were often on the dusty roads for months at a time, conducting their ministry over vast tracts of the inland. Services were held in homesteads, sheds, shire halls and tiny bush churches.

By the early 1980s, it had become evident to the Bishop of Rockhampton, Bishop Bernard Wallace, that with only five priests working west of the Drummond Range—a territory which comprised almost half of the Rockhampton Diocese—the spiritual needs of his parishioners were not being adequately met. In such an area where the distances were too great and roads almost nonexistent, the only means by which the Church could effectively bring a spiritual ministry to the west was by aeroplane. As a result, in August 1982, the year of the Centenary of the Rockhampton Diocese, a Cessna 172—call sign VH-FBD—four-seater light

Father Justin Clare, one of the first flying priests.

aircraft was purchased at auction for $30,000. Two young parish priests, Father Tom Martin and Father Justin Clare, volunteered their services and were enrolled at a local flying school and became the first 'pilot priests' of the diocese.

Father Justin had never been keen on flying. When I met him in 1988, I was training for my unrestricted pilot's licence. He regaled me with stories of near mishaps and warned me about the unpredictable weather.

'Sister,' he told me, 'once you take off, you are really at the mercy of the elements. In summer, it gets really rough out west. The turbulence is incredible. You will find that the air is so hot that there is absolutely no lift in it—you are like a dead weight, a great big stone that can drop out of the sky. When you come in to land and float, it can be very frightening indeed. Best then to fly either late in the evening or at the crack of dawn. If something went wrong I just prayed to God. Flying is certainly a tricky, stressful business. Good luck to you! I'd rather be out fishing than flying any day.'

Father Justin and Father Tom left the Aerial Ministry around the same time. Tom went to work as a missionary in South America while Justin was transferred to another parish. Father Terry Loth was approached by the diocese to become the new full-time pilot priest.

In May 1988, after six years of flying, Terry was ready to retire from the Aerial Ministry. He asked me if I would be interested in working for the ministry. As I had entered a teaching order, I naturally assumed that I would spend the rest of my days in front of a blackboard permanently coated in chalk dust. However, after working as a primary school teacher for almost ten years, I had become aware that I did not really want to invest all my energy into a world of classrooms. Nor did I want to keep upgrading my maths and language skills. I needed a change.

I mentioned this to my Congregational Leader, Sister Andrea McGrath, who gave me the freedom to look into other ministries. Terry's offer could not have come at a better time. He had heard from one of the sisters at the Longreach convent, Sister Cathy, that I was searching for a new ministry. After all, as he explained to me, I was already familiar with this type of pastoral work—visiting people on a one-to-one basis and preparing children for the Holy Sacraments: baptism, first communion and confirmation. My teaching background would also come in handy helping children on outback stations who were studying by correspondence or with the School of the Air. Certainly, the idea was very appealing and I told Terry I would seriously consider his offer.

Then he asked, 'How would you like to learn to fly the Cessna?'

Now that was another question altogether. Me? Fly? Apparently Terry had been unable to find a priest willing to take over from him. Most were put off by the very idea of flying. I already had my car licence and a bus licence—surely I could fly a plane.

Fear was something I had always lived with—I had become aware of this during a personal development course I'd taken through the Institute of Faith Program some years earlier. It immediately struck home that I was being presented with a new fear. But I knew I could handle being a passenger in a plane, so why not a pilot? More questions followed—Was God calling me to this? Is this what my congregation wished for me? Did the Bishop of Rockhampton want this work to continue?

The next few days I spent in prayer. Yes, I felt at peace with the whole idea. I called Sister Andrea in Brisbane who was astonished but supportive of the project so long as it fitted with the bishop's wishes. While I awaited his reply, I continued to pray to God, asking for guidance and courage to make the right decision. The other sisters understood and supported my desire to remain in the west and carry on with Terry's work. I received many letters and calls from sisters all over Queensland saying how great it would be to have a woman in charge of such a ministry. The bishop finally approved the request and it was agreed that the Rockhampton Diocese would meet the costs of my licence.

Holy heck! I was going to learn to fly! I was conscious of the challenge ahead of me, but determined that I wouldn't let my fears take over. This new ministry was an adventure. The flying simply happened to go with the job.

OUTBACK PARISH

A week before my first flying lesson, my Year 2 class gave me a fare-well gift—a photograph of themselves with a large caption which read: 'We hope you don't crash, Sister'. What a confidence booster!

Training for my unrestricted pilot's licence.

I enrolled as a full-time student at Fogarty's School of Aviation at the Maroo-chydore Airport on 26 September 1988. Every Saturday morning I would ride my pushbike from the local convent to the airport for theory lessons on straight and level flying, climbing, descending and turns.

My fellow classmates were, for the most part, gangly seventeen-year-old fellows who had wanted to learn to fly since they were knee-high to a grasshopper. At thirty-three years of age, I was the oldest student. I was also the only woman. It did not seem to concern anyone that I was a Catholic sister. Their only question was, 'But can she fly?' I was beginning to ask myself the very same thing, because for every lesson the others had, I needed two. They wanted to try out all the different manoeuvres, while I would have been happy just to go up, turn the corner, and land again. I was determined not to let my fears take over—until I was shown the tiny two-seater Piper Tomahawk I was expected to fly. Holy heck! I could not believe its size. Once strapped inside, I realised it was not even as wide as my car. I had trouble imagining myself flying in something so ridicu-lously small and flimsy.

After several weeks at the flying school, it became obvious to my instructors that I was having some difficulties with the course. I think the school tried out all their instructors on me. Once up in the air, they had the patience of Job, and were very gentle with me. I completed endless circuits—'going around the block' as I called it—but as for practising forced landings and stalls, I preferred to give that a miss, vowing that I was never going to get myself into a situation where I would need to test these skills. I knew even back then, that I was far from being the adven-turous type. 'Nothing fancy please,' I begged my chief flying instructor,

Captain Peter Fogarty. Even the simplest 360 degree turns made me nauseous.

I often felt I was not psychologically prepared for flying. Determined, yes. Confident, no. Six months earlier I hadn't even imagined that I would one day be sitting behind the controls of a small air-craft. Compared to all the eager young fellows at the school, who had always dreamed of taking to the skies, I was apprehensive

Captain Peter Fogarty

about flying. I was very jealous of how naturally and easily it all came to them. It was hard work for me. The burning question on everyone's lips was, 'When will Sister go solo?'

I always did what my instructors had told me to, even if the situation seemed to require something different. It was Peter Fogarty who encour-aged me, and gave me the freedom, to try different manoeuvres so that finally, on 6 October 1988, I knew I was ready for my first solo flight. What a fantastic feeling it was. Who cared if it took me over twenty-four hours of flying time before going solo? On the downwind leg as I turned onto base and put out one stage of flap, I was anxious and kept repeating to myself, 'You can do it, Anne Maree.' When I landed safely on the strip, the fellows gathered round my Tomahawk and clapped and cheered. The air traffic controllers even radioed in their congratulations.

Rain set in for an entire week after that, which delayed my next solo flight. I was more fright-ened going for my second solo but I faced my fear. Then it was back to the training field for more forced landings and steep turns. The weather was my

In the cockpit

worst enemy. It was wet and windy on more days than it was fine. The crosswind landings were nearly impossible in such blustery conditions, so I had plenty of practice. Too much in fact.

Although I found many of the manoeuvres nerve-racking, there was one incident in particular which, I think, scared the instructors even more than me. It was a Saturday morning and the sky was clear. Sweating behind the controls of the Piper Tomahawk, I was supposed to practise specific take-offs and landings. I fired off from the runway like a stone from a shanghai—so far, so good. I climbed to 500 feet and made a left turn to enter the busy circuit pattern. Now all I needed to do was land the Toma-hawk as I had been taught. As I turned downwind in preparation for the big finish, I executed what is commonly known as a 'base leg' and began to set the aircraft for its initial approach speed. I was so determined to get this landing right that as I flew down the final approach slot, I completely forgot my airspeed. I rounded the aircraft out at a blistering pace about a metre off the ground and closed down the power. Worse still, I suddenly remembered that there was a six-foot deep drainage ditch at the end of the runway. As the nose of the aircraft repeatedly dipped down, I began praying to God that I wouldn't crash. I pulled back on the control column and the Tomahawk—ever so slowly and gracefully, as if in slow motion—lifted into the air, glided over the ditch, and landed safely on the other side. I couldn't believe it, and, as I was later told by the air traffic con-trollers who had their hearts in their mouths along with me during the entire drama, neither could they! Talk about a wing and a prayer! Captain Fogarty called it a miracle.

'Sister,' he said to me, 'I don't know how you did it. You had two chances of stopping in time: Buckley's and none. In my twenty-five years of flying, I've never been witness to such an incident.'

On 22 November, Peter took me for my restricted private pilot's licence test and I passed. This meant I could fly unaccompanied or with passen-gers, and within a five-mile radius of the Maroochydore Airport. I had made definite progress. Even the young fellows were impressed.

The fun and games really began on 14 December, when I started the cross-country navigation exercises needed for the unrestricted pilot's licence. By this time I had graduated from a low wing PA-38 to a Cessna 172. For my first cross-country 'nav' I flew to Gayndah, which was a three and a half hour flight. Nothing was more off-putting than the relentless interrogations from my on-board instructor who wanted me to tell him my exact position every ten minutes. I would glance down at the map on my lap and just that one small movement would send us plummeting 500 feet down and I would lose my heading course. It seemed to take me forever to get straight and level again so I asked my instructor to wait for any further questions until we were safely back on the ground. There was much tension on these navigation exercises as I could not fly the Cessna and do my sums at the same time. I was like a mad woman zigzagging across the skies!

For me, the most terrifying cross-country navigation was flying into Brisbane. If you ever want to feel insignificant, I suggest flying into a busy city airport squeezed behind two large aircraft. In my tiny Cessna, I felt like a little goldfish lost in

Birdsville Airport

an ocean. There was a lot more radio work involved with this nav and I had to keep my wits about me at all times.

Towards the end of January 1989, I went for my last solo cross-country navigation flight before taking my final test. The plan was to fly over Toowoomba, stop and refuel in Goondiwindi and then return to Maroochydore via Oakey. The total flying time was estimated at around four and a half hours. It was a beautiful, clear and cloudless day. It felt eerie knowing that I was flying alone. I remember the thrill of circling over my home town, Toowoomba, because I was sure I was able to see our old house. I was so distracted that I was late giving my radio call. There were no incidents on the return flight so, with my last nav over, I was ready for my final flight test.

It poured with rain in Maroochydore for the next ten days which frustrated me no end. This was supposed to be the Sunshine Coast but it was constantly wet. On 10 February, I took off with Peter for the final flight test. Just fifteen minutes into the flight, it was obvious that I was not flying competently enough to pass the examination so Peter suggested I turn around and return to base. What a crushing disappointment.

More rain. More sitting around the airport. It was another nine frustrating days before I could get back in the air to practise. Eventually Father Terry came to my rescue and suggested that I return west and fly his Cessna as it never rained out there. I arrived in Longreach on 10 March, fifteen years to the day of entering the convent, to thundery skies and torrential rain. Neither Terry or I could believe it. As soon as the weather improved, Terry was keen to check my progress. He was worried that I had picked up 'city' flying methods not at all relevant to flying in the bush. 'No fancy flying out in this here neck of the woods, Anne Maree!' he warned me.

Terry proved to be a very patient and competent teacher. I soon discovered that flying around the Maroochydore area and flying out west involved two totally different techniques. Out here, there were no landmarks, or so it seemed to me. How on earth was I expected to navigate my way across the countryside? As a way of testing what I had learnt at the flying school, Terry insisted I fly his Cessna. One of my first landings was at Roseneath, a property south of Longreach. I had only landed on wide bitumen airstrips before and now I was faced with landing on a rough dirt road beside the homestead. How was I ever going to touch down in such a narrow space? It didn't seem possible.

The manager of Roseneath, who had been prewarned of my arrival and was concerned for my safety, trimmed a tree which stood on my side of the landing strip ('Just in case!' he said). But where was the windsock to show me the direction of the wind? There wasn't one. Instead, I had to guess by reading the tail of a rusty windmill. I have come to love the sight of windmills now, but back then, they were poor substitutes for a proper windsock!

As there was no hope of finalising my restricted licence for at least a month due to ongoing foul weather in Maroochydore, Terry's plan was to take me with him on three of his weekly flying circuits and introduce me to the outback parish. This was to be my first real taste of the work of the Aerial Ministry and an opportunity to familiarise myself with the territory and the diocese's Cessna 172.

I really did not know what to expect for my first month out. The aeroplane was housed in a hangar at Longreach Airport, three doors down from the Salvation Army's 'Flying Padre' headquarters. The first lesson Terry taught me was how to manoeuvre the Cessna out of its berth by sitting astride the tail and pushing down with all my weight, then slowly turning the nose so it pointed out of the hangar making it easier to roll onto the tarmac. This proved to be a very useful trick, one I have kept up over the years because, since I am considerably smaller than Terry, pulling the Cessna out of the hangar by myself is no easy task.

My next lesson was in flight planning. This was fairly complex as I had to learn how to chart a course correctly. Flight Services in Longreach, which helped pilots with plotting courses, were already familiar with Terry's territory which was very handy for me once I went solo. The only problem was that they needed to know the exact time when I would be touching down at any given destination. This was always a rough guess because the winds were never what the weather bureau had predicted and, as a result, I had to constantly amend my SAR (Search and Rescue) time. These days, as a backup, I use a GPS (Global Positioning System)—an indispensable navigation aid for any pilot. It tells me with great precision where I am, how far I am from my destination and when I will reach it. Flight Services have since closed down in Longreach, but I am glad I learnt the old way first.

As was his usual practice, Terry had prepared a Sunday liturgy—which I discovered could be celebrated on any day of the week. This was novel! As he explained, mass was said whenever and wherever feasible. Sometimes it was celebrated in shire halls, under gum trees, or even simply around the kitchen table because there were few churches in the bush. Terry asked me to work on sacramental preparation for children who were soon to receive their First Holy Communion or be confirmed. In the past, I had spent at least half an hour every day with children in preparation for the sacraments. Now I was faced with preparing children whom I would be lucky to see for half an hour every month. Terry had to show me how to condense my instruction into such a short time span.

We took off from Longreach on a Saturday afternoon after Terry had caught up with his footy results. I was baffled once more as to how pilots could find their way in the bush because I could not identify any landmarks whatsoever. Our destination, Isisford, was well hidden on the edge of the Barcoo River and not easy to find for an inexperienced pilot. My navigation skills were fairly poor, especially for flying around some of the more remote and isolated areas of the south-west. Sometimes I chased waterholes because, from up in the air, they looked like homesteads to me. Whenever I found a property straightaway I was ecstatic. With Terry as my passenger, I was never too worried about getting lost, but he had the annoying habit of purposely waiting until the last minute to ask if I knew where I was. This was his way of testing me. I would have to own up to being 'temporarily misplaced' (we pilots never get lost)—to which he always teasingly replied, 'Why, Anne Maree, you must have tunnel vision! Look around, you are at least ten miles off course!'

The people I met during the first few weeks were incredibly generous and welcoming towards me. They had heard of my flying adventure for such a long time: news on the bush telegraph always travels fast. What stands out most in my mind from those early days of flying in the south-west are the smiling faces and those wonderful words, 'Would you like a cuppa, Sister?'

What a soothing ring they had for me because I was always in such a state of nervous exhaustion when I landed. If only they knew what a feat it had been for me to find their property! There is still no better feeling for me than the welcoming sight of a galvanised iron station roof glinting below as I bank, dip my wing, and turn sharply over the homestead to signal that I've arrived.

I don't imagine I was very helpful to anyone during that first month. By the time I had recovered from the flight I had to 'clear the prop' and take off again. To visit so many people in a few short weeks was draining of my energy. Keeping such a strict flying schedule exhausted me at first, but it was great practice for my future circuits.

I helped children on stations to prepare for their First Holy Communion, and Terry baptised a girl on a family property. In the small communities and towns like Jundah, Bedourie and Birdsville, Terry and I spent most of our time visiting people in their homes and celebrating mass in old wooden churches or community halls. Each time, I was surprised by the relatively large turnout—rows of mud-splattered Landcruisers and Toyotas were parked in the bulldust as folk flocked from neighbouring properties to attend mass. I am not sure whether it was the informal settings or the simplicity of the services, but I found them very moving experiences. They were free from formal trappings—so intensely real. I loved the small bush churches, with their school bench pews, their sprays of hand-picked wild flowers in jam jars to decorate the altar and their shining floors carefully swept of sand and dust by some thoughtful parishioner. No-one seemed to mind that the prayer books were in tatters, neither were they distracted by the intermittent crackle-and-zap from the neon Insect-o-cutors which, out bush, seem as indispensable a part of the church equipment as the crucifixes hanging on the walls.

All the women I was introduced to were delighted to learn that a sister would soon be taking over the Aerial Ministry. Chatting freely over morning tea in the kitchen, they told me it was the personal contact with another female that they missed most. Their husbands, on the other hand, eyed me sceptically from underneath their battered Akubras. I don't think they really believed I was going to be the new pilot.

Windorah church

'Where's your habit, Sister?' they kept asking me.

'Betcha she flies like a flamin' chook!', quipped another.

I learnt more in that one month of flying with Terry than in the five months at the flying school. Under Terry's watchful eye, I managed fifty dirt strip landings and clocked up thirty flying hours. In four weeks, I landed on every possible kind of airstrip in the west: plain gravel, red gravel; white, grey and brown clay strips; grassed and black soil strips— you name it, and I landed on it. I felt I had gained in confidence, not only as a pilot but as a person. Terry and I covered over 200,000 square kilometres of the most breathtaking country I had ever seen—a vast expanse of nothingness to the blinded eye, but a land majestic in its ruggedness. However, on the return flight, Terry was amazed that I still remained unable to find my way across the countryside.

'But we were here only a month ago. Don't you remember that hill or that bend in the river?' he would ask.

Holy heck! Although my navigation skills were to improve with time, it took me most of that year to familiarise myself with the area.

Terry and I flew to Maroochydore in March to try and finalise my licence but, once again, the weather foiled my attempt to sit for the flight test so we returned to Longreach for another month. The Cessna had its 100-hourly service and I had the chance to catch up with office work and sacramental preparation. At long last, on 3 May 1989, I successfully passed my final flight test, in Emerald, and obtained my unrestricted licence. The next day, I flew to the town of Moranbah by myself and celebrated my new licence with the sisters. I was overjoyed. My flying career was now officially launched.

The other Presentation Sisters had kept tabs on my progress and sent me letters and cards of support.

'How exciting for you,' wrote one sister. 'It's a wonderful ministry and a great thing you will be doing for the women of the west. But I'm glad it's you, and not me. I'd be scared stiff up there!'

Another congratulated me on graduating from the Victa ride-on mower, which I used to drive around the convent grounds, to a Cessna 172.

'You are moving our congregation with the times,' she wrote. 'From the flying point of view, it's good to see, at long last, that a woman is venturing into what has always been considered a man's territory.'

Sister Marie Therese Corcoran, a 95-year-old sister, thought my flying a marvellous idea. She said if she was younger, she'd love to fly herself. The sisters at the convent in Maroochydore were already used to me reciting my radio calls out aloud in the kitchen as I peeled the potatoes for tea. My parents, on the other hand, had been alarmed when I first told them of my plans to become a pilot, especially Mum, who was very nervous about my flying. But once I explained that learning to fly was a prerequisite for me to continue the work of the Aerial Ministry, they were supportive and even paid for extra lessons—anything to keep their dear daughter safe. Every time a plane flies over the house, my mother now makes a habit of saying a prayer for my safety.

Throughout my training, and even as I fly along today, I have always felt safe because I know I am not alone. My faith is absolute and I trust that God will look out for me. Nevertheless, God must have been temporarily distracted that day I nearly landed in the ditch at the end of the runway!

In October 1989, Terry and I flew the Bishop of Rockhampton, Bishop Wallace, for his annual trip west to visit the diocese. Although Terry did most of the flying, I flew the bishop to Marmboo and back just to prove to him that I could fly the Cessna on my own. I executed a near perfect landing, much to the bishop's relief, and delivered him safely back on the ground.

As the year drew to a close, Terry wanted to make sure that I could navigate by myself so he asked another priest from Longreach, Father Terry Stallard, to accompany me on one of the runs. The new Terry was wonderful company. He boosted my confidence no end when he fell asleep minutes after take-off. He would even be asleep when I came in to land— a blessing for any pilot. I much prefer having passengers who doze off rather than wriggle nervously in the front seat. I remember a neighbouring parish priest who flew with me on one occasion felt moved to confess his fear of flying when we were in the air. It was an unusually rough and turbulent flight and the Cessna was buffeted about. Pale with terror, the priest was convinced that because of all the turbulence, a wing might tear off, or worse still, we would fall out of the sky!

Terry Loth completed his final flying circuit with me in November 1989. There was a farewell every place we went. The people were sad to see him go, and it was an emotional time for him.

Terry officially retired from the Aerial Ministry in December 1989. We had flown together for the best part of that year and I was going to sorely miss his presence in the Cessna, not to mention our Friday evening squash games followed by a round of Five Hundred. When he left Longreach, I presumed that I would be the full-time pilot who would chauffeur the new priest around the west. However, due to a shortage of priests in the Rockhampton Diocese, I was warned that it could be a long wait until a priest was found to fly with me. Other arrangements had to be made. Eventually a priest from Quilpie in the Toowoomba Diocese, Father Jeff Scully, agreed to accompany me for a weekly circuit every second month. Father Terry Stallard from Longreach was asked to fly with me in the local area, while Father Chris Schick from the Barcaldine parish would cover the Birdsville region with me for a week every third month. For all the 'in between' time, I would be working by myself.

Today, despite clocking up almost 3,000 flying hours, I don't consider myself a born or natural pilot. I have had to work hard at my flying. The prospect of flying into any controlled airspace still scares me, and I dislike having to land under the watchful stare of another pilot. I'm happy to be just a modest bush pilot and fly around the west.

I obtained my night licence a few years ago, not that I'm particularly keen to fly at night—there is little to see in pitch darkness—but simply to allow me to return home to Longreach when I've been delayed and need to take off in the dark. I'm aware of the dangers but I try not to let fear overcome me, especially when I lose my way or get caught unexpectedly in dust storms.

Claypan

I've had more than my fair share of scary moments in the air. Once, flying from Innamincka Station in South Australia to Cooks Well in Queensland, the Cessna was suddenly engulfed in a cloud of red dust so thick that I couldn't see a thing except the ground directly below me. I radioed Charleville for help and was advised of a course to follow. But, because of the dust, it was impossible to identify any landmarks or determine my precise position. I was thankful to be alone—at least I did not have to worry about any passengers. Flight Services at Charleville eventually suggested I fly to Mount Leonard and advised me to land wherever I could. I touched down on a dirt road near a homestead only to be placidly greeted by a woman, Del Henderson, who immediately offered me a cup of tea, just as if it were a daily occurrence for her to have a sister executing an emergency landing in her backyard! She had no idea of what I had been through. Shortly afterwards her husband, Allan, arrived home. The Birdsville police had been alerted that I was in the vicinity and radioed him to check if he could hear or see my plane. When the dust storm cleared several hours later, Del and Allan refuelled the Cessna and sent me on my way to Birdsville.

Another time, a wall of dust hit just minutes after taking off from Palpara. Fortunately, I was flying over the Diamantina River when it happened, so I immediately descended to 500 feet and followed the winding river. There was no need to worry about obstacles in my path or losing my way.

As any bush pilot will confirm, some of the most frustrating moments are when mechanical problems occur far away from a hangar. From the very start, I was not, and still am not, the most skilful mechanic, but over the years, through trial and error, I have learnt the basic workings of my Cessna. I discovered that it has a 24 volt battery because I accidentally left the master switch on when I was staying overnight at a friend's property. The battery also went flat in the air once and I lost all radio contact.

I was pleased to find out that two magnetos can keep me in the air—if the first one gives up the ghost, I can still fly home in relative safety by temporarily relying on the second one.

After my much loved and trusted mechanic, Laurie Curley, was killed

Laurie Curley, my mechanic.

in a light aircraft crash just outside Roma in late 1996, I had to struggle on my own for a while. When Laurie set up shop in the original 1921 Qantas hangar at Longreach Airport, I could conveniently fly home late on a Friday afternoon, let him give the Cessna a general check-over, and then, thanks to his efforts, I would be airborne again by early Sunday morning. If I had engine trouble, Laurie would always be there on the radio, at any time of the day or night, talking me through whatever problem I had until I felt secure enough to limp home. I thank God for bush mechanics like him because it is their skill and dedication that keep me in the air.

My call sign is FBD: 'Foxtrot Bravo Delta', or as a jackaroo once joked, 'Friendly Bible Deliverer'. I try to visit everyone in my parish, irrespective of their religion, as I see the main thrust of my ministry as pastoral care of the isolated families. I'm thought of as a local because I share so intimately in these people's lives. But whenever the need arises, I am just as happy pulling a sheep out of a bog or lending a hand mustering as I am in providing religious instruction to children or conducting a communion service.

When I first started flying around the bush, I suspect people expected to see a 'traditional' nun, dressed in a black habit and veil, landing on their property. But as I always say, 'I'm sorry to disappoint, but times have changed.' So has the Church. My congregational ring and a small badge identify me as a Presentation Sister, rather than my attire. I still wear a veil, but it's a fly veil as protection against the flies.

People certainly have very funny ideas about nuns (who take solemn vows and are an enclosed monastic order such as the Carmelites) and religious sisters (who also take vows but devote their time to being with people), vesting us with some sort of supernatural powers. Once I was asked by a jackaroo to bless his Landcruiser!

Windorahites

Thanks to all the people who share their life experiences with me, I am in constant touch with reality. For the last couple of years, I have been a regular at the Spring Carnival race meetings in Birdsville, Bedourie, Betoota and Windorah. I always attend the Birdsville Races on the first Saturday in September, which raise much needed funds for the Royal Flying Doctor Service and the Birdsville Hospital. I fly in early in order to beat the rush of some 300 planes that touch down for one of the nation's most celebrated race meetings. This outback town of one hundred people swells in a weekend to a staggering 5,000. Accommodation is wherever you can find it, mainly camping out along the track to the racecourse. It's a hectic time for the few locals, thus, for the last nine meetings, I've helped out wherever I can—catering, cleaning and babysitting. These race meetings are exhausting work, but I see them as valuable occasions where people can get together. They come from all over the bush and there is a lot of catching up for many. It's an ideal time for me to participate in the life of the outback community, mixing with tourists and locals alike as they swap yarns. For them, it's a joyous occasion which provides a welcome break from the hardships of everyday life.

When I joined the Aerial Ministry, I'd never set foot inside a pub. Now, not only have I been inside a pub, I've pulled beers at one! I've served behind the bar at the Noccundra Hotel—a famous watering hole on Nockatunga Station near the Jackson Oilfields—to enable the publican's wife to get on with other hotel work. I must admit that sometimes I'm not too keen on serving people who already have had a little too much to drink! What I enjoy most is having the chance to chat with the station hands who call in for a beer. As for the tourists, I'm not sure what they would think if they knew that they were being served by a nun!

I do not talk 'religion', nor do I try to convert anyone. I don't even like the thought of it. On the properties I visit, it is more important that we just talk over a cuppa. At the end of a long, hard day, sitting out on the verandah surrounded by the quiet of the bush—that's where life is. As for the rest, people know who I am and what I stand for.

I visit 130 families on a regular basis, some people I see once a month, some only every two months, but it can also be merely three times a year. Now that I am well into my tenth year of flying, I've noticed that I seem to be staying longer at each place. This is not intentional, it just naturally developed that way over the years. The real challenge, I believe, is to be sensitive to each situation. These people lead busy lives and I would hate to add extra stress to their already exhausting schedules. During my stay, I will get out and help with mustering, shearing, and feeding lambs and poddy calves as well as doing chores in the kitchen and the classroom.

I remember one occasion back in the early months of flying when it rained for almost a whole month. It was the year of the Charleville floods. Road and rail links to Longreach were cut and I was grounded at the convent. I did not know what to do with myself. I felt I should be out with the people but, instead, here I was, stuck in town. The only assistance I could give was ferrying stranded teachers in and out of the town of Emerald. Back then, I had no real idea of the significance of badly needed rain for the people living in the bush. I now realise that they would much rather see rain than me. These days, having observed first-hand the damage drought has wreaked in the bush and the enormous strain it places on families living on privately owned properties, I would gladly suffer months of gloomy exile in Longreach in exchange for a few inches of rain out west.

The magnitude of my bush parish was brought home to me when I chauffeured Father Michael, a visiting priest from Ireland, on one of my three, weekly circuits. February was certainly not the coolest or most comfortable month for an Irishman to be flying around the outback, but he survived the heat well, much to my surprise. Father Michael's parish covers no more than 25 square kilometres of lush green midlands. Travel and distance took on a whole new meaning for him after a month flying with me! On one of our first stopovers, he asked me what size the property we had landed at was.

'Father,' I coolly replied, 'this place is only small. It's 25,000 acres.' Father Michael's eyes widened. As we continued our circuit around the parish, the size of properties kept growing—from 7,500 square kilometres (a little under two million acres) at Naryilco, to four million acres at Innamincka. Father Michael was flabbergasted. A substantial property in his parish, he explained, was 200 acres. The size of a small paddock out here!

Father Michael used to record his thoughts on a portable tape recorder as we were flying. At one point I had to stifle a giggle when I heard him say out loud in his thick Irish accent, 'Now we are flying over the desert.' We were actually flying over some dry country between Longreach and Isisford—hardly what one would call desert.

'He doesn't know what desert is yet,' I thought.

When we touched down at Sandringham, a large company station brinking on the edge of the Simpson Desert (real desert!), Father Michael quickly updated his recording.

It amazed my Irish visitor that he could shake the hand of every child at the Birdsville State School in between the first and second bell—there were only thirteen pupils. He himself was the principal of a school with over 700 students.

Like myself, Father Michael delighted in the company of the people of the west, sharing meals in their homes and swapping yarns. He was moved by their spirit and their generosity. After celebrating mass in one shire hall, he was presented with an Akubra hat which did not leave his head for the rest of the trip. Often the managers on the large company stations would lend us a ute so we could explore their properties. Father Michael could never get used to the fact that he would not be greeted by the sight of another property over the next rise or around the next bend, or that he had trouble spotting cattle, especially on the larger stations. It tickled his fancy to see a sign outside the town of Windorah stating that the next fuel stop was 228 kilometres away or that the town of Betoota had a population of one—yes, just the publican!

When he returned to Ireland several months later, Father Michael wrote to me explaining that his experience in the west had served as a real eye-opener. Now he realised more clearly how much the Church had changed over the years. He also admired the fact that the Aerial Ministry crossed all boundaries, reaching out to people of different faiths. He was right. Denominational tags are not so important in the west.

I love my work. These have been some of the happiest years of my life. I work on contract with the Rockhampton Diocese. The diocese pays for all my fuel and aircraft maintenance but, unlike the Salvation Army's Flying Padre who sells cinnamon donuts  at the Birdsville Races to keep himself airborne, my ministry is entirely dependent on the goodwill of the people of the bush. These people give me food, hospitality and friendship.

In recent years, a group of professional women, the Gold Coast Zonta Ladies, have been a great support for my ministry as well. Each January I meet them for brunch at Jupiters Casino and give them a report on my year. They offer me some financial support and also supply me with magazines and other reading material that I can distribute to the women I visit.

I can't imagine not flying. Once, when the Cessna underwent a major overhaul and was out of operation for a month, I borrowed the parish priest's four-wheel drive and travelled on some of the western roads. The novelty of being on the ground rather than in the air quickly wore off after countless bogs and stalls in bulldust, blown tyres, and the constant dodging of potholes and roos. I sorely missed my Cessna. It took me ages to drive from station to station—I would never be able to continue with my ministry if I had to carry it out from behind the wheel of a car.

Of course there are some disadvantages in my type of work. It can be very lonely. Although I am in constant contact with people, I am on my own when I fly. Also, it's not always easy to share my frustrations. Working as I do means that I am forced to live out of a suitcase for weeks on end. I sleep in a different bed every night and I have few moments to myself.

Since 1989, my daily prayer time and Office (the official prayer of the Church) with the other sisters of my congregation has become a 'prayer on the run'. I can no longer participate, as I once did, in a community life with the sisters because I am rarely home, nor can I share in the daily Eucharist. My annual spiritual retreat is probably the only occasion when I can really unwind, reflect and put things back in perspective. It is a time to withdraw and listen to God in one's own life. This is another reason why my weekends in Longreach are precious to me.

Also, Saturday is the only day when I can catch up with my correspondence, pick up spare parts for the plane, wash and iron my clothes and, if there is still some time, quickly run the mower across the lawn—an old habit I've retained from my early convent days and which is a wonderful therapy of sorts.

By Saturday evening, as the screen door clacks open and shut with the comings and goings of visitors and just as the sound system cranks up next door at the line dancing club and the first strains of 'Achy Breaky Heart' come floating through my bedroom window announcing the start of an evening's boot scootin', I'm packing my suitcase again in preparation for another weekly flying circuit.

THE WOMEN OF THE WEST

Women need to talk, and for the women I visit every week, I'm essentially a listening ear, a shoulder to lean on in a tough world of men. For most of these women, I am the only female they may have seen in the past few months. Generally all other visitors are male—from the truck drivers and station bosses, to the mailmen, refuellers and stock agents. But it's the women who have the interesting stories to tell. Many came to the bush as governesses or nurses. They married the men on the land and stayed. The men are more predictable. Raised in the bush, they are at home here. But many women, when they made their marriage vows, also committed themselves to a strange life—a lifetime of isolation, loneliness, flies and dust storms.

Leah Cameron

Their roles have changed over the years. Nowadays, they are not just wives and mothers, but also educators, nurses, bookkeepers, financial managers, electricians and mechanics. To me, they are the driving force within the family and the mainstay of the wider community.

On my regular visits, I have listened to a middle-aged woman who knew she was dying and who confided her anguish in me as she watched the distress of her family. I have sat with a young wife whose husband had just been killed in a plane crash while mustering on the property—I was by her side as she received the phone call. I have helped a couple bury their seventeen-month-old baby on the family property—one of the hardest things I have ever had to do.

But it would be untrue to say all is doom and gloom. In fact, the reverse is true, as I have also been part of so many joyful celebrations in their lives—baptisms, weddings and the breaking of drought. I've even been privileged to be present at the birth of the baby of one of my mums in the local hospital. Her husband, who was miles away at mustering camp at the time, was not able to be with her. I knew she was anxious—mind you, there were four women present in the labour ward, none of whom had had babies, telling her how to have her fourth! I was just holding her hand.

Since I myself have come from a different environment—I'm more of a suburban kid—I am always amazed when I see these women accepting their extreme isolation as if it were something quite ordinary. It is simply their way of life—no big deal. Their isolation means that, for most of them, they are usually deprived of all the amenities, resources and services, the permanent availability of which we generally take for granted. Their nearest town or city may be more than 1,000 kilometres away. Just to find a hairdresser, chemist or newsagency would require a seven-hour bumpy drive down unsealed dirt roads. Most of their shopping is done by mail order catalogues or, these days, over the phone. Fresh bread, fruit and vegetables can take two days or more to reach them by mail truck. There is no such thing as running down to the corner store. If an ingredient is missing in the pantry, they learn to make do and compromise.

Many stations are still not connected to electricity, and the water—what there is of it—varies from place to place in smell, colour and purity. It took me a long time to get used to cleaning my face and teeth in brown water. Now I don't even notice it.

'Chumpy' delivering the weekly mail and perishables to Windorah.

There is no daily mail service. No daily newspaper. There are no book-shops or libraries at hand. No cinemas, no theatres. However, most of my women would say, 'We aren't isolated. We have the television, radio—even a telephone.' Prior to September 1992, they relied on a radio or RAD phone, or the 'party line', where they shouted themselves hoarse just to make them-selves heard. It was impossible to have a private conversation since all their neighbours, or the rest of the State for that matter, could listen in. Today, the old HF (high frequency) radio has been replaced by the connection of standard telephones which is a significant but costly improvement to their lives. However, many miss the 'galah' sessions on the radio which used to keep them in touch with their neighbours. The intermittent crackling and humming from the black box in the homestead kitchen also kept them company when they were home alone. Now the radio waves are silent.

These women are geographically cut off from essential services, such as schools and doctors. If not living in a small town, children start their schooling with distance education and School of the Air. Families working on company stations can be lucky enough to have a governess in their employ, but for many families, especially on the smaller, privately managed properties, mum is the home tutor. Although this adds to her already busy workload, I don't know of a woman who would begrudge her time and energy when it regards her child's education.

Once children reach the age of twelve, they are sent away to boarding school. In my experience, every family who has a child away at school

Jeannie Reynolds

asks the same question at the start of each new year—'What are we doing out here?'—because boarding school is the biggest wrench in family life. Families are used to doing everything together. There are no such things as babysitters or day care centres. Children play an important role in station life because they are expected to pitch in with the work. When they leave the property, it means one less pair of hands to help. During the month of February I spend a lot of time with parents who are sending their children back to school. I've noticed that it is always an emotionally trying time which affects the entire family. But in this current grim climate, the hard dry times and the bleak future on the land, parents know they cannot deprive their children of the chances which only a proper education can secure.

In matters of health, the isolation of the bush means that the nearest GP or hospital is often hundreds of kilometres away. Instead, people have come to rely on the Royal Flying Doctor Service (RFDS), and if it wasn't for this unique life saving medical service—as they will tell you themselves—many would not be here today.

Check-ups by doctors and dentists usually become part of the annual holidays. Clinics are held once a month in community halls. A visit to the clinic also provides one of those rare occasions to swap stories and catch up with what has been happening in the past month.

In the event of a serious accident or illness, the flying doctor—who is on call around the clock—will fly out to the trouble spot. During emergency night evacuations, kerosene flares, battery-operated lights, even car headlights are used to guide the plane safely onto the dirt landing strips.

Outback grave

Back in the days of radio, the women manned the wireless and were taught morse code to summon the flying doctor because they were the ones minding the homestead while their husbands were out at camp. Out of sheer necessity, it is the women who have become adept at diagnosing symptoms and describing them over the phone, as well as administering basic first aid from the flying doctor medical chest. There are more than 2,000 of these 'outback pharmacies' distributed around Australia—half in my parish alone. In the last five years, there has been a resident nurse in the town of Bedourie which has a population of one hundred. She told me that a doctor had once requested she take a blood sample from a patient.

'What's the use?' she lamented. 'There's no way of getting it to Mount Isa for you to analyse.'

Isolation from proper medical care is of enormous concern to the people of the outback and the social life of all the women I meet is centred on fundraising—car rallies, race meetings, ride-a-thons, all these just to keep the flying doctor in the air. But it's not easy. With successive governments shifting priorities, rural health care is still lagging far behind the city. Alas, it verifies too often the grim truth 'out of sight, out of mind'.

Isolation also bears hard upon the women when they need counselling for a marriage breakdown, grief, IVF program or when dealing with an alcoholic partner. Fortunately, the work carried out by the flying doctor has extended into counselling in recent years. In some instances, women can share their concerns with the district nurse, but for many, it would be too difficult or too long a trip to drive to the nearest clinic. Therefore, they learn to bottle up their emotions, but sometimes, I am afraid, this is not a healthy solution.

Small communities like Jundah and Isisford have no public transport, thus, unless you have your own car, there is no way of getting out of town. Furthermore, the type of vehicle one needs out here has to be reliable. Toyotas and Landcruisers are essential components of outback life because of the poor road conditions and long distances between towns and stations in isolated areas. When a breakdown or an accident occurs, there is no roadside assistance or service that can be alerted, and no mechanic at hand. I know of one woman who was in such a hurry to get back to her property in order not to miss her favourite TV soap that she rolled her Toyota. She ended up having to walk for four hours to get back home.

On these roads, people are few and far between. A roo bounding into your headlights can cause serious damage to a vehicle—not to mention severe physical injuries. In the event of a family crisis, the time taken to travel the enormous distances makes it difficult for anyone to attend to the emergency or even make it to a funeral. I admire the women who travel hundreds of kilometres on their own. They are used to driving over huge distances. One lady travelled six hours to help with the catering for a car rally and when this chore was over, she drove straight back home. She told me she did it to raise money for her child's education.

To visit a next-door neighbour can easily entail a three-hour journey over rough dirt roads that are often corrugated and choked with dangerous bull-dust. When it rains, the roads wash away. Over the years, there has been some improvement with roads in south-west Queensland, but many are still haz-

Colleen Girdler

ardous. In the Diamantina Shire, the majority of the 1,683 kilometres of roads are still only dirt and gravel with a mere seven kilometre stretch of bitumen in the entire shire.

Politically, once again remoteness means neglect and the people have learnt that, in the eyes of politicians, they hardly exist since their numbers are too small for their votes to count. Yet their environmental concerns, particularly the proposed World Heritage Listing for the Lake Eyre Catchment area, are important. A proposal to grow cotton on Cooper Creek has led to a new water management plan for the Cooper Basin. Added to this is the whole Wik issue which, for a time, has brought confusion and uncertainty.

I can see the distress which some of these issues are causing to families who have lived in these areas for generations. Being part of a minority group, they need courage to stand up and fight for what they believe in. Though few in number, they do not give up, nor wait passively for things to happen. Instead, they have rallied together and voiced their views at every opportunity. When the former State Labor Government proposed discontinuing the railway link to the Quilpie, Yaraka and Winton areas, local families mobilised themselves to demonstrate their opposition. Individually, they speak of this bond of solidarity that is so evident in the bush. They unfailingly support each other in times of need. They work hard for their livelihood and their genuine love of the land cements the whole community.

Perhaps the most striking change I have noticed in the bush over the last ten years is the dramatic reduction of permanent staff on properties. Previously, each station formed a sort of self-sufficient community, with its managers, overseers, stockmen, ringers, jackaroos, cooks, nannies, cowboy-gardeners, fencers, mechanics and dam sinkers. Now, because of the hard times in the economy, stations have been forced to tighten their belts and to operate with only skeleton staff. Mustering with motorbikes and helicopters has replaced men on horseback. Contract staff are substituted for permanent employees.

Telecommunications and modern media have opened up the west considerably. There are televisions and video recorders on all the properties and

Maree Morton

many managers now use fax machines and email to help with the daily running of the station. But despite advances in modern technology which have made station life easier, the reduced staff numbers still mean an increased workload.

Both the downturn in the economy and the prolonged drought have taken their toll on the women I visit. For seven years I helped an elderly widow, Mrs Rogers, on her drought-affected property, Belmore. She managed the 24,000 acre sheep and cattle station on her own after her husband's death. Together, we have worked side by side clearing scrub, looking for feed for her sheep and praying for rain to fall. On the property next door, which is managed by a husband and wife team, the situation doesn't look much better.

Not long ago, as I completed another year of flying, I could still envision

Mustering

a picture of hope for all these people who were waiting for rain. As I started the new year, I felt an overwhelming anxiety that the 'big wet' simply was not coming. Added to this are the problems of low market prices for wool and beef, the high cost of commodities and the longer hours that must be borne by fewer staff. No-one has the resources to carry out improvements on their property. Funds are drying up and hard work seems to bring no reward. With all that, often the heat is such that one can hardly stand outside. And then comes the final stroke—an invasion of grasshoppers, which manages to finish off what scanty feed remains.

I have sat and prayed for rain with these people. In front of their frustration and despair I feel so useless, as I can only mumble a few words of comfort. All I can do is ask my God to give them the strength and courage to go on.

I know how strong, adaptable and independent these women are, but I have also witnessed their disappointments, frustrations and anger. At times, I have seen their vulnerability as they struggle for survival in such a harsh country. Most of them do not try to escape from the problems or crises in their lives—the death of a child, the death of a spouse, terminal illness, accidents which suddenly cripple the breadwinner of the family, a mother's anguish at having her only son in jail far away in the big city, parents worrying for their young children in a distant boarding school. There is financial insecurity, or simply a crushing workload and not enough hours in the day to do it all.

My list could go on endlessly, but I would not want to paint a picture of unrelieved wretchedness or despair, because this would not be doing justice to these women. After ten years of flying around the bush, I have become intimately involved in their lives. My role is first and foremost one of a friend. I am someone who is willing to take time out and listen. But I know my limits. I do not imagine for one moment that these women really could not do

without me—in fact they have already learnt to deal with their problems on their own. And that is precisely why they are still there. They are true survivors. I am simply grateful that I can go to my God with their worries and pain. Although I cannot take their problems on board, at least I can be with them. I don't have all the answers and neither do they expect this of me. But for them it may just be of some comfort every now and then, to have a female friend by their side.

Cheryl Geiger

CIRCUIT ONE

CHERYL GEIGER—WINDORAH

My first port of call each month is Windorah. It's about a one and a half hour flight from Longreach, or a four-hour drive over rough, potholed roads. With a population of less than one hundred, the community here is like an extended family. 'Windorahites', as they often refer to themselves, have an amazing community spirit and will always help and support each other in times of need. However, with everyone in Windorah knowing each other, it can be difficult discussing problems with other locals for fear that one's personal woes will become part of the town gossip.

The role of a sister like me—as I see it—is, among other things, to act as a sounding board for women who need to talk. And in the small towns, as much as on the remote properties, this seems to be just what the women want—a chat over a cuppa.

One of the first women I usually touch base with is Cheryl Geiger, who I met during my first week of flying in 1989. Under the watchful eye of Father Terry, I had managed twenty dirt strip landings and my confidence as a pilot was slowly growing. However, Windorah will remain etched forever in my memory—unlike the other towns and properties I had landed at, Windorah's airstrip was bitumen!

In the last six years, I have been staying with Cheryl and her husband Merv in their house in town. They always make me feel completely at home. Cheryl is very sociable. A true Windorahite, she devotes much of her time to various community activities. Together we've worked side by side in the catering tents at the annual race meetings and flying doctor fundraising events where I have been able to admire the full range of Cheryl's practical talents.

I have shared in the tragedy of her eldest daughter Karol's car accident, and the death of Cheryl's young niece. Luckily for Cheryl, she receives wonderful support from her family, especially Merv. Merv can put his hand to anything. If you ever want to know about cars or auctions, just ask Merv! In his spare time, he is renovating their new home on the outskirts of town. He may not have much time for books, but Merv is certainly not an uneducated man.

Cheryl has an open invitation for anyone to drop in at her home. I've met many people at smokos at the Geigers'. In 1997, I spent Christmas with the family. Three other single people in town were also invited to share their Christmas dinner. That's Cheryl for you. This sort of generosity comes so naturally to her. She is forever thinking of others and never of herself.

Windorah kind of grows on you. We have an old saying out here—once you cross the Cooper Creek and come to Windorah, you will always return or never leave.

In a bush town like Windorah, there is always plenty of gossip. It can't be helped because everyone knows what everyone else is doing, or at least likes to imagine they know. If not, they'll just make it up. If it sounds good, it will be around town in a flash. It's always been my policy to try and ignore the gossip.

One of the hardest things I found when I first moved to Windorah in the late 1960s was the old-fashioned attitude of the locals. I'll never forget the first time I went swimming. I put on my bikini, and off to the creek I went. Everyone was staring. Why? I couldn't figure out. Apparently it wasn't the done thing to wear a bikini in Windorah. Instead, folk went swimming fully clothed! It was something I could never get used to.

You were thought of as a bit of a hussy if you got around town in a skimpy top and shorts. No matter how hot it was, girls were never allowed to wear revealing clothes. I'll never forget the day when one of the local girls showed up at the annual tennis tournament in a sexy little tennis outfit complete with frilly knickers. Folk thought it was outrageous. Everyone commented on the fact that you could see her knickers. The poor thing! I think a few of the blokes' tennis games were a bit off that day.

I was born in Brisbane on 10 November 1950. My parents, Bert and Oriel Schloss, were married when Dad was still serving in the Second World War. Dad was a carpenter by trade, and we travelled the country a fair bit, mostly in Queensland, because of his work.

I left school at the end of Year 10 and started work at the Red Seal Potato Chip factory in Brisbane. Several months later I took a job in Fortitude Valley as a machinist, but as I hated sewing I also gave that the flick. Then a job came up at a hospital as a domestic. I cleaned floors, filled

Me, aged thirteen.

water jugs and took the patients their meals. I was told that when I turned seventeen I could begin training as a nurse. I'd always wanted to be a nurse, so this was great news indeed. Unfortunately there wasn't much work for Dad in Brisbane so he decided to take the family to Warwick. Both he and Mum thought I was too young to be stopping on my own in the city, so they carted me off with them as well. This meant that my nursing career was temporarily put on hold. After Warwick, we moved to Roma, which is about 630 kilometres from Brisbane. I went to the local hospital looking for a job as a domestic because I was still too young to begin nursing. They put me on as a cadet nurse but I only worked for one year because Mum and Dad packed up once again and moved to Windorah.

Poor Mum! As soon as she set foot on the red dirt, she hated it. She hated Windorah and everything about it—the heat, the flies, the dust storms and the isolation. But above all else, she hated the water. Our mum flatly refused to drink the water which was pumped straight out of the Cooper Creek. As we didn't have a rainwater tank, we carted drinking water from a lady's place down the road for Mum. Sometimes, if Mum woke up in the middle of the night with a thirst, one of us kids would have to go back down to the neighbour's house and cart water back up for her.

We lived in a tent when we first moved to Windorah. After a while, Dad built a bit of a lean-to with three rooms, which made things slightly better for Mum. Our mum never once got behind the wheel of a car so she never went anywhere. She just stopped at home.

Although the sign on the outskirts of town says 'population approximately 65', there's probably a hundred people living in Windorah today. There's a shire hall, pub, shop, garage, two churches and a small school. That pretty well describes Windorah! There isn't much else, and it hasn't grown very much since the day our family arrived. In the last three years about eight homes have been shifted into town and two new Aboriginal homes have been built. There's a small Aboriginal community, and we get on well together. There are Aborigines on the local committees and their children attend our four-room school. Sometimes things get a bit heated but that happens everywhere. You can't have a perfect town.

Windorah is one of those typical bush towns that is too far off the beaten track to attract many tourists. Mind you, we still get our fair share, especially during the winter months. Usually they are retired folk doing the big tour of the outback towing caravans and trailers. We've also had several film crews come out, mostly to make television commercials. Once, a convoy of semitrailers and trucks rolled into town to film an ad for IBM. The crew spent a week burying hundreds of computers and keyboards in the sandhills. The whole town turned out to watch the filming. Today, if you go for a wander in the dunes, you can still see the odd keyboard poking out of the red sand. They're a strange sight, but I kind of enjoy seeing them there. It's something to show the tourists.

There wasn't any electricity when we came here. The folk who could afford it had their own motor to run power to their homes, but the rest of us used kerosene lights, gas irons, and had little motors attached to our washing machines. The water was something else which I had to get used to. Muddy water was pumped into the town's overhead tanks from the Cooper which is eight kilometres away. If you were a little late getting into the shower you'd miss out because the water was gone and the pumps were off. But all this is thankfully in the past. Today we have a new pipeline and bigger tanks.

To help make ends meet, I worked for many years at the local telephone exchange, which was in the same building as the post office. In those days, there were just two other girls and myself. The exchange hours were 8 am to 10 pm, Monday to Saturday and 9 am to 12 noon on Sunday. We had our own motor to generate power. There was only one trunk line into town, so when the exchange was closed, a line was plugged from the police station directly to Longreach in case of an accident or an emergency.

It wasn't long before I became engaged to a local boy. It's a small town! Merv was employed on the roadworks. We'd been good mates for about six months when he popped the question. By that time, my parents had moved back to Brisbane because

Our wedding day.

Mum had been diagnosed with a heart complaint. I went down to Brisbane to stop with them so Mum could help me pick out my wedding frock. We must have visited every single bridal shop in the city! I tried on thousands of frocks until we found one I liked and Mum didn't, and one Mum liked and I didn't. In the end, Mum won and we bought the one she liked. The frock I wanted had short sleeves, but Mum argued that no-one in their right mind ever got married in a short-sleeved wedding frock. Anyway, it wouldn't have been considered right by Windorah standards, despite the fact that my wedding was set for the hottest time of the year.

The night before the wedding, I stayed at the post office residence. On the big day, the postmaster and his wife served me breakfast in bed and promised me a leisurely day. Merv and the boys were supposed to bring the cars around to the post office by midday so we could decorate them before heading off to the church. As it was starting to show signs of being an unusually hot day, Merv and his mates decided to go swimming at the creek. By two o'clock, there was no sign of the cars or the boys, so someone had to be sent down to the creek to fetch them. The relaxed day suddenly turned into one of frantic panic. When I was finally dressed in my long-sleeved frock and ready to leave the post office, the temperature was well in the forties and there was a strong, dry gust about. As I hobbled down the steps of the post office, the wind whipped off my veil. I gathered up my skirts and ran back inside the post office. The small crowd of well-wishers waiting outside thought I'd suddenly had a change of heart! Ten minutes later, back I came on the arm of my dad, and we set off for the church. I was an hour late for my wedding, and the boys were late as well. Mind you, in a town like Windorah, nobody minds—there's not too many weddings. Mine was only the third.

The local ladies did all our catering. As there was no running power, the beers had to be stored in fridges at a property seventy kilometres out of town. The cars which brought the grog to the reception had boiling radiators by the time they chugged into Windorah. By late afternoon, the heat was so awful that I changed after the speeches. The blokes were lucky as they could take off their jackets and shirts. Despite the extreme heat and minor setbacks, it was a beaut wedding enjoyed by all.

Merv and I lived out of his caravan near the roadworks, where we both worked for several years. Merv was a grader driver and I was employed in the office doing the pays and paperwork. When I became pregnant with my first child, Merv and I decided that a move to Toowoomba would not be such a bad thing. Merv had never lived in a real town, so the idea was tempting. I stopped with my mum in Brisbane while I was waiting to have Karol. After a week in the hospital I met up with Merv in Toowoomba, where he was scouting around for work. In the end, we only stayed in Toowoomba for four months. Merv didn't like it one bit. There wasn't much work for him there, and I think he found the whole experience unnerving.

You might not have much work or money in a little bush town like Windorah, but the folk are still very friendly and welcoming. In a big town, no-one wants to know you. The shopkeepers refuse you credit if they've never met you before. We found it very difficult paying off our car and meeting other financial commitments. Added to this was a newborn baby, so finally we just packed our bags and returned to Windorah toward the end of 1975. A new section of the road had just opened so we went back to our old jobs with the roadworks. We upgraded to a forty-foot caravan which had its own bathroom, toilet and kitchenette. When the roadworks were completed, we packed our bags again and took ourselves to South Galway Station. We were both excited about the move and looking forward to station life. Merv had been offered a position as maintenance man and I was expecting our second child.

Tony was born in September 1976. In my time, you had to go away to the city six weeks before the birth. To make matters worse, I was never on time—always a fortnight past the due date. The telephone became my best friend, but it was costly and hardly a substitute for actual presence. If you are leaving toddlers behind it's even worse. It's difficult for everyone, not just for young mothers.

The year after Tony's birth, a vacancy opened up as station hand for Merv, and cook for me, on Tenham Station, a property some hundred kilometres from South Galway. By this time I was expecting again—a real glutton for punishment. Number three, Peter, was born in Quilpie. I developed pleurisy and pneumonia and had to stay in hospital an extra ten days. I was very weak on my return to the station and it took quite some time to recover fully.

Merv and I enjoyed our time at Tenham. The homestead is on the edge of Kyabra Creek which is beautiful in the summer and a great place for kids to go swimming. We found station life very rewarding. I soon fell pregnant again with number four. In my third month of pregnancy, it started raining cats and dogs and there was severe flooding at the station. The cars had to be moved three or four kilometres away to high ground and we canoed down the channels to reach them. This was the only way we could get to town for supplies. One morning I awoke to find I was haemorrhaging. There was not much anyone could do because of the floods. The flying doctor gave instructions over the phone and I was told to stay put. I lost my fourth child that day.

I never had the time to visit the doctor to check if everything was all right and kept putting it off until six months after my miscarriage. As the flying doctor comes out only once a month, medical problems are often neglected. You know you have a problem but you don't do anything about it until it's too late. Fortunately, I was able to fall pregnant again, and gave birth to a healthy girl, who we called Ann. My dad was thrilled to bits that he and Ann shared the same birthday, and we made a pact that the day she turned twenty-one, we would throw a big party. Sadly, Dad and Ann only ever shared her first birthday together. Not long afterwards, he was drinking in his local when he suffered a stroke. The flying doctor flew in the next morning but it was too late. Dad had a blood clot on the brain, and by lunchtime he was dead.

You learn to cope with death better out here than in the city. People will call in and comfort you, and there's not much time to grieve. You just have to get on with life. Just before the fourth anniversary of my Dad's death, my brother Warren was killing a beast in the yards when he had a heart attack. He was buried on the same day Dad died. Warren was only thirty-nine, and left behind a young wife and four kids.

In 1990, there was another tragedy. My oldest daughter, Karol, who was only fifteen at the time, was driving our ute down to the creek for a swim. Like most teenagers out here, she learnt to drive at a very early age. There was a group of kids in the car—my two daughters, their cousins and a few of their mates. On their way home from the creek, Karol rolled the ute and her little cousin was killed. The lass had only recently celebrated her tenth birthday. Any death is tragic, but when it involves a young child it seems so much worse. It was awkward facing the neighbours, particularly Deb, the little girl's mother. I felt very uneasy dropping in at her place as it was my daughter who was the driver of the vehicle that killed her little girl. Plenty of townsfolk called in to spend time with Deb and help her get through it.

Sister Anne Maree would always fly in if there was a death anywhere in the district. She flies down at the drop of a hat to see what help she can be. She comes to town once a month so we Windorahites can go to church, but we don't think of her as someone who just holds a religious service. She's not that kind of person. She's someone we can all have a bit of a yarn to. I can tell her things I would never tell anyone else in town. She might not have the solution to my problem, but just having a chat gets it off my chest. I also know that she won't be spreading it around town.

I don't know if I would call myself religious, but I have a strong personal faith. Although I look forward to Sister's church services, they're not really that important for me. We all have our own beliefs. I don't think going to mass makes you a better Christian or person. Religious belief is personal, and Sister respects that.

Anne Maree has been wonderful with my kids. She's prepared all four for their sacraments—First Holy Communion and confirmation. The preparation's never been a hassle for them because she's not pushy like some of the clergy who have visited us. Years ago, visiting priests used to come to town. Most folk didn't like spending time with them because they only talked religion. If you weren't Catholic, they wouldn't speak to you at all! Once, a priest even refused to visit a sick gentleman because he wasn't Catholic. This same priest didn't appreciate women reading in our church and only ever talked to the blokes. Sister doesn't have this problem. She can relate to all kinds of people. She never preaches. I should know because she stays with us when she flies into town.

Merv is a bit of a non-believer. He likes to ask Sister all sorts of questions when she's stopping at home with us. Merv says he has sung out a few times to the 'Old Fella' above, but never got a response. Sister and he can argue for hours about the Church but it's always friendly. A good mate of ours always pops in when she's here because he loves to pick an argument with her. She's wonderful at holding her own. I've only seen Sister come close to losing her cool once. Our local policeman, a Mormon, came round for a barbecue. Sister and he began a heated discussion about religion. She became quite cranky. But she's learnt not to take the bait.

The best thing about Sister is that she can go into anyone's home and fit in. I like to think of her as being like my own sister. I can confide in her and know I won't be judged. I think the women of the west, like myself, are just so pleased to have her here. I would never have told Father Loth some of the stories I've told Sister. I count her as one of my best friends.

I think women are the real backbone of the bush. We hold the fort when the blokes aren't around. We do it because we want to, not because we have to. Otherwise, we would pack our bags and leave. Blokes who were born and bred in a small town know what they want and wouldn't have it any other way. Merv would hate to leave Windorah and move to the city. His family have been in this district for years. There are four Geiger families in Windorah. Everyone is related to each other in some way. Many years ago, we took the kids to Sydney to have a look around. By the time we arrived in what we thought was the city, but in fact was only the outer suburbs, Merv had had enough of all the traffic and noise. He stopped, turned around, and drove us to a garage to fuel up and head back to Windorah. Luckily there was a motel in sight and we stayed there overnight. Everything looked a bit better the next morning and we spent a day there seeing the sights. The closest the kids got to Sydney that time was the Campbelltown turn-off!

I feel I have a great marriage. Merv and I get along very well and we are proud of what we have achieved, especially with our four kids. I've always considered education as important for myself and for my kids, but Merv thinks otherwise. He went to school in Windorah. He's hardly passed an exam in his life and left school as soon as he could. He doesn't hold a degree in anything, yet I don't think there's anything he can't do. But in today's world you must have it on paper to say you are qualified. Peter left school in Year 10 and has the same attitude as Merv—he's his father's son all right. He's a strong believer that an education won't get him anywhere. But when he applied for a job as an apprentice electrician, he discovered quick smart that he needed a year ten pass which he didn't have. There's still hope that one day he may go back to school if he really wants to. More and more people in the bush are going back to get an education. I think you need to have the basic skills of reading and writing to get on in society.

My two boys will never leave the bush. They may not have big ambitions, but they are happy in their jobs and love living here. Tony is employed on the local council and Peter works on the Dingo Barrier Fence. Our oldest girl lives in Longreach and is now a young mum, while the youngest is finishing off her last year at school and hoping to go to Toowoomba after graduation. She won't live in the bush. I don't think she knows what life in a big town is really like, but if that's what she wants, we won't stand in her way.

Sometimes it makes me a little sad when I see how the outback is changing. Although we still don't lock our back door or take the keys out of the car, I don't think we're quite as secure as we used to be. Nowadays, there's also a tendency for folk to keep to themselves. Not as many people will show up for social functions as they did in the past. Television and video recorders have destroyed social life in the bush. Before they came along, there was a real effort to socialise and catch up with friends and neighbours. Since television invaded the west, hardly anyone goes out anymore. Or if folk do decide to go out, you can be sure that they will rush home the first chance they get so as not to miss their favourite show on the box. Well that's becoming 'citified' in my opinion, because it's controlling their lives.

Christmas day down by the Cooper.

When Merv and I first married we bought ourselves a little boat. We would get up early in the morning and waterski on the Cooper. Everyone would have a turn and chip in for fuel. Folk would come from far and wide bringing playpens for the littlies and shift them around following the shade of the trees to shelter them from the sun. On Christmas Day we would have Christmas lunch at home, but Christmas tea would happen down on the banks of the Cooper. We'd set up such a feast. It was always a grand evening, and the whole town would join in. Now everyone does their own thing.

I remember my favourite event was the Sunday night flicks. A movie used to be screened at the shire hall. Everyone would take a pillow and blanket and lie on the dusty floor. There was a big screen fixed to the wall and an old sixteen millimetre projector. If the movie wasn't that interesting, you could always have a bit of a cuddle and hold hands with your boyfriend instead. This would only happen when the lights went out, because the blokes are a bit shy out here. The movie arrived on the mail truck each Thursday and would be sent back on the following Monday.

Sadly, the Sunday night flicks became too costly for the small number of people who used to attend. Video recorders had just started to take off in the bush and fewer people bothered to show up at the hall, so eventually the screenings stopped altogether. A real shame in my opinion.

Apart from the flicks, what we really looked forward to were the dances, in particular the gymkhana and race balls. We would save our money so as to outdo the next person—the best dress, long gloves, new shoes ... the works. All the girls wanted to be the 'Belle of the Ball'. It didn't matter what age you were—fifteen to ninety—because there was always a 'Belle of the Ball' and a 'Matron of the Ball' and we'd all compete with each other for the titles. Today, when the young ones go off to balls they wear jeans and riding boots. They don't dress up like we used to twenty years ago and it's no longer a family event. In my day, we'd take the kids with us. Everyone packed blankets and pillows, and when the kids were sleepy we'd make up a bed for them in the supper room. Drinking alcohol was also more moderate back then. Naturally, there would be a bar at some functions, but not always. Now it's a must—if there isn't a fully stocked bar at a function, you won't get a soul turning up. I've been lucky with all of my kids—they haven't taken up drinking. Unfortunately it's become the main hobby for young people out here. Since there isn't that much to do, they go out and drink themselves stupid. Alcohol is a real problem in the bush and it's not about to go away.

Merv and I will never leave this area. Although we thought about moving near Toowoomba, the hustle and bustle seems to get worse every year, so we've decided against it. If the kids move away, we can always visit. It's good to stop somewhere else a while and then come home again. Merv is currently employed full-time with the council. In his spare time he works as a mechanic fixing tourists' cars which have broken down. He's due for his long service leave soon, so we are looking forward to a holiday.

Hopefully our tragedies are all behind us now. For a while, it wasn't easy, but I think we've coped well. The town will always rally behind us and, gossip and discontentment aside, I

Our new house.

think we're lucky to have such a strong community spirit.

Last year, Merv and I moved an old shearing shed twenty miles into town. We are slowly renovating it and hope to eventually make it our home. My dream is to one day open up a snack bar beside it. Nothing flash or special, just your sangers, pies and whatnot. We'll serve a few tourists and tell them what our town has to offer—sandhills, fishing and great hospitality. It looks like we'll be stopping out here in the peace and quiet. That will do me.

CIRCUIT ONE

ANNE KIDD—OURDEL STATION

A surprising number of the women I visit are trained nurses and, because of the shortage of doctors in the bush, all are called upon from time to time to attend to injury or illness in their communities. Some, like Anne Kidd, have taken it upon themselves to offer, as much as training and the law allows, a regular medical service in areas without resident doctors.

Anne, like Cheryl, was one of the women I had the pleasure of meeting in my very first week of flying out west with Father Terry. She regularly attended the monthly church service in Windorah and she and her husband, Sandy, kindly invited Terry and me to stay with them at Ourdel Station.

Ourdel is a family-owned property in the Channel Country, ten kilometres from Windorah. It's hard land. When not struck by drought, it is devastated by floods. I became a regular visitor to Ourdel during my first few years of flying, but nowadays, as I need to spend more time with the children at the small State school in Windorah, it's more convenient for me to stay in town with Cheryl and Merv Geiger.

Anne trained as a nurse in Brisbane and now runs the Windorah clinic. The clinic has only been in operation since 1992. Before then, the people in Windorah and on neighbouring properties who had a medical emergency had to drive to Longreach or rely on the flying doctor. Thanks to Anne's perseverance, the town has, at long last, access to proper medical care.

Anne's husband is something of a legend around these parts. He is very outspoken on all the community and environmental issues which affect his shire, and loves to argue. Whereas Sandy is outgoing and exuberant, Anne is more reserved. Sandy is forever inviting people he meets over to Ourdel for tea. He starts the entertaining but then hotfoots it to bed, leaving Anne with his guests and a stack of dirty dishes to wash! But Anne takes it all in her stride. She is one of the most gentle and competent women I know.

I was born in Cunnamulla, a small country town on the banks of the Warrego River in south-west Queensland. In its heyday, Cunnamulla was known as the 'wool centre of the west' and quality fleeces fetched 'a pound a pound'.

My parents managed the Tatts Hotel, which was one of the best pubs in town. In those days, pubs were more than a place just to drink. They were pleasant establishments which provided decent room and board. Mum ran a smart dining room, serving wholesome country fare, while Dad worked as the publican. Men labouring on the railway line would doss down at the Tatts, but we also had quite a number of travellers passing through. Our family lived in the staff quarters in the pub. I recall it was a little cramped, but comfortable.

When I was seven, we moved to Nambour on the Sunshine Coast, and later to Nanango, near Kingaroy, where Mum and Dad continued to lease and manage pubs. It was very exciting to be constantly on the move, going from town to town and from one pub to another. I attended three different convent schools, but I was always getting in trouble for acting up and 'wagging' school. Finally, my parents decided I needed some sort of stability and discipline, and sent me to board with the Brigadine nuns at Soubirous College in Scarborough, on the Redcliffe Peninsula.

Much to my surprise, I enjoyed boarding school and became an exemplary student during primary school! I adored the Brigadines because they were kind women. The Mercy Sisters had frightened me, but the Briga-dines treated me like family. Although they forced us to attend daily mass at six in the morning, the sisters never drummed religion into us. They weren't the kind of nuns who would push religion down your throat until it came out your earhole!

Dad died when I was fourteen. It was a difficult time for the entire family. He had been sick for months with cancer, and was constantly in and out of hospital. My older sister Erin, whom we called 'Chick', had been

Me with my younger sister Mary.

working for a bank in Brisbane but she came home to help Mum in the pub. Our youngest, Mary, was still at school in Childers. After Dad died, the three of them packed up and moved to Brisbane. I think Dad's medical bills must have eaten up any savings my parents may have had because Mum and Chick were desperate to find work and put a roof over their heads.

To make ends meet, Mum worked various odd jobs, mostly cleaning rooms and doing some bookkeeping at one of the pubs in town. I was still away at boarding school. The Brigadine nuns who had, of course, heard about the upheaval in my family life were very kind and helpful to me and I shall never forget their generosity.

I left school after 'Junior' (Grade 10) and worked as a junior clerk and typist in a small Brisbane office. As soon as I turned seventeen, I started nursing. On my first night duty shift at the Mater Hospital, Mum unexpectedly showed up and told me that Chick's husband, Mick, who was part of a volunteer fire crew, had been severely burnt in a sugarcane fire. He was not expected to live. Mum caught the train to Childers to be with Chick and after Mick's death, she brought Chick and her daughter back to Brisbane to live with us.

In 1963, after completing my training at the Mater, I started looking around for work. I was offered a private nursing position with a family out west. I was attracted by the idea and accepted the job for a couple of months. A 'couple of months' stretched into thirty-three years. I've never left!

There is an old song which goes something like—'Where creeks run dry or ten feet high, it's either drought or plenty.' This pretty well sums up the Channel Country in outback south-west Queensland. Because it is so flat out here, heavy rains can cause beneficial flooding. Droughts or floods—there is never one without the other!

When I first arrived in the Channel Country they were experiencing a 'record' flood in the Cooper. My future employers—pastoralists Jim and Mary Kidd—met me at the small airport in Windorah. Their only son, Sandy, was also there. He later confessed to me that he had come to Windorah not to see me, but my plane! Sandy was passionate about flying. He had his own Cessna 172, and he never missed a plane coming in or taking off. He would help with the refuelling and hang about the airstrip chatting with the pilots. My first impression of him was that he seemed quite odd!

The Kidds are one of the oldest pioneer families of the Channel Country. When I arrived at the age of twenty-one to nurse Fanny Kidd, Sandy's grandmother, the family was living on the other side of Windorah, on a sprawling 55,000 hectare sheep property called Mayfield.

Mayfield was a magical place. Sandy's grandfather built it in the early 1900s. The homestead comprised three buildings, but was unpretentious. The armchairs were spilling their springs and it wasn't surprising to see the legs of a table glued haphazardly together. Jim and Mary Kidd, Sandy and his sister Margaret lived at Mayfield's out-station, Ourdel, which was eight miles from the main homestead. It had been built for Jim and Mary after Tom Kidd was killed playing polo. The name Ourdel is actually an anagram for Lourdes, but without the 's'—Mary Kidd's idea.

I lived up at Mayfield with Grandma Kidd, a Miss Hammond and Sandy's three unmarried aunties, Bub, Kitty and Meg—the 'Mayfield Ladies' as they were known in the district. Kitty was the oldest. She did all the bookkeeping and cooked the meals. Bub was the 'handyman'. She loved working in the large garden. Meg, the youngest, was the lady of the house.

Like Sandy, the three Mayfield Ladies never modified their behaviour for anyone—king or beggar. They were devout Catholics and religion played an important part in their lives—although they were the only women I knew who were game enough to take the dog and a picnic lunch for the kids when they went to church!

Old Grandma Kidd suffered from fits and high blood pressure. My days were spent nursing and keeping her company. She had long hair which she always wore up in plaits. When I was sitting with her during the day, I would ask after her grandson. Sandy was a real character. He was straightforward with a good sense of humour. He had never once set foot outside of Ourdel, except to go to school in Brisbane. He worked with his father managing the property which, in a good season, ran 15,000 sheep and about 1,000 head of cattle.

I liked Sandy and got to know him well. So well in fact, that just six weeks after our first meeting on the airstrip in Windorah, we were engaged. He took me flying in his Cessna and as we were gliding over the

Cooper at 2,000 feet, he proposed. He told me if I didn't agree to marry him he wouldn't land the plane!

Living on an established family property took me into a completely new world. I had never had any contact with the 'real bush' before then. The closest I had ever come to wildlife were cats and dogs, but I still had a lot to learn about them too! Horses and cattle frightened me, and I was terrified of insects—sandflies, stink bugs, and especially grasshoppers! One day, I was told to go out to one of the paddocks and feed the horses. I'd been warned not to get too close, because one horse was notorious for kicking and biting. Well, that just about did me. It was starvation time for the horses whenever I was in charge! Only the thought of Sandy's scorn could make me enter the paddock and give them their feed. Sandy's mother was a saint. She came to help me and was as patient and kind to me as

Our wedding.

she was with the animals. Like myself, she was not born or bred in the bush. She was a generous woman who dedicated her life to her home, her family and to helping others. She kept the local post office busy with all the letters she wrote to friends. She was such a dear, sweet woman and I owe her much for educating me in the ways of the bush.

Sandy continued to work on his family's property while I was busy giving birth. I had five children—two boys and three girls—all in six years! My lessons with the sheep and cattle started when our youngest, James— or 'Dude' as we nicknamed him—was old enough to start helping Sandy. I was also called upon to lend a hand in the yards. Working with sheep was not as difficult as I'd thought. Apart from shearing, I was taught about lamb marking and mustering. I found the cattle work pretty straightforward too—just brand and sell, or buy and cross brand. Fortunately cattle out here do not require any chemical treatments such as drenching, spraying or dipping. Also, since we haven't many sheep anymore—we only keep a few for mutton—the workload is much lighter.

For the last four years I have been working as the resident nursing sister at the Windorah clinic. I love my work, especially now that my kids are all grown up and I have more time. Before the clinic opened, medical emergencies were a real problem. For years, getting any sort of medication was a nightmare. The prescriptions had to come from Charleville, 450 kilometres away, or you had to wait until the flying doctor could bring them in, which usually meant a delay of several days. Most properties have a Royal Flying Doctor Service kit with a basic supply of medications, but if two people needed the same medication, only one got it, while the other had to wait until the next mail.

Before the Windorah clinic was established, if someone had a medical problem he or she would call on anyone in the district who had any sort of nursing experience. Quite often, I was the one and, I am afraid, a lot was expected of me. 'Bush medicine' had little in common with the medical treatment I had experienced in the city hospitals, where doctors were always on hand and nurses simply did as they were ordered. Suddenly, I had to learn to diagnose and make on-the-spot decisions. The bush nurses of today are better equipped for this type of work and actually receive special training for rural and remote area health care. In my time, you just did the best you could.

As a registered nurse, I can be useful to the flying doctors, because they can quickly get an assessment of a patient's condition from me and I can advise them as to whether or not an evacuation may be necessary. However, working on my own has often been problematic, especially in the early days when all surgery was carried out on my kitchen table! I tended to broken bones and minor accidents, and stitched up cuts. As there was no proper lighting, I used to go through a few 'torch holders'—people who were obliging enough to stand over the patient with a battery-powered torch. This was fairly useless because it only took a few seconds before they too would be flat on their backs—in a dead faint!

The idea to establish a proper medical clinic came from the Central West Regional Health Services in Longreach. Dr Murphy, a local doctor in Longreach, also had a hand in the setting up of the clinic—a small, three-room house, with a waiting room as well as a consultation room. Although I work part-time, I sometimes spend the entire week at the clinic, depending on the needs. I conduct health assessments, check-ups for kids and the elderly, pregnancy tests and treatment for minor illnesses, falls off horses, station accidents, road accidents—you name it, and I have treated it! I suppose I'm a little like a substitute GP.

Doctors days—set days when the flying doctor flies in to hold a special clinic—are held here twice a month. It's a busy time because people drive from all the outlying properties to see the doctor. I assist the doctor in the clinic runs and do whatever I can to help out. Medically, things are looking much brighter in the bush, and I hope the future will bring even better facilities for the people of the outback.

I am often asked if I feel isolated. I tend to think of isolation as being on a desert island and not seeing a soul for months! Sandy and I probably have more contact with other people than most city dwellers. We have visitors coming and going all the time. We also have proper power now, thanks to an electricity generator in town. The water has vastly improved, although not in colour. It's still muddy brown, but at least it's pumped straight from the river which has saved one local the headache of having to manually pump it from an old windmill! I guess the one thing I did miss when I first came here in the sixties was music. The only radio station we could pick up at Ourdel was the ABC, and it never played popular music. I almost missed out on the Beatles!

Faith is important to me. As I see it, what Anne Maree is doing for the Church is a bit like what the Beatles have done for contemporary music. I am a practising Catholic, but for many years I didn't have the possibility

'Dude'

of going regularly to mass or belonging to a church community. Thanks to Anne Maree, I now have both. The Rockhampton Diocese was lucky to get Anne Maree to learn to fly—with much trepidation on her part, but compensated for by dedication. These days, when she flies out west, she comes on her own and organises the children in Windorah as well as the adults—although they tend to be disorganised—to run our own liturgy. She has even got us singing hymns by bringing out a portable tape recorder—otherwise we wouldn't know any!

Sandy

Anne Maree is one of the most easy-going, flexible people I know. My fondest memory of her is when she came out to visit Sandy and me at Ourdel when we were loading sheep to truck away. As we were leaving early the next morning, I asked one of our local legends, 'Wingy', to take Anne Maree to the airstrip in Windorah. Instead of taking her to her plane, he took her to the shed and she was put to work with the sheep because he didn't think she could fly!

I think Anne Maree's ministry is what the future holds for the Church. We need more people like her. Few men are entering the priesthood these days, let alone training as pilots. Anne Maree offers a completely new approach. I don't see her as a religious sister, but as a friend. For me, she is a real bridge between the organised Church and the people. Personally, I wasn't that surprised when I found out she could fly a plane. Out here, flying is no big deal. Many stations used to have their own planes until money got tight. Sandy of course thinks she is brilliant—anyone who can fly a plane is all right in his books! Anne Maree's Aerial Ministry is very important not just to those living in the Channel Country, but for the entire Queensland outback.

Sandy hopes that Ourdel will remain in the Kidd family for many years to come, although he feels that the pressure of life becomes harder for every new generation. Our two boys, Tom and Dude, have stayed on the land and are both working at Ourdel. Tom and his young wife, Jane, are now occupying the small cottage where Sandy and I first lived after we were married. Dude is just like his dad and has both a pilot and chopper licence. However, two of our girls—Catherine and Helen—have left the bush. They are living happily on the Gold Coast and Adelaide respectively.

Sandy is a true bushie. When I met him, he was a lively, wiry bloke who just couldn't keep still. Age has thickened his waistline a bit, and slowed his movement. Back problems don't help much either. But he still rides horses and gets the cows in for milking. He was always an early riser—a habit that won't change, worse luck! A good friend on a neighbouring property who has known him since she was a child describes him as the most untidy person she has ever met. His shirt tails permanently hang out of his trousers and he has this habit of never wearing socks. But he can tell stories like no other, and everyone from miles around loves him for it. He sometimes gets upset if you don't agree with him, but he is the first one to give you the shirt off his back. He was elected to the Barcoo General Council in 1965 and is very outspoken on matters concerning this shire. He has the ability to stir people into action and fight for their rights. Flying has continued to be his great love. Because of his passion for planes and his willingness to drop anything to help others in need, he was awarded the BEM (British Empire Medal) for services to the community during the great floods of '63. He had flown to the rescue of a man with a ruptured appendix, who was marooned on a sand dune.

I can understand that some women can hardly bear living out here. As for myself, I am so busy that I don't really have the time to stop and think about the problems of isolation. Certainly, I don't have things like stress going through my mind because hard work takes it all away. I am quite happy to stay on in the Channel Country, as long as I can get away every now and then. My dream is to travel around Australia one day in a comfortable campervan, and visit our eight grandchildren. I don't think it will take too much convincing to get Sandy on the road with me. I'll just have to steer him away from Ourdel and his beloved planes.

CIRCUIT ONE

JEANNIE REYNOLDS—
MORNEY PLAINS STATION

In these remote areas, husbands, wives and children are very close and depend upon each other's help and love. While some children, like Ann's daughters, may leave for greener pastures, family ties always remain strong. Without these, it would be hard to cope in the bush; Jeannie Reynolds is one woman I know who really has learnt self-reliance and confidence without the support of a mother or even a full-time father.

My first impression of Jeannie was that she loved a good argument. When we first met, she had very set ideas on religion, and on what her children should be taught. She enjoys discussing issues concerning the Catholic Church. I think it helps her to think things out clearly. I prepared her two older boys, Ashley and Jason, for their confirmation and First Holy Communion, and later on, her two youngest children, David and Shannon. Jeannie is grateful for this kind of assistance.

Jeannie has known tragedy in her life but she carries on bravely. Every month, without fail, she comes to our small prayer service at the Windorah church.

Jeannie is forever complaining that her days are too short. She loves it when the men go out to camp because, then at last, she can have some free time to herself. She is also very involved with community activities. These days, when I touch down at Morney Plains Station at sundown, I wonder what new project she has launched since my last visit. As I have observed how generous she is with her time, I am not surprised that she finds she has never enough of it.

I was born in 1957 in Toowoomba, the last of seven children. At that time, the eldest was eighteen and the youngest nine, which meant there was a fair gap between them and myself. You could say I grew up on my own. I spent most of my childhood at Moothandella, which is a family property, now in its fourth generation, about forty-five kilometres east of Windorah.

I don't remember much of my early childhood. There was a fire at Moothandella in 1960 when I was three years old. In that fire I lost my mother, my grandfather on my father's side, and two sisters. Of the elder of the two girls, Joycelyn, I have no memory at all. As for the younger one, Thora, for many years I disliked her because she had, or so I felt at the time, tried to drown me in the sea. I don't hate her anymore of course. In fact I haven't any feeling for her because I never really knew her. I hated the sea then. I still do now. I don't like the sand, the smell, the wind or the waves. The very taste of salt water gives me the creeps.

The only picture I have of Mum and me.

I have no memory of my mother at all, except for her pushing Dad and me out of the homestead. I realise now that it was the night of the fire. I was locked in the car—I have no memories of anything else about the fire whatsoever. As a child, whenever I tried to talk about the fire the subject was quickly changed, so I learnt from a very early age not to ask questions about the past. I met with the same silence regarding my mum. Every time I tried to ask about her the subject was changed. No-one wanted to talk about her. Maybe they were just trying to protect me. I don't know. But it meant that I grew up with a terrible sense of loss.

As I grew older, I didn't worry about it as much. I never missed not having a mum as a child. I never knew what it was like to have a mother, so I guess what you don't have, you don't really miss. I had plenty of other things to occupy me. In my teen years I began thinking about what life would have been like if she were alive. I also thought more about my two sisters who died. I guess I'll never know. The older I got the more I began to miss my mum. I think the time I truly missed her was when I married and had my first child. I suddenly felt a strong need to ask people who had known her what she was like. They would tell me what a wonderful woman she was and then the subject would be dropped. I'm fairly used to it now. No-one speaks about her anymore.

Dad and my eldest brother, Chas, worked on Moothandella running 7,000 sheep. I spent most of my time on neighbouring stations. I was sent to Mayfield for the weekends, which was a fabulous rambling property managed by Dad's first cousins—the 'Mayfield Ladies'. They were three spinsters and real ladies. They were terribly proper and polite. They were also very generous and couldn't do enough for me.

I started school in Windorah as soon as I turned five and boarded with the postmaster and his wife. I think I was packed off to school just to keep me out of Dad's hair. After just one and a half years the postmaster was transferred, so I started studying Grade 2 at home by correspondence with the help of a governess. The governess and I didn't get on, so when she left I was sent off to Charleville to live with my sister.

Dad remarried when I was eleven. My stepmother seemed a strange lady. I felt I was never allowed to become close to her or befriend her. The day Dad married, I was told that she was my new mother, and that I was to treat her as such and call her 'Mum'. Because I didn't know what it actually meant to have a mum, I found this very hard to do. I have always considered my stepmother to be a very jealous person and, sadly, we have had a very strained relationship.

I was sent to Rockhampton for high school and lived with my stepsister. I enjoyed school, but I missed Moothandella. I'd count the days till I could go home. After graduation, I returned to the south-west to look for work. My best friend from Windorah, Barbara, and I decided that we'd become mechanics. Of course, in those days it was unheard of for girls to study mechanics, so that idea was quickly dropped. The next brilliant idea I had was to join the police force. In the end, Barbara and I applied to become nurses. Barbara quit after six months, but I persevered with the course and went on to the Royal Hospital in Brisbane for my aide's training.

As a young girl growing up on a family property, I can't say I was ever bored. When you live in the bush, you make your own fun. Every Sunday was spent down at the creek. There was always someone who played a musical instrument so there were plenty of parties and dances. As there were hardly any girls in Windorah, we'd have to invite girls from nearby Jundah because it was unheard of for the boys to go to a dance without any girls. Barbara and I considered ourselves very fortunate to have all these young men hovering around. The trouble was we never really got involved with any of them. They were only ever good mates or 'big brothers'.

It was while I was nursing in Brisbane that I met up with Warren. We'd been friends back in Windorah. We married in 1976 when I was only nineteen. We moved straight back to Moothandella and worked for Dad until Warren died in 1986. I was at the homestead when Dad walked in and told me that Warren had collapsed in the yards. He'd had a heart attack while slaughtering a cow. When I reached the yards and saw him lying in the dirt, I knew straightaway that he was dead. I recall someone going to fetch our local nurse. Over the next couple of days many people called in at Moothandella. My sister-in-law, Cheryl, was a great help, attending to whatever needed doing. I went into shock. I couldn't believe Warren was gone. Nothing seemed real.

Warren's death was the biggest nightmare of my life. We were so close. We lived out of each other's pockets and had no secrets from each other. We did everything together, and when our children were born, I finally felt complete because I had my own family. It was perfect. When he died, my dream was shattered.

I guess all I really ever wanted out of this life was to have my own little family and live by ourselves some-where out here in the sticks. I think this comes from having only 'half-fam-ilies' all my life—being half a part of this family, or half a part of that family, but never really fitting in any-where. Dad and I were never close. I grew up feeling I wasn't wanted. I was always in the way. It's not his fault. I guess being on his own he couldn't

Warren and me on our wedding day.

cope with me, especially after losing Mum and two daughters in the fire. After Warren's death I began to better understand what my Dad went through.

I had four children with Warren, three boys and a girl. The boys were all born close together, but there is a four-year gap between my last boy, David, and my daughter Shannon. After David's birth, I felt I'd had enough. No more kids I'd promised myself, but deep down, I desperately wanted to have a little girl. Because I'd never known a mother–daughter relationship, somehow I got it into my head that I could have the relationship in reverse by having my own little daughter. Now, after ten years, I've started asking myself why I'd tried so hard. I'm constantly being told Shannon is so like myself—wilful and pig-headed. This may explain why we don't get on. Maybe when she's older things may improve between us. I hope so, for both our sakes.

After Warren's sudden death, it was decided by family and friends that I move to town. My sister was living in Charleville and one of my brothers managed a property close by. I couldn't stay on at Moothandella because I couldn't handle the horror of what was left behind. Warren is buried at Moothandella, as well as my mum, my two sisters and my grandfather.

When I moved to Charleville I felt totally alone. Looking back, I think had I moved to Windorah I would have coped better. I wouldn't have felt as isolated. Although Charleville is not a big place by any stretch of the imagination, it was still too big for my liking. Town life was completely foreign to me. I used to hate going out into the garden, which was tiny compared to what I'd been used to. I was always terrified of disturbing the neighbours. There was not enough space to roam. If I went to any of the social functions, I rarely took the children with me as it was not the done thing. I'd never left my children on their own before as we'd never had babysitters on hand. I felt uneasy about leaving them with a total stranger.

To me, city people are more isolated and lonely than what we are out here. If we go to town to a function, or even to the pub for a counter tea and a drink, we will talk to every person we see. Ninety-nine per cent of the folk you'll already know, and the one per cent you don't know, you'll talk to anyway. You go out of your way to make them feel welcome. If you live in the city and go out—whether it's to a restaurant, movies, wherever—you probably wouldn't even speak to another living person except maybe when ordering your meal. The same goes with your neighbours. You don't speak to them. You wouldn't even know what they did for a living. That is something I discovered when I lived in Charleville after Warren died. No-one bothered to take the time to say hello. Out here, you make a point of getting to know your neighbours. People are more genuine.

The kids and I spent three years in Charleville until Peter came along. The funny thing is I used to date Peter before I went out with Warren. They had been good mates before I knew either of them. Even when Warren and I married, we continued to see a fair bit of Peter. After Warren's death, it was a real comfort having Peter around because I could talk to him about Warren and he'd understand. He knew what I was going

through. I don't think you could do that with a total stranger. I think there would be feelings of jealousy. With Peter, there wasn't any of that. We merely picked up from where we'd left off.

When Warren died, I promised myself that I'd

Mum, my two sisters and Warren's graves at Moothandella.

never let the memory of him disappear, especially as far as the kids were concerned. It's been hard talking to the kids about him, and I've found that the memories I have of him, I want to cherish for myself and not share with anyone. I've had to force myself to talk to the kids about their dad. They went through the same problem of not wanting to talk about him which didn't help matters much. Because I never knew my mum and nobody wanted to talk about her, I didn't want the same thing to happen to my kids. The real tragedy is that Shannon will never know her own father. She's lucky if she even smiled at him before he died.

One of the most important decisions I have made in my life was to marry a second time. Warren used to joke that if anything ever happened to him I would go back to Peter. At first marriage seemed the only solution to save me from my lonely life which I hated so much. Yet I felt uncomfortable about the whole thing because as far as I was concerned, I was already married. My sister was horrified that I didn't want to marry in the church, but I felt I couldn't go back as I had already been down the aisle once before and made my vows before God. As much as I tried to tell myself that it would be what Warren would have wanted, it still felt like a betrayal of sorts. Finally, Peter convinced me that I was making the right decision, and we married in a simple garden ceremony with only our families and close friends present. Peter was crazy taking on me and four kids but we moved to Morney Plains Station to begin a new life together.

Morney Plains is 126 kilometres west of Windorah. Station life at Morney was totally different to what I had known as a child growing up on Moothandella. Now our closest neighbour was an hours drive away. Inviting a friend to tea was something I really missed when we first moved to Morney. At Moothandella we used to do a lot of entertaining, asking friends over and making a night of it. If I want to ask a neighbour to tea at Morney, I'm obliged to invite them to overnight at the station because it's just too far for them to drive back home.

When we came to Morney, the most terrifying thing was not having a telephone. Instead, I had an old HF radio. All messages from the outside world came via the flying doctor base and any phone calls had to be made through the base. With the radio, you couldn't chat about anything personal because the rest of the State could listen in on the conversation. The local galah sessions on the radio were held twice a day so the neighbours could call in and report that they were fine and didn't need any help. You knew exactly what was happening in the district. If someone was away having a baby you went through it with her. You lived as one big family. You helped each other out. To me this is what's wrong with the world today. Nobody goes out of their way to help anyone anymore. The telephone has made life easier but the contact with neighbours has gone. As much as I hate to admit it, I do miss the galah sessions.

We have seven men and a governess working for us at Morney. I suppose we are luckier than some of the privately managed properties because we have a regular incoming wage. Still, my dream is to live by ourselves. I find it especially hard here at Morney having strangers constantly coming in and out. Usually at our dinner table you will find the head stockman and his wife, the governess, and up to a dozen ringers if the stock camp is in. This means that I can't sit down and have a personal conversation with my family or talk about family problems at the dinner table. It's the privacy I miss most, but I've learnt to compromise.

The men stay out at camp when the mustering is on. It would be impossible to muster a paddock in a single day and return home by dusk for a meal and a sleep. It's just too far. To give an idea of the distance involved, from Morney's homestead to one boundary fence is well over one hundred kilometres. The men go out to camp two to three weeks at a time, so I'm left by myself to manage the station with our governess. I must confess I love it when everyone's away because it gives me time to myself. I work as the station cook and I'm usually on my feet from dawn till dusk. I rarely get the time to do little else except cook, clean and wash clothes.

It would be lovely to have real power but I don't think we'll ever get it—not in my lifetime anyway. Instead we have a generator. We turn it off at night before going to bed. I find it hard to sleep with the noise of the generator going. Maybe it's a subconscious thing, but it makes me think of fires. I prefer to sleep knowing that nothing can short-circuit and cause a fire. The other crazy thing I do is organise the cupboards in such a way that in the event of an emergency I know everything is within easy reach. I also make sure that there is never anything blocking the doorways. I realise this behaviour is the result of having lost so much in the fire at Moothandella. I can't help it. The sadness is still there.

You would think being born and bred in the bush would help you adapt to this kind of lifestyle, but it doesn't. Ashley, my eldest son, is a true city boy. Unlike his two brothers, Ashley has never been much of a bush kid. At boarding school, all his friends were city boys. The day he left school he stayed on in Brisbane. He's not in a hurry to come home. It's hard for any mum to cut the ties and accept that her son's living in the city. I can't help but worry about him. Shannon on the other hand, well I can't work her out at all. She's still at home, but looking forward to going away to boarding school. I think she needs the company of other girls her age. Thankfully the school is only a four-hour drive away. It would be cruel to keep her at home any longer than necessary.

In my opinion, the west is the best place to bring up children when it comes to their education. The School of Distance Education is excellent because it is conducted on a one-to-one basis. The children's work is set out in papers, in plain English, so that even mum can understand it. It's combined with School of the Air classes where the child can talk to a teacher and about six or seven other classmates over the radio. Our kids did maths, reading, social studies and sciences over the radio. When we first moved to Charleville after Warren's death, my children went to 'normal' schools. I found it difficult following their progress because when I spoke to their teachers there seemed to be little response and concern. With distance education, parents are so much more involved with the teachers. We also have the itinerant teachers who come out for a couple of days every year to meet the children and their family.

Boarding school is a whole different kettle of fish. It's difficult for mums as well as dads, especially when you have an unhappy boarder on the phone crying hysterically that no-one loves them, they don't have any friends, everything is terrible and all they want to do is to come back home. I'm lucky that my kids were all outgoing and not too miserable being away from the station. Yet I still had my fair share of sleepless nights, worrying how my boys were coping. Just when I thought I had recovered from one child leaving home, then it would be time to send the next one off. I think I was so wrapped up in packing the boys off to school that I forgot all about Shannon. It's the child left behind who suffers the most. The expense of boarding school is another major concern for many families living in the outback. There's the travel, uniforms, and books to consider. Travel is our biggest problem. The closest bus is in Charleville which is over 600 kilometres away, and then it's on to Brisbane which is even further.

The worst thing about sending children to boarding school is feeling that you, as a parent, miss out on seeing your kids grow up. I've seen friction build up between teenagers and parents who live under the same roof, but in our case, because the boys were away for five years, when we saw them in the holidays or spoke to them on the telephone, we were always on our best behaviour. I think the main advantage is that you end up becoming good friends.

It bothers me when people talk about isolation and how awful it must be for us living so far away from everything ... Everything? In the west, you simply learn to cope with not having things automatically on hand.

When I go to town I always take an esky for frozen goods. Fruit and vegetables are expensive, but you learn to buy in bulk—we keep them in a coldroom. I found it impossible when I lived in Charleville to go to the shop and buy just one tin of peas. I just couldn't do it. Out of habit, I would have to buy at least a dozen tins.

You learn to stock up in the summer months for when the Cooper is in flood. Most of our holiday time is spent shopping. I get some very strange looks from the cashiers at the large shopping centres when I arrive at the checkout with my overflowing trolley. They all think I'm crazy. Sure, there are things we lack, but once again, you learn to compromise and make do with what you have.

Medically speaking, I believe we have a better health care program than what's on offer in the cities. Our doctor is always at the end of the phone and he can be reached day or night for medical advice. I've become quite good at describing an illness or pain over the telephone. I've learnt to be as descriptive as possible. In the city, you can be rushed to casualty in a matter of minutes, but then you can just as easily wait hours before anyone comes to your assistance and then, it would be someone unfamiliar to you. In the bush, we can't complain about our flying doctor service. Dr Bob is fantastic. The nursing staff are wonderful as well. Sympathy is something you won't find in big city hospitals. Even when Warren died I found the support from the medical staff incredible.

Some people keep their pain too much to themselves, and that's where Anne Maree comes into the picture—this is where she shines. I first met Anne Maree when the first flying priest, Father Terry Loth, brought her along on one of his rounds. Father Loth occasionally dropped in at Moothandella and later at Morney Plains, but I'd never felt comfortable confiding in him. Perhaps it was his personality, or the fact that he was a man. At any rate, he looked and acted very much the 'man of the cloth' so I never felt quite right telling him my personal problems. Anne Maree is different. She's the exact opposite to the priests we had coming round.

Religion in the bush has always been friendly. You went to church because it was generally considered more of a social outing and not just a matter of going to church. I was baptised a Catholic and grew up a practising Catholic. As a child I looked forward to the visits of the Rosary Sisters, who always looked so saintly in their habits. The time I spent with the Mayfield Ladies was always filled with little religious rituals. They used to make a habit of reciting the rosary in the car. I wouldn't dare cry, 'Watch out for the kangaroo!' when one came bounding our way for fear of disrupting their 'Hail Marys'. In church, the Mayfield Ladies would bring a picnic basket and a thermos of cordial while we kids amused ourselves pulling the wings off blowflies and lining them up along the pew.

When I left school I went through one of those phases where you just up and leave the Church because you simply don't see any use for it anymore. At the time I said I would never go to church again, but then as I settled down and had my own family, off I went back to church. When Warren died, the shock was so great that I cursed God. It was the Church's fault and it was definitely God's fault. Why did God take him from me when I needed him most? I seriously contemplated suicide after Warren's death. I couldn't live without him. The more I thought about it, I knew I could never leave my kids on their own. The kind of childhood I'd experienced made it impossible for me to leave them by themselves without a mum or a dad. The Church preached that suicide was a sin anyway. A mortal sin if I recall correctly. Reason thankfully took over before my emotions got the better of me. It wasn't until years later that I was able to rediscover my faith. Once I got past the stage of cursing God, I turned to the Church looking for some kind of answer to all the madness I'd been through. I had to learn to be 'friends' with the Church before I could be a part of the Church.

Anne Maree coming into my life changed everything. Straightaway I knew she was one of us. I'll never forget when she took over the Aerial Ministry and flew in one day and almost landed on the road. She had just gained her pilot's licence and was still trying to find her way around the bush. Morney's dirt airstrip runs alongside our main road to Brisbane and as Sister was flying in, I saw her coming in to land on the road, obviously thinking it was our airstrip. When she suddenly realised that there wasn't a windsock in sight, she pulled sharply on the throttle and flew across the road to land safely on the other side. We still joke about her little 'mishap' today.

Anne Maree relates to our way of life. She must have the biggest shoulders and ears of anyone I know because she has to put up with all our problems and carrying-on. She's part of my family. I confess that I do worry about her. Because she has become personal friends with the women she visits, we all depend on her. If anyone deserves a long holiday at the end of the year, it would have to be her. I think she really needs to go away and unwind. Her job may seem fairly straightforward—flying around the countryside, visiting people and 'overnighting' in their homes— but there's a lot more to it. It's an incredibly draining job. I know I couldn't cope with sleeping in a strange bed every night, let alone shouldering so many people's problems. Even though Longreach is her base, you could never call it her home. Her home is her Cessna. That's where she practically lives.

Anne Maree and I can talk about religion—how the mass and the sacraments have changed over the years—and she always keeps me informed as to what is happening in the Church today. She's prepared all my kids for the sacraments, which is important to me as a practising Catholic. But she doesn't come around to preach religion. Don't think for an instant either that Anne Maree only flies in to see us women. She's also here for the men. Peter looks forward to her flying in. She's someone he can talk to when he's got a worry or a concern he wants to unburden. She'll watch the rugby with him and then they'll talk shop. Men can relate to Anne Maree and if there is ever a problem, they feel happy to talk it over with her.

People say that life in the bush has changed dramatically over the years and I agree with them. Television is something I think is slowly destroying life out west. On Sundays, we used to go to the pictures in Windorah. It didn't matter what was showing, it was just an occasion to socialise. Nowadays, everyone has a telly, a video recorder and an air-conditioner. Why on earth should they leave their lounge room to go out in the heat and travel the distance to see a movie they didn't really want to see in the first place? When I was growing up, distance was never really a problem. We'd go out to Cunnamulla—a four-hour trip—for a game of football and camp the night on the banks of the creek. Today, if folk can't go somewhere and be home in a couple of hours, then they won't bother going at all. In my opinion, things are getting too fast to suit the outback life.

I don't necessarily wish for my kids to stay in the bush. At this point in time, Jason is the only one who's happy to work on the land. It won't be easy for him because the way things are shaping up, I can't see there being much of a future in the outback. He's keen to own his own property, but having seen it from both sides, I think he's crazy. My experience of living at Moothandella as well as managing a large station like Morney tells me that he'd be far better off working on a company station. It's just too risky trying to make it on your own. If you are employed as a manager on a company station the wool and cattle prices don't influence your income as drastically as if you were managing a private place. It's also not that easy going from station hand to becoming a manager. You can wait years for a manager to retire before being promoted. Jason really hates school. I can't say I blame him, as I too would prefer to be out there driving a tractor or building cattle yards rather than sitting in a classroom learning about Shakespeare, which is something he'll never need. But it worries me that if, in a few years time, he did decide to do something and needed to have school subjects, then it would be my fault because I didn't give him the education he needs. I just hope my boys will do well and that they are happy.

I think I've been lucky having two husbands who've both been very patient with me and are good listeners. Your husband needs to be your best friend. When I think about it, there aren't too many marriages out here that fall apart, because you learn quickly to establish a strong mateship. Men in the bush relate to women easily. I for one can't handle sitting around in the kitchen drinking endless cups of tea nattering about the kiddies or the latest fashions. I'd rather talk about cattle prices or motors. Even growing up, perhaps because there were more men around and so few women, I always felt more comfortable with the blokes.

Peter and I often talk about where we will retire to. Truthfully, we

Peter and the kids.

haven't a clue where we will end up. To start with, I can't find the right climate to suit me. I hate cold weather and rain, although we don't have much of that out here. If I had to live somewhere other than Morney, it would still have to be in the bush, because this is where I have my roots. I couldn't stand living in the city. I'd hate to have to lock myself in a small house, with no space to move, inside or out. I live here because I want to, not because I have to. It is the kind of life I want and chose for myself and my family. It's the companionship of my husband and such people as Anne Maree that makes my world run smoothly. The bush is definitely changing and although I'm sometimes saddened by all this so-called progress, it's where I intend to remain and live out the rest of my days.

A CALLING

As I consider Jeannie's remarkable strength and self-reliance, I am thankful that I was raised in a close and loving family. It is from my family—from my parents in particular—that I received my faith, as well as the courage to enter religious life, and later, to start flying.

As a child, I remember Dad telling us to turn off the telly and the radio when he came home from work. We were told to keep it down and make as little noise as possible. I found out later that this was because his nerves had been affected by the Second World War. Dad hated noise. I never understood why until he told me about the horror of Changi. Dad was twenty when he enlisted in the army. Plenty of his mates died in the camps and he helped bury them in unmarked dirt graves. He never seemed bitter or angry when he talked about his ordeal as a prisoner of war. In his own discreet way, he taught me a lot about courage. The courage he showed all those years ago just to stay alive continues to inspire me in my work today.

Mum says that Dad and she met at the end of the war through their love of tennis. During the war years she used to wait on tables at the Catholic United Services Association on Saturdays, and afterwards attend the dances in the memorial hall in Toowoomba. Cheap meals were served to the returned soldiers and they were entertained with sing alongs around the piano. When Mum met him, Dad was working for the Jensen Bros grocery store, in partnership with his older brother, Ron. She knew that Dad, like most of the prisoners of war, had suffered at the hands of the Japanese, especially on the infamous Burma Railway Line. It was hard for

Mum and Dad's official engagement photo.

Dad to get back into civilian life. Mum and tennis were just what he needed. They 'kept company' for three years, despite the warning from Dad's mother not to let a Catholic girl 'get him'. A Catholic girl had already 'got' one of her sons. Naturally, this advice was ignored and the marriage took place on 31 January 1949, at the Mary Immaculate Church in Brisbane.

I was born five years later on 4 December 1954, at St Vincent's Maternity Hospital in Toowoomba—the first daughter and second child. From all accounts, it was an easy birth compared to what Mum went through with my older brother, Peter, four years earlier. My parents decided to christen me Anne, but the aunties on my mum's side strongly advised against it, complaining I would be nick-named 'Annie'. As a compromise, I was given two names—Anne Maree—to keep the family peace.

Ten days after my birth, I was baptised a Catholic by our local parish priest, Father O'Dwyer. As Mum tells it, an argument broke out as soon as I made my appearance at the baptismal font when the extended families caught sight of my red hair. Both Mum and Dad denied that there were any redheads in their immediate family and flatly disclaimed all respon-sibility. After some clever detective work and scouring of the family albums it was eventually traced back to Dad's side.

Within eleven months of my birth, my brother Anthony arrived feet first. My sister Bernadette was born thirteen months later, and in October 1958, my youngest brother David. This meant that Mum had her hands full with four active toddlers under the

Our house at Toowoomba.

age of four. Her doctor, Dr Hickey senior, wanted to know if we were all trying to break a record!

We lived in a pleasant, raised, two-storey timber house at 267 West Street across the road from a golf course. From our sunroom we had a magnificent view overlooking Toowoomba. The house had four large bed-rooms and two toilets—the pink one and the blue one. There were four palm trees in our front yard as well as a huge Norfolk Island pine in which we strung coloured Christmas lights every December. You could see them from miles away, and people used to slow down when they drove past our house to admire them.

Dad bought his own little corner store across the road from our house which he managed with his brother-in-law, Frank Quinn. During their thirty-year partnership, the store, like their families, continued to grow.

The Jensen, Bowdler and Quinn cousins with Santa.

After each new extension to the shop Mum and Aunty Clare would despairingly declare 'enough'. But I suppose Dad and Uncle Frank's business acumen proved sound, and the Gumleaf Food Centre, as it was officially called, did a wonderful job of feeding, clothing and educating the twelve children from the two families.

Thanks to Mum's sister and brother, we had a bevy of cousins from two even larger Catholic families. The Quinns, like ourselves, lived within cooee of the shop so we grew up as an extended family of sorts. Altogether there were twenty of us and my siblings and I were very close to our cousins. We all went to the same schools and celebrated our birthdays and Christmases together. With so many cousins on hand, I was never short of someone to play with. We used to ride around on our flashy Malvern Star pushbikes and go fishing for yabbies with just a line and a Coke bottle. If we were really lucky, as a special treat we'd be allowed to cram in the back of the rickety shop ute and tour the town with Dad or Uncle Frank at the wheel.

I was a tomboy as a kid and always joined in the games with my brothers and boy cousins. My sister, Bernadette, liked to play with dolls, while I preferred toy guns. Although we are the best of friends now, we used to fight when we were kids. Sometimes we would divide our bedroom

Dad and Uncle Frank's shop ute.

into two sections—hers and mine—so we wouldn't have to talk to each other. I always felt I conformed while she bucked the system.

Our family lived a religious and disciplined life. We grew up with a roster system for sweeping,

washing up and taking out
the garbage. We were a
very close family, but there
was a lot of freedom in our
closeness. We all loved the
fact that our dad owned a
grocery store. Although it
wasn't an easy business
and seemed to be a con-
stant worry for Dad and

Promotion day at the Gumleaf.

Uncle Frank, from a child's point of view it meant that we were the envy
of every other sweet-toothed kid in the district. I felt quite privileged
having lollies and other goodies virtually on tap. However, taking anything from the shop without Dad's permission was forbidden. I remember
confessing to Father McMorrow in Saturday morning confession about
stealing lollies on more than one occasion. To my relief, I would be wearily
dismissed with just one 'Our Father' and five 'Hail Marys' as penance for
my crime.

My brothers and I loved helping out in the shop after school, stocking
shelves and sweeping floors. When it was approaching closing time, we
could even ring up the customers' items on the cash register. If we found
any coins on the lino floor, they were ours to keep. We never guessed at
the time that this was how Dad paid us.

We also enjoyed hanging around with the staff. They were quite a collec-
tion of characters and were, in a way, part of the family. If one of them had
to be fired, it was most unpleasant for all of us. Dad prided himself and his
staff on giving exceptional customer service. He was always telling us how
crucial it was to acknowledge the customers with a little nod of the head, a
smile and a 'Good morning, Mrs Jones'. While Uncle Frank seemed to enjoy
being out the back looking after the financial side and chatting to the 'travellers' (salesmen), Dad would rather be exchanging greetings with the customers and making sure the shelves were well stocked.

In summer, when temperatures soared and the shop fan did little more
than churn the sticky air, we would help fetch watermelons from the back
of the shop and carry them to the front display. Dad's rule was that if any
fruit or produce fell on the floor we could claim it as our own. Somehow

we always managed to have at least one watermelon a day. We'd lug the bruised fruit back home and sit out in the cool of dusk on the front lawn seeing who could spit the pips the furthest.

As the shop expanded, Dad hired five new cash register girls. There was one in particular whom I really admired. Her name was Dell. She was promoted to chief cash register girl within weeks of being employed and instantly became my heroine. The way Dell so deftly and expertly rang the till with her long painted nails greatly impressed me. That was what I was going to be when I grew up—a glamorous register girl in my father's shop.

The only time Dad got a real break from the shop was during our two annual holidays to the Gold Coast. Each January we would spend a week in a motel, and each May, three weeks in a rented house opposite the beach. These were the highlights of the year for me. We would all be bundled into the packed Zephyr station wagon and impatient Dad would drive like a man possessed, speeding so that we would arrive at the Coast on time. To make things more interesting, there was always a good chance that one or more of us would start feeling carsick. The family named a creek after me when I managed to throw up at the same spot two years in a row. It must have really frustrated Dad to know that while we were parked beside the road with one of us vomiting, those slow trucks and hopeless drivers that he loved to overtake were going to get ahead of us again.

It was magic falling asleep at night listening to the sound of the surf. I loved Surfers Paradise back then, with its sand dune beaches, in the days before all the skyscrapers sprung up. In the last week of the holidays, we made regular excursions to the Currumbin Bird Sanctuary and Jack Evans' Porpoise Pool. We weren't allowed to go into the surf without being supervised. I always remember Mum panicking and yelling out to us when she thought that we had gone too far, even

David, Peter, Bernadette, me and Tony at Surfers Paradise.

though we were still quite close and swimming between the flags with hundreds of other holidaymakers.

It was at home that my faith was first nourished. Religion has always been important to my parents. Dad, who was raised as an Anglican, converted to Catholicism before he married Mum. Both he and Mum gave us the value of a God in our lives. They were firm advocates of 'the family that prays together stays together'.

The Jensen family.

Mum had a habit of saying little prayers as we were driving along. I remember begging her when we were leaving for our annual holidays to let us have a break from the usual family practice of saying the rosary. I pleaded with her to recite all twenty-one on the drive to Surfers Paradise so as to avoid saying them for the rest of the holidays, but Mum never gave in. Instead we always got three extra rosaries in on the drive up to the Coast. These were recited out aloud— one at the beginning of the three-hour drive for a safe trip, one in the middle for good measure, and one towards the end in thanks for a pleasant trip. As much as I disliked being interrupted in the midst of a good comic book, I always felt that these rosaries were quite important. Given Dad's frustration on the road, driving at what seemed to us to be only a hair's width behind the car in front and poised ready to overtake at a moment's notice, perhaps what we should have prayed for was a stress-free trip. Not just a safe one.

We also recited the rosary each night after tea, kneeling around a lighted candle. Slouching down on the couch was tolerated for about ten minutes. Because there are five decades to the rosary, it was ideal that there were five of us. We each had our own decade. Mine was always the second. It was a great challenge to see how fast we could say our parts without Mum sternly warning us to recite properly. Each decade was offered up for some special intention. Actually, everything you could possibly think of was prayed for in our household. We prayed that we would make the right decisions. We prayed for the dead and the dying. Passing exams was always a popular one, as well as praying for a good recovery whenever one of us happened to be sick. My brother Tony was too embarrassed to mention to any of his non-Catholic friends that we had to say the rosary every night. If we had visitors staying, he found it mortifying when we suddenly had to excuse ourselves and retreat to the next room for our prayers.

We used to say grace before meals, and grace after meals—when Mum remembered—but it was always in a quick, painless, non-meditative sort of fashion with everyone already buttering the bread or adding salt to their dinner. In my early childhood we went to mass four times a week and we always sat in the same pew up the front. When I was older, I went every day. Back in the 1960s, mass was said in Latin and women had to wear a hat when they entered a church. Many a time I didn't have one, so I would have to put a handkerchief on my head instead. If I didn't have a hanky, I thought that putting my hand on my head would do just the same.

Every Tuesday night, Mum would go off to novena—a type of prayer gathering. I was supposed to be sound asleep in bed, but instead I would sneak out and Dad and I would watch *The Rifle Man*, starring Chuck Connors. As soon as I heard Mum's car pulling into the driveway, I'd guiltily race back to bed. This meant another visit to Father McMorrow in the confessional and several more 'Our Fathers' for penance, but I thought it was well worth it at the time.

Me, aged fourteen.

I believed very much, back then, what I was taught about purgatory and hell. If you died with a mortal sin on your soul, then you were going to hell forever and ever, amen. Venial sins were not quite so bad, as you were still able to get to heaven after doing time in purgatory. The best thing about confession was that it wiped your slate clean. It was very common for practising Catholics to wear a medal engraved with the words: 'I am a Catholic. In case of an accident, please call a priest'. As my brother Tony used to joke, 'Forget the doctor. It's far more important to get your soul saved!'

I completed my entire primary schooling with the Presentation Sisters at St Anthony's in Toowoomba. The sisters there wore long black robes, and a tight white collar and a headpiece with a pointed peak. Huge wooden regulation rosary beads dangled from their belts. The only skin we ever saw belonged to their faces and hands, not that we could imagine that they had skin anywhere else! One of the questions visiting sisters always asked was, 'Hands up who wants to be a nun?'

All the little girls would shoot their hands straight up into the air, myself included. But, of course, at that early age I didn't take it all that seriously. I liked and respected the sisters at my school, but I never thought, back then, that one day I would join their congregation and devote myself to religious life.

For my secondary schooling I rode two miles on pushbike to St Ursula's College—a school for girls run by the Ursuline Sisters. My mum was one of the foundation pupils at the school so it was only natural that my sister and I should follow in her footsteps. I took the commercial subjects as I could not cope with the academic ones. I am forever grateful to my parents for their attitude of 'just do your best'. Despite the extra tuition in some subjects, I still had to struggle to keep up with the other students. Somehow I was never overly concerned with studies and boasted to the other girls that I was going to leave school at the end of the Junior year to work in my dad's shop. That, or play tennis professionally.

Under 18 State tennis champion—I won 150 trophies!

Tennis, by this stage, was a major part of my life and I was seriously contemplating the idea of turning professional. Playing tennis had developed from an enjoyable pastime to a passion which I carried throughout my childhood right until the day I entered religious life.

I'd first become interested in the game when I was seven. Peter, my oldest brother, was already playing and his coach, Mrs Turner, suggested that I come along with him. And so began my Saturday afternoon coaching lessons. During the week, I would practise by myself hitting balls against the brick wall of the shop, in between the parked cars of customers. This held me in good stead for tournaments in later years when I became known as a good 'brick wall' player—I just kept returning the ball. At the age of ten, my parents proudly drove me in their new car to my first tournament in Allora. I won, and was on the road to many wins after that. By fifteen, I'd collected more than 150 trophies for my efforts, as well as every age title in Toowoomba and the under-eighteen Queensland title.

Dad eventually bought a block of land across the road from the Gumleaf Food Centre and built our own tennis court, complete with lights so we could play at night. He always liked to joke that 'the family who played together, stayed together'. All my spare time was taken up practising serves and volleys with other local players. Training for, and competing at, tournaments around Australia and New Zealand meant there was little or no time for anything else. Once I played in a tournament against a future Australian champion, Wendy Turnbull, and I'm proud to say that I gave her quite a run for her money. Wendy, of course, went on to make tennis her very profitable career while I entered the convent. My dream back then was to play at Wimbledon one day. All my time and energy were focused on that goal. I eventually made it to Wimbledon, twenty years later, but not as a player, only as a tourist. It was the year Boris Becker won, and I've had a soft spot for him ever since.

I graduated from high school in 1971 without a clue as to what I would do next. I had abandoned the idea of working on Dad's cash register and there were not many options for girls at the time, especially in a country town like Toowoomba. It was a toss-up between teaching, nursing or secretarial work. Perhaps because many of my classmates from St Ursula's were going on to study at the teachers' college, I too decided to follow suit and study for a diploma in education.

As I had outgrown the pushbike, Dad let me borrow the shop ute to drive the two kilometres to the Darling Downs Institute of Advanced Education. I never enjoyed college. From the very start, I knew I'd made the wrong decision. I think I was too young and immature, and my shyness didn't help matters much. My first year was full of frustrations and disappointments. Study was tedious and the classes in practical teaching were a nightmare for me.

My growing dissatisfaction and unhappiness were also due, in part, to having passed into the open bracket tennis tournaments. Pitted against more senior, professional players, I saw clearly that I could not make a career out of competition tennis. My life, which previously had centred almost completely on tennis, began to lose direction and focus. It was a con-

Sportsgirl of the Week, 1969.

fusing time and I started to think seriously about what I wanted to do with my future. So, on a Friday in October, when I received an offer of employment with the Commonwealth Bank, I considered it carefully. I spent the weekend talking to my friends and parents about whether or not I should leave college. Luckily I had finished my first-year exams at the institute, so I already had something behind me and the year of training did not seem like a complete waste.

The bank wanted my reply first thing on the Monday morning. I can still remember the song that came on the radio as I drove back from the institute after telling my lecturers that I was leaving the course. It was, 'The Happiest Girl in the Whole USA' sung by Donna Fargo. Without a doubt, I was the happiest girl in Toowoomba that morning.

The Commonwealth Bank gave me my first taste of the adult world and real work. Earning my own money made me feel free and independent, and I liked seeing my bank balance grow each week. I was responsible for collecting withdrawal and deposit slips from various small businesses and agencies scattered around town each morning. I always enjoyed the pleas-ant early morning stroll before the bank opened its doors at ten o'clock for customers. When they came to the counter it was usually to write in their pensions or child endowments in their bankbooks. This was way back in the days before computers and I had to check any discrepancies between bankbooks and statements. I came to enjoy my fifteen months with the Commonwealth Bank, and although still painfully shy, I seemed to get on well with most of the staff.

Every Wednesday afternoon after work, I would drive up to St Ursula's College and become the 'eyes' of an elderly blind sister, Mother Kevin. I read to her and kept her company in a small, cramped office at the convent. I like to think now that she may have already envisioned a religious life for me.

It was some time in June of 1973 that, out of the blue, a Presentation Sister from Brisbane wrote me a letter that was to change my life. The sister, Pauline, had been stationed at St Anthony's parish in Toowoomba several years earlier. We had become good friends while we both worked with The Children of Mary Sodality—a religious group which encouraged parishioners to attend monthly communion. After she left Toowoomba for Brisbane, we only corresponded at Christmas. In her letter, she asked if I would be interested in meeting a novice, a young sister in her second year of religious training, who was in Toowoomba doing community experience at the Presentation convent. It all seemed ordinary enough, a simple and common request. I had, in fact, glimpsed the novice, Sister Glenda, at daily mass and wondered who she was. She looked beautiful and so serene.

The idea of religious life had already taken hold somewhere in the back of my mind, but it was not until receiving Sister Pauline's letter that I acted on it. I was seized with a terrible panic. How could I bring myself to talk to Sister Glenda? What would I say to her? Would she think me ridiculous? It took a lot of courage just to pick up the phone and call her to make an appointment. Apprehension made me sick in the stomach.

We agreed to meet on a Saturday. When the day finally arrived, I could not concentrate on anything before my visit to the convent. What would the other sisters think of my coming to see Sister Glenda? I had never talked to anyone about religious life. Would the sisters be expecting me to enter? I was met at the convent door by Sister Kieran, the superior of the house. She took me into the parlour and introduced me to Sister Glenda. It was all so formal. There was an elegant polished table and four straight-backed chairs in the room. It lacked the homely touch of our lounge room, which added to my anxiety. I had no idea of what sort of questions to ask. I just assumed, or hoped, that Glenda would do all the talking about what it was like to enter religious life. What do you ask someone when you really are unsure of why you are there in the first place? When I think back to that momentous meeting, it seems that Glenda talked mainly about herself and her life in the novitiate, but it wasn't what she said that was important. I kept thinking, 'This is what I want for myself.'

Something within me just clicked and everything suddenly made sense. I know I definitely came away from that meeting with the overwhelming certainty that I wanted to enter religious life. I felt on top of the world. Other people might have made such a move by themselves, but I am someone who needs a bit of a push and some encouragement. It may sound like a well-worn cliché, but God works in many different ways, through many different people and situations. How does anyone know what is the right thing to do? Each one of us makes his or her particular response to what I see as a universal invitation to discover reality and say

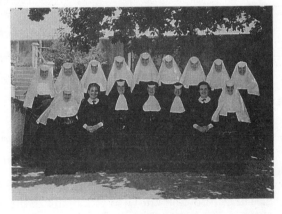

The Presentation Sisters

'Yes' to life. Some people ask me how I could decide to give up my 'freedom', to forgo marriage, children, even sex. It is difficult to recall my exact attitude at the time—I just knew that I wanted to enter religious life. I never saw it as 'losing my freedom'. As for sex, back then it wasn't talked about so bluntly—you hardly saw it on the TV or even read about it. I didn't have a steady boyfriend at the time and although I mixed easily with boys and enjoyed playing tennis with them, that was as far as it went.

The calling to religious life is different for each person. I grew up with the knowledge that God had given me the gift of life. This gift of life, this gift of faith—for it really is a gift—was further nourished at home by my parents. Along with my three brothers and sister, I was supported and encouraged to practise my faith in the Catholic Church. I went to Catholic schools where I was taught exclusively by nuns who were, in my eyes, gentle and holy women.

The meeting with Sister Glenda was truly a beautiful moment—one that was to change the entire direction of my life. It revealed to me a desire which had been within me for quite some time—the desire to enter religious life. I wrote to Sister Pauline indicating that I wanted to join the congregation of the Presentation Sisters of Queensland. I confessed to her that I knew nothing about religious life, nor had much real understanding of the Bible or God! She wrote back telling me that I would learn—the real question which I had to ask myself was whether I was emotionally ready for such a commitment.

Weeks later, I drove to Brisbane to meet with Sister Pauline. I had never ventured very far from Toowoomba. I was the real country kid making her way to the big smoke. I prayed for every traffic light to turn red so I could check the directory, which was on my lap, to find the way to the Clayfield Convent. As was the general practice back then for young women considering entering the Presentation Order, a meeting was organised with the Mother General to discuss why one wished to enter religious life. Sister Pauline introduced me to Mother Gabriel Hogan, who asked me many personal questions. She wanted to know how I related to my parents, brothers and sister, my feelings about teaching (at that stage the Presentation Sisters worked either as primary or secondary school teachers) and my life in general. She talked about the history of the sisters and about life in a religious community. She also wanted to know what some of my interests were. When I told her about playing tennis professionally, she wondered how I would cope with giving up competitive sport. To this day I still do not know how I made it through that interview. I was so shy and terrified, but somehow I must have given satisfaction, since a few months later I was accepted as a postulant (a candidate for admission into a religious order).

Back home in Toowoomba, the letters began to flow between Sister Pauline and myself. All my insecurities were coming to the fore. She kept reassuring me that I would learn and grow in my love of God and that I should stop worrying. I asked her how I should go about breaking the news to my parents as I had been agonising over the easiest way to tell them.

One Saturday morning, when Mum and Dad were still in bed, I walked into their room and calmly announced that I was going to become a Presentation Sister. The news certainly got them out of bed. I don't think they knew what hit them! Their first reaction was one of complete astonishment. Mum burst into tears. Dad just scratched his head a lot. Poor Mum! Her concern was that I was not mature enough to make such a commitment for life. She did have a point, considering I was only eighteen at the time. She was also worried that I would be kept cloistered with other sisters in a convent and that she would never see me again! I had to reassure her that joining the convent was not like serving a prison sentence and I was sure they would be allowed to visit me. I explained that I had been accepted as a postulant with the Presentation Sisters, and that I had thought long and hard before making my decision. I had never felt as determined and resolved about anything before in my life. What I needed now was their support and approval. As it turned out, I need not have worried myself sick before telling them.

Once they recovered from the initial shock, they were very supportive—in fact, Dad was secretly thrilled. We talked an awful lot that morning and by the end of it all, I felt exhausted, but also giddy with relief and happiness because I had the full support of my parents.

That same day I told my parents about my decision to enter the convent, I drove over to St Ursula's to break the good news to Mother Kevin. I wasn't sure how she would react, since she herself was an Ursuline Sister and might have wished me to join her congregation. Actually, I had wondered whether I should be entering the Ursuline order. After all, I knew more Ursuline Sisters than Presentation Sisters, or 'Pressies' as we called them, and had more contact with them. Indeed, Mother Kevin did not hide a certain disappointment, but all the same I sensed she was glad to know I was entering religious life.

I have a photograph of myself and my cousin John which was taken by my father when we appeared in a play together in primary school. I am about eight, chubby, dressed as an angel in a tutu with coathangers and cellophane for wings. John is standing next to me disguised as the devil. John loves this picture as much as I do because, as he likes to joke, today he is a mischievous rebel while I am a nun! We live by the choices we make and mine was to dedicate the rest of my life to a religious calling. Looking back, now more than twenty-four years down the track, I know that the hand of God was working in all of this, as there was no way I was ever going to do anything about it myself. I needed a push. God gave me a shove.

CIRCUIT ONE

COLLEEN GIRDLER— NOCKATUNGA STATION

While it must have been difficult for my mum to contemplate 'losing' me to the convent, she fully supported me in my decision to enter the order. It is fairly common out west for mothers to suffer enforced separation—when their children go to boarding school or when a sick or injured family member has to be transferred to a far-off city for treatment. But the hardest separation of all has perhaps been endured by Colleen Girdler.

I was introduced to Colleen at a mass gathering at the Noccundra pub in August 1993. A pub may be an unusual place to hold a church service, but out bush, it's as good as any! I had flown to the Noccundra pub with Father Frank Anderson so Frank could celebrate mass in a small room behind the bar. Colleen was a friend of the publican's wife, Leah Cameron, and would occasionally lend a hand with the bar work.

The following afternoon, as Frank and I were getting ready to fly out to our next destination, Colleen told me how much she had appreciated being able to attend mass and how she missed singing in church—so much so that I later sent her a tape of the hymns we sang.

I didn't catch up with Colleen again until the following year when I landed at Bellalie Station, where she was then living, to say 'g'day'. I stayed three nights due to engine trouble and it was during this time that I came to really know Colleen and her story. She told me how she had turned to God after hitting rock bottom.

I was able to meet her again when she moved with her husband, Allen, to Nockatunga Station. It was here at Nockatunga that she learnt that her only son had been arrested for an alleged involvement in a double murder. Colleen bears this anguish with a straightforward courage that amazes me.

'Pete's* in jail. He's been arrested for murder.' The telephone connection, as bad as it was, could not disguise the hysteria and panic in my daughter-in-law's voice. 'The police have arrested Pete. A double murder.'

I dropped the phone. No-one can fathom what effect those words had on me as a mum. The total shock, horror and disbelief. The anguish. What could I do? I was living and working on a 2.5 million acre property smack in the middle of nowhere, with my daughter-in-law crying over the telephone, telling me that my only son had been arrested. Accused of murder. Thousands of miles away.

Over the following weeks the details of what had occurred slowly fell into place. There was a mention on the news late one night. The bodies of a couple who had been missing for some time were found by police, each at a separate location. The victims—apparently a drug dealer and his wife—were already known to the police. Two men were subsequently arrested on suspicion of murder. It was reported that a vehicle belonging to one of the suspects was spotted at the scene of the crime and another bloke was picked up later after a tip-off. Various statements were made to the cops and one of the suspects implicated my son. No-one can say even now that Pete was involved except this one bloke. Ironically, this same bloke is now out on bail while my son has been held in remand for over two years awaiting trial and his chance to tell the truth.

Pete's wife was questioned by the cops. When she called me at Nock-atunga Station she was in a state of shock. She seriously believed the cops would take her boys away because she thought she would be implicated as an accessory and go to jail as well.

When Pete was a young tyke, if something troubled him he would have nightmares and often sleepwalk. That was always the telltale sign that something was troubling him. Later, when I asked my daughter-in-law if she'd noticed Pete behaving strangely before his arrest—Did he have nightmares,

My son, Pete*

drink more than usual or seem on edge?—she told me 'no'. There'd been nothing of the sort, no indication whatsoever that something was upsetting him.

I don't believe my son has the ability to murder another person. Pete is no saint, but he's no murderer either. You would have to be a hardened criminal to take someone's life. My son could never do that. He claims he is innocent and I believe him. I'm dealing with a person I know—my son. As a mother, you can't not stand by your kids. No matter what they do, it's your duty as a mum to be there for them.

The natural reaction is to apologise. Months after the murders I wanted to call or go round and see the victims' parents and their families. Face to face. Friends had to say to me, 'Colleen, don't go and see the parents of these people to apologise for their pain.' Yet I still can't help wondering what the parents are going through. I can't imagine what they must be feeling.

The first time I visited Long Bay jail in Sydney was a real shock. Nothing prepares you for going into a maximum security prison. Seeing your kid in a white jumpsuit—zipped up the back with a lock on it—is pretty hard to take. Shut away in the remand centre, which is supposed to be for those awaiting trial, but being treated like a criminal without any dignity or rights, is the picture of my son that I'll never forget. Pete in a white jumpsuit saying, 'Believe me, Mum, I didn't do it.'

If you aren't familiar with Long Bay, from the outside it doesn't look like a jail at all. In fact the gardens out front make the place seem almost pleasant. Inside, the visiting area is quite attractive. They have tried to make an effort with sun umbrellas, lunch tables and chairs. You'd almost believe you were somewhere else. In fact it could be anywhere, until you take a closer look and see that all the tables and chairs are screwed into the concrete and on the surrounding high wall walks a guard toting a gun. That's the ugly reminder which catapults you back to reality.

It's a long, hard drive from Nockatunga Station in outback Queensland to Long Bay Correctional Complex. On one occasion I brought Pete's youngest boy, my grandson, with me to see his dad. At the end of visiting hour, after we'd said our goodbyes to Pete, my grandson decided to hide the key to the visitor's locker where I'd left my handbag. I asked him to tell me where he had put it, but, thinking it was some kind of game, the kid wouldn't say. Exasperated, I turned to one of the wardens and jokingly said, 'Look at that innocent little face.'

'Yeah,' the warden replied, 'look at the blokes down there. They all have innocent little faces too.'

If I wasn't such a lady I would have given her a piece of my mind. I've learnt to hold my tongue because I know full well that Pete could cop it later on.

If Pete is sentenced, he'll be sent to a maximum security prison. For the past fifteen years I have been living and working on cattle stations in outback south-west Queensland. Since Pete's arrest, I've driven down to see him a number of times because the courts like to see a member of the family present. It helps the situation. My second husband, Allen, came out with me once, but for a bushie who has never strayed too far from the outback, to have to come to a city, let alone Long Bay jail, was a truly horrific experience.

Allen Girdler is a true bushie. He's the one responsible for showing the outback to me in a whole different light. Like most blokes raised on the land, he's not much of a talker, but through him I've learnt to believe in myself again. The same goes for Anne Maree. She arrived at a time in my life when I was really at a crossroad. Throughout this entire ordeal she has supported me as only a true friend can, and has never judged me or my son. To other people I may appear strong and self-reliant, but only Allen and Anne Maree know how much pain I carry. I rely on them to help me stay balanced. I think they treat me like one of those old scrubber bulls that you hear the stockmen joking about, 'Don't force them, just poke 'em along and you'll get them to go wherever you want.'

I grew up in a small town in New Zealand. My parents were middle-of-the-road, ordinary people. Our mum was a gentle soul with a wonderful sense of humour. It was through her, no doubt, that I came to believe in the Lord and to know that no matter what happens to me, He never sends me more than I can bear. Dad, on the other hand, was a government worker, quite successful in his particular department, but not, I feel, a very good father. With a brother four years my senior and a sister four years my junior, I was that middle child, the one that is not old enough to do *this*, but definitely old enough to know better than *that*.

With my brother Terry in New Zealand.

My early memories of childhood are mainly of being on the road, constantly on the move from one town to another. To gain any sort of a promotion, my father had to be transferred every few years. This was hard going on Mum who was quite a sickly lady, but I never once heard her complain. It was from Mum that I learnt to put down roots and make a home wherever I go.

I came to Australia on 17 July 1963, just four days after my marriage. Nineteen years of age, with stars in my eyes and a husband I was proud to stand beside, my only goal in life was to be a good wife, mother and homemaker. I thought everything else would fall into place. Looking back, I realise just how young and naive I really was, but at the time I thought myself extremely worldly and wise.

The first five or six years of married life were spent living in a caravan, travelling from one construction site to another, mainly in the State of Victoria. Our first child, Pete, was born just one day after our first wedding anniversary. Our daughter, Marina,* arrived four years later. As to be expected, there were the usual problems experienced by young people adjusting to married life but my husband, Greg,* and I seemed to survive them. It was only in our sixth year that things seemed to be veering from my grand plan. Our marriage began to break down.

Our first home was in Canberra. Pete had started school and I wanted him to have the stability I'd never known as a child. My dream was for us to stay in the one town so that the kids could complete their education in one school. But after a few years in Canberra, we were on the move again. Greg was offered a position in Melbourne which was too good to refuse, but by now our marriage was falling apart. I pleaded with him to leave me with the children so that we could make a life of our own, he surprised me by buying a block of land on the Mornington Peninsula. He promised me that we would build a new home and settle down. Naive and trusting as I was,

I really did think at the time that our problems were over and that we were headed for a new beginning.

The house in Mornington was duly completed—a lovely home built exactly the way we wanted in a new suburb surrounded by families starting out like ourselves. With both the children happy in their schools, life took on the normality of suburbia. Greg won by tender a government job in partnership with two others. He was a clever, charismatic man able to convince people that he was the only one who could do the job. I still remember the excitement that was caused by his win. Ten thousand dollars! It seemed like a small fortune. In no time at all, other jobs rolled in, one after the other, and as they got bigger, so did an all-consuming urge to be even more successful and wealthy.

As our finances grew, our home life deteriorated. Once again Greg and I were drifting apart. Pete was at an age to realise that things were not as they should be between his father and me. It seemed no matter how hard I prayed, God wasn't listening to me. This time I knew I was going to have to cope with it on my own. We decided that I would take the children and return to New Zealand until Greg could sort out the mess. What a sham it all was, but when it came to my kids I refused to fall apart.

Eventually Greg drifted back into our lives, but he was never completely the same person with me again. I returned to Australia and our business took off. Contracts were won and money was plentiful. Despite the emotional turmoil, Greg and I worked side by side, and were to all intents and purposes a happily married couple. Strange as it may seem, we were good mates and when it came to the running of our business worked well together.

As a last resort to try and patch up our marriage, we planned a holiday overseas. I had to obtain a new passport and as I didn't have a copy of my birth certificate, I applied to the Births, Deaths and Marriages Office in New Zealand. When the certificate arrived, to my utter amazement I discovered that I was adopted. The sense of loss I felt was indescribable. The document I held in my hands wiped away any sense of security I'd previously had. Now, I felt literally on my own. Discovering that I was adopted was yet another blow to my self-confidence and esteem. By this stage I was starting to feel like I was a mistake in every sense of the word.

Depression and despair consequently led to a nervous breakdown and a long stay in hospital. After many weeks shut up in an institution, I persuaded the doctor that I would never recover locked up like that and convinced him to allow me to return home. He agreed on the condition that I would report to him on a regular basis. I began to look for a way out of my misery.

The day Greg won a large part of a contract working on the Jackson to Moonie pipeline in the outback, I welcomed the news hoping that it would help the relationship and our marriage. This contract brought me out to the south-west corner of Queensland. I travelled by myself to a remote area to look at a cafe that Greg thought would be a good buy as it came with a permit to build a motel on the site. With the discovery of oil in the district, more accommodation in the nearby town of Thargomindah was becoming a necessity. To build a motel became my personal project, and so began, quite by accident, my love of the outback and all it has to offer.

I've always believed that Greg must have had his own reasons for doing what he did. I don't believe that he ever deliberately set out to destroy our marriage. When I think back to our years together, however traumatic things were between us, my feeling is that Greg just fell out of love with me but could not bring himself to sever the ties. I'd always told him that he was free to do as he wished, but he had to be the one to make the decision to separate. I had been the one who begged and pleaded for him to go but when the moment finally came and Greg ended our marriage, I wondered how I was going to cope. I spent many hours driving to Thargomindah to check on the construction of my motel. 'Thargo' was a small bush town and the people there were very warm and friendly. Nobody judged me or seemed to care about my past, so slowly I was able to regain my self-esteem and make a fresh beginning for myself.

The motel in Thargomindah provided me with a decent living for several years but, best of all, life soon took on some sort of quality. My daughter Marina had by now grown into a beautiful young woman who gave me much needed moral support. We worked together in the motel, until she met and married a wonderful man and moved to a small family property on the outskirts of town. They have had their share of sadness— trying to make ends meet during the ongoing drought, as well as the death of their three-month-old baby boy from cot death. In this isolation, situations like these seem to be so much worse. To see your son-in-law forced to drive the distance to the small outpatients hospital only to have his son declared dead is truly tragic. No-one can remove that pain. You can only pray to the Lord for strength.

The tragedy of a disastrous first marriage is that it robs you of all trust. When I met Allen Girdler in Thargomindah, he too was the casualty of an unhappy marriage. He was newly divorced and struggling to raise a son on his own. His ex-wife, a local girl, had taken off with their daughter. This was hard for him as his children were his life.

Allen was born and bred in Thargomindah. His parents were drovers who spent all their time on the road. When Allen's mother was seven months pregnant with him, she was kicked in the stomach by a cow. She went into labour and was taken to the bush hospital in Thargo where she gave birth. Allen was rubbed over with olive oil, wrapped in cotton wool, put in a shoe box and kept in an airtight room. Nobody thought such a frail, sickly baby would survive. The doctor's name was Dr Allen—hence the name—and his advice to Allen's parents was not to take this baby on the road droving. But, ignoring his advice, they took their premature son on the road with them. Months later, when they returned to Thargo, the same sickly baby had miraculously transformed into a healthy, chubby little boy.

When there wasn't any droving work, one of the best ways for Allen's dad to provide for his large family of fifteen was by shooting brumbies. In the late fifties, brumbies were an enormous problem in the bush, coming in from the Simpson Desert and breeding in the thousands. In a record eighteen months, Allen's uncle, George Girdler, shot more than 6,000 brumbies, earning him a place in bush folklore. Following the family tradition, Allen started droving with his father at the age of eight. Allen was keen to stay on at school and get an education, but his

Allen, Nockatunga Station

father just said, 'If you're old enough to roll a swag, you're coming with me.'

All Allen ever wanted out of life was an education. It's been his dream. Since he was deprived of an education, he's been determined that his own kids get one. It's taken every penny from us to see this happen, but now both his son and daughter have graduated from high school. He is so proud of them.

After eighteen months of yes's, no's and maybe's, Allen and I decided to live together. Marriage was not on the agenda at this stage, as we had both been badly hurt. I gave up the motel and we moved to Norley Station. Allen was the overseer on a property that was roughly a million acres. Station life was something I had only ever read about in books or heard about from Allen. I never, ever imagined that I would be living on a property as large as this. The manager and his wife made us feel welcome immediately and I soon turned our modest two-room sandstone cottage into a real home. I was lucky to be employed by the company, working two days a week cooking for the stockmen and cleaning the manager's homestead. Breakfast before sun-up, the clanging of bells to summon the blokes for smoko and meal times, and tea in the early evening made for a very simple and happy lifestyle. The meat, as I quickly discovered, never came from a shop or supermarket. I had to learn to butcher a beast, bag it, and then try to find many different and inventive ways to cook it up for the blokes' tea.

That first year at Norley was a time of learning and adjusting to station life. The general isolation took some getting used to, and I felt very lonely the weeks Allen spent out at the stock camp. Still, there was plenty of work on the station to keep me busy so I knuckled down and quit feeling sorry for myself.

On Australia Day 1990, Allen and I married. I think Allen had been holding out, testing my attitude and adaptability to station life before he made any commitment. The wedding was held in the garden at Norley with only family and close friends attending. What we didn't bargain on was the hot weather. It was 48.3 degrees in the shade! Apart from the minister almost collapsing from the heat, all went well and the knot was duly tied.

When our time was up at Norley, Allen applied for a job as assistant manager at Bellalie Station, 250 kilometres from Thargomindah. When word came through that he had been accepted, we were thrilled, but my only reservation about moving to Bellalie was leaving Marina behind. Since the death of her baby son, she had isolated herself from most people. Once again, the Lord was to show me to trust in him, and prove that He was looking out for me.

For as long as I had been out in this country, I had often overheard people talking about a Catholic nun who had an aeroplane and flew around the bush visiting families living in isolation. They called her the flying nun, which amused me no end as the only nun I knew who 'flew' was the actress Sally Field from the TV show called *The Flying Nun*.

A pub may be a strange place to meet a nun, but that's where I met Anne Maree for the first time. To earn some extra money I worked from time to time cooking at the Noccundra pub, a family run hotel on Nockatunga station, which is a Kerry Packer property. Anne Maree flew in one Sunday afternoon to hold a religious service out the back of the pub. My first thought was that she didn't look like a nun at all, what with her cotton shorts and baseball cap! The following month she called in at Bellalie for a cuppa and a chat. I was elated. Allen was away at stock camp, and I was feeling terribly lonely. Before Anne Maree's surprise visit, I was having problems—financial and emotional—and was seriously thinking of leaving the bush and going back to New Zealand. The morning Anne Maree flew in was literally a godsend. We hit it off immediately and chatted nonstop for the entire day. There was so much I needed to get off my chest and she was a great listener.

The Lord must have realised that I was in dire need of company that morning, because three days later Anne Maree was still with me. She was about to take off, and the engine was clanking and making a right racket. I remember thinking to myself, 'I'm glad she's got that fella on her side because I wouldn't want to be flying in that!'

Luckily, she taxied back up the airstrip and after much cranking, revving and not really getting anywhere, we decided to call her mechanic, Laurie Curley, in Longreach. She was, fortunately for me, grounded. From that first meeting I knew there was someone there for me—a flying nun.

Like myself, Anne Maree is not originally from the bush. She's come from somewhere different and, like me, she's grown to love the outback. I have never thought of Anne Maree as anything else but a very dear friend. She's someone I can have a laugh with, as well as a cry. She has never failed to comfort me and give me hope, and for that I shall be eternally grateful.

Anne Maree fits in wherever she goes. Several years ago, when she was on one of her flying visits to the Noccundra pub, the publican's wife needed an extra pair of hands to help serve behind the bar. Without hesitating, Anne Maree came to her rescue. There she was, this tiny woman, pulling beers like an experienced barmaid and not a single soul in the pub, not even the blokes, guessed they were being served by a Catholic sister! I always say that Anne Maree quenches everyone's thirst out here! She does a good job all round and is loved by all the women in the west. I think a flying nun is far better than a flying priest. I think it's what we need, and that's the advantage of having her here—the women have someone they can relate to so much easier.

After three contented years at Bellalie, Allen and I moved to Nockatunga Station. We were fortunate to be taken on as the drought had just started and work was not easy to find. Allen was employed as the boreman. He was disappointed not to be working stock, but as far as he was concerned, Nockatunga was the best piece of dirt in this corner. Nockatunga is a 2.5 million acre station nestled in between the Wilson River and Cooper Creek, forty-five kilometres from the Jackson Oilfields. In a good season it carries some 16,000 to 18,000 head of cattle. During our time here we've seen this number dwindle to 5,000 because of the drought.

I don't think anyone, unless they have lived on the land, can imagine what it is like to watch the water in the dams dry up, the cattle die, and the country around you just blow away like dust. Drought means that you count every penny—if you need new clothes you go without. It means that your kids have to be taken out of boarding school because the fees can no longer be paid, the fatty meat on the table is now lean. It means a man tries to hide from his family how bad the situation really is and a son who grows up thinking he's going to work on the family property is going to work elsewhere, because he can't earn a wage from the land. Above all, drought means the killing of this country.

The bush is slowly dying. Years ago, if you couldn't sell your cattle because of bad feed, at least you didn't have to watch them dying from starvation. Several years ago, wool prices had dropped to virtually nothing. Allen came home after shooting thousands of sheep—shooting stock because there's not even a dead twig to feed them is heartbreaking for a stockman.

The people of the bush are proud and will never let on about their problems. They'll always tell you they're 'managing' because no-one wants to ask for a handout. Drought forces you to swallow your pride. It humbles you. For men like Allen who have spent all their lives working in the outback, drought spells disaster because it destroys their livelihood. These blokes have never had the chance to learn anything else. Station life is all they know, so that is why they stubbornly refuse to give up hope that eventually it will rain. If I took Allen away from this corner, he'd shrivel up and die. His love of the outback is genuine. His spiritual bonding is with the earth.

As much as I have come to love the west over these years, another real sadness for me is the damage caused by alcohol. Alcoholism is a huge problem in the bush. There's a bar at every rodeo or race meet these days and, of course, every town has a pub. The tragedy is that you can't go anywhere without there being alcohol. It's responsible for breaking up families and relationships in the bush. I know of plenty of women who through isolation, and particularly being with just men, have started to drink. In the bush there are no support groups in place that cater for alcoholics. At least in the city, if you have a drinking problem you can find help. I think the isolation is to blame, as well as a faster lifestyle and too much outside influence. The pressure of running a property during a drought does not help things, but drowning your sorrows in drink only makes the situation worse.

It was here at Nockatunga that I found out Pete had been arrested for murder. I don't think I could have coped if it hadn't been for the understanding and support of Anne Maree and the staff at Nockatunga. Throughout this entire ordeal Anne Maree has listened to me, prayed with me and, more importantly, reassured me that I did not fail as a mother.

Jail is such a dehumanising place. People automatically assume because you're in there in the first place, you must be guilty of the crime. Pete's been in remand for over two years now, with no date set for a trial. He's just waiting, like me. At least he's been able to study for his High School Certificate, which is something he never had. While in Long Bay he's also learnt to use a computer so I guess he's not wasting too much time. But when, and if, he gets bail and is eventually released, he'll carry the stigma of having been in jail for the rest of his life.

As his mother I can't, and never will, believe that my son is capable of murder.

My years spent on outback stations are not many compared to the other women out here, but I feel that I have found a way of life no-one could ever understand unless they themselves have lived on the land. Yes, the days are long and physically hard, but at night you are rewarded with clear skies awash with milky stars which hang so low you feel you can almost touch them. As I sit on the verandah in the cool of the early evening and watch the changing colours moving across the sky, it renews my faith in God. Suddenly, I understand what Anne Maree means when she speaks of gliding over the vast country and how she can't help but believe that there is a God when she sees a sunset. The peace and solitude that welcomes me after hours spent hunched over the industrial stove cooking for the men, or working out in the yards with Allen, makes up for all the heat and dust of the day.

The bush has taught me a lot about myself and to look closer at people and realise that we all carry scars. Some of them are just easier to see than others.

Thirty years ago, I would never have imagined that I would be living in such a remote area in the outback with a bushie for a husband. I'll always remember, back in the early days at Bellalie, when I first heard a dingo howling. It was late at night and I was sitting on the loo when suddenly, there was the most chilling, eerie wail floating down from the hills. I screamed out to Allen, 'What's that?'

There was quiet, then he yelled back, 'Just sit there, sweetheart. It's the call of nature.'

Recently, Allen was offered the position of manager at Mt Howitt, a large Stanbroke Pastoral Co station far from Nockatunga. It's a great opportunity for him to manage such a large and important station—one he can't refuse—but it's with enormous sadness that I'll be leaving the place that has given me more than I can ever repay, which is a belief in myself again. The only good news at the moment, if I'm reading my calendar correctly, is that in a month's time, Sister Anne Maree should be landing on the dirt airstrip at Mt Howitt for a cuppa and a chat. I thank God we're still on her flight path.

Mount Hewitt Station

*Names have been changed.

Postscript: Pete, Colleen Girdler's son, has since been released from prison with a not guilty verdict.

CIRCUIT ONE

LEAH CAMERON—NOCCUNDRA
HOTEL

M any of the women in this remote corner have come from a completely different world. Some followed their husbands, while others were simply pushed by a desire to live in the bush and escape the city. Leah Cameron, like a number of other women I visit, started life out west working as a governess.

I met Leah when I flew off course on my first trip to Quilpie. I was flying two priests to an annual review meeting. Visibility was poor, but I didn't feel particularly nervous. About half an hour before we were due to arrive, one of the priests, Father Chris Schick, peered out the window and told me he could see Quilpie in the distance. The place he saw was too small to be a town and, when I checked my map, I realised we were nowhere near our destination. I decided to fly above the road, thinking it would take us to Quilpie, but when it suddenly vanished, I had to admit that I was lost. Eventually a property with an airstrip came into sight. As I taxied in, I could just make out the name on the station roof—Nockatunga. I had flown right off the map!

A heavily pregnant woman was already at the strip. She introduced herself as Leah Cameron and said she'd only been living at the station for a week. She was not expecting any visitors and was astonished when she discovered who we were. The last people she expected to meet in this isolated corner of the bush were a nun and two priests!

Leah had been on her own for the last few days and was delighted to have company. Her husband was away at camp and her two children at boarding school. After a cuppa, she refuelled the Cessna and we took off again for Quilpie. (I carefully followed the map this time and had no problems.) The Lord must have meant for me to fly to Nockatunga that day, as it enabled me to make a new friend.

How typical. Whenever I look for a quiet spot to reflect and meditate, everything seems so loud because of the generator thump-thumping away in the background.

This morning, on a rare visit to my home town, I sat in the small church which was so much a part of my earlier life. It was like being with an old friend, and as I looked towards the side door, I could almost see us, the Bensein family, all those years ago, pouring into one of the long pews. Dad would lead the way, choose a seat, and stand by as we all filed in. He would then take his usual place at the end and sit down, with his stiff leg jutting out. His stiff leg was the result of a motorcycle accident when he was in his twenties. He had to have a metal plate put in his knee which he said slowed him down—'Enough for your mum to catch me', as he liked to joke.

We loved to hear stories about our parents' romance. They were so much in love. Our mother was very beautiful and we children adored her. As the story goes, Dad looked across a crowded room, caught the eye of our mum, and straightaway knew that she was the one. They were married in this very church—St Mary's—in Maryborough in October 1950. They had five children, all close in age, who played with and cared for each other.

We grew up twenty miles from the beach. The sea has always meant a great deal to me. Now, after more than two decades of living in the outback, I still yearn for the sea—to walk in the soft sand, hear the waves break against the shore, and to feel the salt air on my face. I try to have a holiday every year by the beach. On the last day, I always walk along the shore and cry, because I know it will be another year before I'll return. When I first went out west, I used to lie awake at night and listen to the wind and pretend to myself that it was the sea breeze. There are times when I swear I can still hear it.

When I left high school, I wanted to be an artist. But it was the sixties, and girls were discouraged from having original ambitions. Instead, the vocational

The glamour days of hairdressing. With Nanna, 1971.

guidance officer advised me to take on an occupation which involved a rather different form of creativity—hairdressing! I had just turned fifteen when I was offered an apprenticeship in a small suburban salon. But where was the glamour I'd hoped for? My feet and legs ached from standing up all day on the hard cement floor. I was dog-tired from sweeping up enormous piles of hair, and my knuckles were rubbed raw from laundering hundreds of towels. I shampooed scalp after scalp, prepared the ladies for the older, more experienced girls, and eventually conned friends into letting me cut and style their hair on weekends—all the while dreaming of running off to the glittering life of the city.

The closest I came to city glamour back then, was when there was a ball. I would start work at the crack of dawn and continue right through lunch until late at night. Then the other girls and I would rush around in a frenzy doing each other's hair, race home to get all dolled up and attend the ball ourselves.

Saturdays were our busiest days in the salon because of all the weddings. Our wages were very small so, to earn extra money, I took on several babysitting jobs. I don't know why, but I still had this crazy dream of living in the city. Maryborough just wasn't big enough or exciting enough for me. I wanted to spread my wings and see what the world had to offer. When my four-year apprenticeship was successfully completed, I packed a suitcase and went to work in Brisbane.

I took a flat with my best friend in Coronation Drive and thought that all my dreams had come true. For two nights every week, I worked the evening shift at a salon. Every other night, I went out dancing. After several years in Brisbane, I finally felt that I'd had my fill. Although I had made some close friends, I began to perceive the shallowness of life in the city. Dancing at some stranger's birthday party in a borrowed frock and hairpiece, I happened to glance down at my partner's shoulder and realised that it was my false eyelash stuck on his lapel that was winking back up at me. It was then that I knew it was time to move on!

Somehow I got it into my head that a break in the country would put things back into perspective, so I started buying the Queensland *Country Life* newspaper. There were several advertisements asking for private governesses which appealed to me. I applied to a family living on a property outside of the township of McKinlay, in a remote corner of far north-west

Queensland. It seemed perfect. I packed my suitcase once more and bade farewell to the curlers and the city forever.

The year I spent as a governess on Milgery, a privately managed sheep and cattle property in the open downs country, was a great adventure and an invaluable learning experience which has stayed with me to the present day. However, when I first set foot on the property I was terrified. I thought it terribly isolated—more than 1,500 kilometres from Brisbane—and with nothing but scrub stretching for miles and miles. I was shocked to discover that all the roads which ran to and from the property were mere dirt tracks. The family had a total of nine children. They made me feel very welcome and quickly taught me the standard lore of country women. During the week I was kept busy in the station schoolroom teaching the two oldest children. On Saturdays, I joined in the flurry of cleaning the homestead and generally helped out wherever I could. Once it was discovered that I had trained as a hairdresser, women from neighbouring properties began driving over to Milgery for afternoons of shampooing, hair setting and styling. It was all great fun.

I looked forward to the weekends when we would gather at other stations or have picnics down by the banks of the McKinlay River. 'Some river,' I thought, because there was never any water—it was always dry! I loved these social events. There wasn't a grain of pretension, only bush sincerity and, I might add, a good deal of tolerance for my lack of outback experience.

It was at one of these weekend gatherings that I met Ian Cameron.

He was a handsome young jackaroo who had grown up in the bush and was working on a property 'next door' to Milgery. When I was introduced to Ian—or 'Splinter' as everyone called him owing to his height and physique—he wasn't much of a talker. He was reserved. He was the opposite of the men I had known in Brisbane, and I think this is what attracted me to him in the first place. There was nothing insincere or phony about him.

'Splinter'

'So what if he is a man of few words,' I thought. 'He'll improve with time!' We were engaged eight months after our first meeting. I was twenty. In February 1974, we tied the knot in my hometown church where my parents had wed. The aisle seemed so very long as I walked down clutching my father's arm. It was a big step both for Splinter and for myself—a commitment for life. It meant living far away from my family and accepting the bush as my home. Once the decision was made, there was no turning back.

Our first home was a corrugated iron cottage in McKinlay. There were only fifteen people living in 'town' and apart from a small church, schoolhouse and a cluster of houses, the only other building of interest was the pub! This remote and forgotten place was put on the map thanks to the movie *Crocodile Dundee*. But twenty years ago, McKinlay was not half as colourful or romantic as Hollywood would like to paint it.

Every morning, Splinter would leave for Bull Creek, a cattle property eighteen kilometres away, where he worked as a station hand. The running of the household was left to me. He had hoped he would make a good cook and bushwoman out of me. Wishful thinking! If I ran out of ingredients, there was little chance of rushing down to a local shop. All the roads were unsealed, which made driving anywhere uncomfortable and difficult. The nearest town, Julia Creek, was more than eighty kilometres away and on such bad roads, it would take me at least three hours to get there. I was still ignorant about the ways of the bush and those first few months of married life were quite a test of patience for both Splinter and me.

Sometimes things are not easy for either of us. As happens in most marriages, Splinter and I have our ups and downs but, looking back, I can honestly say that I made the right decision. Splinter and I are really good mates. We have worked hard at building our relationship and I would be incomplete without him. Couples depend enormously on each other in the bush. There are few distractions in these parts, therefore you learn to enjoy each other's company. You also know when to give each other space. I am thankful that our marriage is strong, otherwise life would be miserable out here.

In 1974 I fell pregnant and had to be sent away to a hostel in Mount Isa two weeks before the baby was due. The fact that I didn't know a single soul and would have to get to the hospital by myself was depressing. The only other alternative would have been to remain at home and risk driving out to the nearest hospital which was three hours away. Fortunately for me, my stay in Mount Isa was a day short of two weeks. When our son, Andrew, was born, a nurse telephoned Splinter and he drove the 200 kilometres in record time to inspect his son. He was pretty pleased with himself. After a week in hospital he came back to collect Andy and me and we returned home to begin our life as a family.

When Andy was a toddler, we moved to Lagaven Station, a 35,000 acre cattle property in the McKinlay district, and remained there for the next three years while Splinter continued to work at Bull Creek. Our new homestead wasn't anything flash, just a simple bush-timber house, which I tried to turn into a home. There was no real power when we first arrived, only the outdated thirty-two volt and only when the motor was running. Our fridges ran off kerosene, which made the house stink. We had no lights unless the motor, which was too difficult for me to start, was running. Whenever Splinter returned late, I had to either sit in the dark or burn wax candles. It was the loneliest time I'd ever experienced in my entire life. Even the flocks of corellas squawking overhead at dusk seemed to be mocking my misery.

Apart from Andy, I didn't know or see anyone. I tried to establish a garden but the black soil was rock hard like cement. Instead, I taught myself to sew on a borrowed Singer treadle, and started to paint. Anything, just to keep sane.

As a toddler, Andy was the dearest little boy you ever saw—quiet by nature, but very adventurous. Whenever he got the chance, he would immediately wander off into the bush. I used to dress him in red, otherwise I wouldn't have been able to find him in the dried grass, which was the same colour as his hair. I could never believe how quick and quiet he was at getting away. One day he really outdid all his previous escapades by wandering off at dusk. I searched high and low, calling out to him until I was hoarse. Finally, seized by panic, I tried to call a neighbour on the phone. Typically, the 'party line' was down. In desperation I got into the ute. As I drove slowly down the dirt track in the dark, I noticed cattle in the bottom paddock running away as if something had scared them. Upon closer investigation I saw Andy happily trotting behind the cattle with our labrador, Jay. I made him walk back to the homestead, and smacked his little bottom all the way, while shedding tears of anger and relief. His wandering ceased after that.

After a year at Lagaven, my loneliness came to an end. I began meeting people—women from neighbouring properties, who were very sympathetic and gave me plenty of moral support. They offered me plants for my struggling garden and comforted me during my lonely times. Eventually I was given the opportunity to open a hairdressing salon in Julia Creek. I would get up early on a Wednesday, drive the eighty kilometres over dirt roads and work through till Friday evening, and then drive back home again. The women were pleased to have a hairdresser in Julia Creek and generously helped Andy and I out with accommodation, meals and babysitting. It was all great fun and my loneliness vanished. It also provided a small income which enabled me to at last make my dream purchase—an automatic washing machine!

Working in Julia Creek meant that I could bring home fresh supplies of milk, fruit and vegetables. Before that time, we had to rely upon deliveries that came only once a week on the mail truck, and these consisted of just pumpkins, spuds and carrots! The one disadvantage of working part-time was that Splinter and I spent less time together. But he understood that my new job meant a lot to me so we just did the best we could.

In 1978 I gave birth to our second child, a girl, whom we christened Kirsty. It was a long and difficult labour, and both Kirsty and I were worse for wear by the time it was over. I could barely walk, and it was later discovered that a nerve at the base of my spine had been damaged. After a week at Lagaven, the pain became so unbearable, that I drove myself thirty kilometres over unsealed roads to see the bush nurse. Apart from the injury to my spine, she also diagnosed a nasty infection in my uterus. I was sent straight to the hospital in Julia Creek. The next couple of months were a very stressful time for our family. Specialised treatment was required for my spine and the doctors advised that I be flown to Brisbane. Andy and Kirsty flew down with me, and everyone took an active part in getting me back on the road to recovery. Needless to say, I was relieved when 1978 was finally over. Splinter took me to the beach at the end of the year and this was really balm to my soul.

At the end of 1979, we were on the move again. Splinter's employers at Bull Creek had built us a new house on the station's home block so Splinter could be closer to his work. We were both happy to move somewhere new. At long last, we were all able to spend more time together as a family. Andy had started school by correspondence and I was his home tutor. I disliked it, but not as much as Andy, who could never understand why he had to spend so much time cooped up inside studying books instead of roaming the bush, as was his habit. It was a terrible struggle with plenty of tears and frustrations. Apart from teaching, I started painting again. Finally, the bush was beginning to agree with me. I was so busy that I did not have any time to get lonely or bored. The soil was relatively fertile and there was dam water instead of the usual bore water, so my garden thrived. I'll always retain a fond memory of that property.

In 1985, Splinter was offered a job in the Northern Territory at Newcastle Waters, a large company station owned by the Consolidated Pastoral Company. Splinter loaded up the truck with all our worldly possessions, while I was left to drive the kids the 1,000 kilometres to our new home. We moved into the original old homestead, a sandstone building with cool cement floors and eighteen-inch thick walls. It was a great old house. We also inherited the previous owner's dog, a Great Dane called Humphrey.

Kirsty was my constant companion and helper, and the thought of losing her to boarding school was unbearable. We had already sent Andy away to a school in Brisbane. Splinter and I drove down to help him settle in. As it was the school's policy not to allow parents to contact their children for two weeks, the separation was traumatic. Andy was very unhappy and homesick, which distressed me no end. I cried all the way home to Newcastle Waters, much to Splinter's annoyance. Once the settling in period was over, Splinter telephoned Andy and told him that he could leave if he found the experience too awful. Luckily Andy decided to stick it out. I wanted my son to have a sound education and this, only boarding school could supply.

I worked as the gardener at Newcastle Waters. The following year I helped set up Meals-on-Wheels and other community services for elderly Aborigines in the nearby town of Elliott. This was a real eye-opener for me. I enjoyed the company of the Aboriginal women and learnt more about their culture, of which I knew so little previously. I also took up painting again and even began to sell some of my work in the town.

In 1990, I received the shock of my life when I discovered that I was pregnant. At thirty-nine, I thought I was too old for such a thing to happen! In the midst of all this emotional upheaval, we left the Northern Territory and moved back to Queensland. Splinter was offered work at Nockatunga Station, a cattle property in the heart of the south-west, on the Wilson River. This decision to return to Queensland was prompted by our desire to live closer to Andy and Kirsty. Their boarding schools were just too far away from Newcastle Waters. We were also worried that they might be growing apart from us and that we would be missing out on many precious years together as a family.

Right from the beginning, Nockatunga Station felt like a mistake. It was still very isolated—over 1,000 kilometres from Brisbane—and with both children away at school, I found myself, once again, lonely and unhappy. Splinter was employed as a contractor machinery operator and also did some aerial mustering on the station, which kept him away from home. The drought had kicked in, making the situation even more depressing. No woman had lived in the homestead for some years, so there was plenty of women's business to attend to. I was heavily pregnant and desperate for female company. I had not met any of my female neighbours because the nearest one lived at least a three-hour drive away. The future looked bleak. I remember lying in bed one night, in a state of depression. I began questioning God. What was He thinking when He brought me out here? This wasn't a nice place, there were no families living nearby, no friends. Nothing—just me and the cattle. I couldn't even be with my kids.

Well, I got a right rap on the knuckles, because the very next day, a small plane landed at my doorstep in a great cloud of dust. When I heard the droning of the plane's engine coming in to land on the airstrip opposite the homestead, I rushed out to see what was going on. Out hopped a nun and two priests! I could barely believe my eyes. I thought I was hallucinating! The woman introduced herself as Sister Anne Maree. She apologised for the intrusion and explained that she had been on her way to Quilpie with the two priests to attend a meeting, but had somehow managed to lose her way. She politely asked me if she could use our RFDS radio to notify the priest in Quilpie that she was lost and would be running late. This was my first introduction to the Aerial Ministry. From that time on, I was included in the monthly visits and welcomed, so to speak, to Sister Anne Maree's outback parish!

Anne Maree's monthly visits give me something to look forward to. She brings news from outside, from other women on distant stations, but best of all, she is a connection with the Church. My religion is very important to me. As a practising Catholic, it hasn't been easy for me to maintain my faith while living in isolation. For many years I had been accustomed to living without Sunday mass or the support of a parish. Thanks to Anne Maree, I can once again feel a part of a wider Church community. I now have access to monthly communion, a prayer service, or even mass when she brings a priest with her. I no longer feel that I am alone or out of touch with my religion.

Noccundra pub, circa 1940.

Had Anne Maree not strayed off course, I am not sure how I would have coped on my own out here. Since our first meeting, things took a turn for the better. Soon after, I gave birth to a baby girl, Court-ney. Splinter came to the hospital bringing all of the station's bookwork for me to do. I did the right thing, for once, in his eyes, managing the books and the birth over one weekend! Courtney's birth was extra special because of the twelve-year difference between her and Kirsty. Splinter and I marvelled again, after all those years, at the miracle of life.

Splinter has always been persuasive by nature, but the day he took me to see a dilapidated old sandstone pub and announced his intention of taking on the lease, I thought he had really gone loco! Not only was the pub in the middle of nowhere, but it was practically in ruins. Furthermore, I didn't know a thing about barwork. Splinter kept pointing out the sand-stone blocks to me as we walked around the grounds. 'It'll scrub up well, Leah,' he insisted. 'These are the original blocks!'

Courtney

At least someone could see the potential because, quite frankly, I couldn't. Originally built in 1882, the Noccundra Hotel had been the site of a small store which supplied goods by pack camels to the surrounding stations. As Splinter took me on the grand tour, the mess of corrugated iron sheets, glass bottles and other rubbish strewn around was hardly a comforting sight. Inside, the walls were plastered with a mud mortar and covered in graffiti—the legacy of past patrons. I was not keen to take on the lease of a rundown old pub, but was outvoted by the rest of my family. So here I am today, the cook and fellow publican of the Noccundra Hotel! Over the last seven years we have lovingly restored the pub. With generous finance from our landlord, help from builders, and our own sweat and blood, you would never believe the transformation.

As Splinter has spent the best part of his life working for other people, his dream has been to try his hand at managing his own business. Together, we have looked upon this lease as a challenge. It has been a long, hard slog building up the business. It may still not be your 'country manor' but it has gone from being a rowdy bush pub to a pleasant meeting place for the locals and an example of outback hospitality for tourists. We now have ample accommodation and powered van sites. Camping down by the Wilson River is also popular with tourists. The flying doctor holds a clinic here once a month and the flying dentist also flies in regularly.

Despite being constantly run off my feet, I love it here. Winter and the annual race meets, which are held on the Saturday of the Queen's Birthday weekend, are our busiest periods. Whenever Anne Maree flies in, she stays for the night. She fits in as easily here as she does wherever she goes. She appreciates how busy things can get, and the difficulty I find in trying to be everything to everyone. She encourages me, chides me for overdoing things and reminds me to take time out. These days, when she flies into Noccundra, she will help me in the kitchen, make sandwiches, dish out meals, even serve behind the bar! The first time she worked behind the bar, I don't think any of the men who had come in to wash the dirt down with an icy-cold beer knew that the smiling barmaid was a nun!

These days, nuns seem much more like normal people. They are approachable. I am not being disrespectful to the traditional nuns from older days, but I could never feel close to them at school. I had the feeling they were there only to teach and keep us in line, whereas Anne Maree is a friend, and I can count on her in any situation. Splinter is very fond of her, like a lot of other men I know. He and Anne Maree share a common interest in light aircraft and can talk for hours on end. He appreciates that she is a friend who genuinely cares for me and for all the other isolated families she visits. I always tease her, saying that God must have fiddled with her GPS navigation equipment many years ago when she executed the emergency landing on my doorstep. For me, she is, quite literally, heaven-sent!

I believe the bush puts things into perspective. I still have my fair share of dust storms, floods, flies and mosquitoes, but after the rains, I see the beauty of the country unfolding. The combined run-offs from the rivers turn the land into a huge watery jigsaw. The sunrises and sunsets are our daily rewards and the stars out here seem so close and bright. Whenever I think I have something to complain about, or if things seem to get a bit out of control, I just go for a walk down to the Noccundra waterhole and spare a thought for the publicans' wives who lived here at the turn of the century. I read somewhere that one woman gave birth to ten healthy children over a period of eighteen years. Six were actually born in the pub. No sterile birthing suite for her! In her time, there were no proper ceilings, only a hot tin roof, and plenty of spiders dangling from the bush-timber beams. The washing was all done by hand in a copper, with brown water drawn from the river. I still have the brown water, but at least it churns through a large automatic washing machine. I also have the luxury of proper floors, airconditioning and plumbing!

One day I will go back to my beach and live by the sea, but for now, I am happy to stay put. I will always thank God for these years spent in the outback, and for the goodness and kindness of people like Sister Anne Maree, who have helped me along the way.

The silent wisdom of the women of the bush has taught me how to live.

CIRCUIT ONE

DALE BROWN—
NARYILCO STATION

As I leave Leah and head off south-west to Naryilco Station to visit Dale Brown, I think about the hardships faced by the women of the west. While it is perhaps easier for women like Dale who were raised in the bush to cope with the isolation, they still have many adjustments to make after they wed.

Most of the women I meet take their workload in their stride, but all suffer dreadfully when they have to send their children to boarding school. It is such a wrench on family life, but parents realise that boarding school is the only way to give their children a decent education and a chance to mix with their peers. While many mothers hope their children will eventually settle on the land, none would ever want to deprive them of the choice of living elsewhere.

As well as raising her young family of three, Dale works as the station cook and is co-manager of Naryilco, a Kidman station on the Queensland–New South Wales border. We met in March 1989, when Father Terry and I flew in to baptise Dale's youngest daughter, Emily Rose. Since our first meeting ten years ago, Dale has welcomed me into her home every month. Mind you, she sometimes manages to forget the day I am due at Naryilco, but this is never a problem—she just fits me in with the rest of her busy schedule.

Working as the station cook, Dale must look after a large number of staff. She's up at the crack of dawn and is flat out until late in the evening. Our walks down to the creek bed give her a chance to unwind and take some time out for herself. Lately, her concerns have been for her second oldest boy, Bernard, who finds it very difficult to adjust to the life at boarding school and wants to come home. It is hard for parents, this constant worry for their children far away from home. Dale is no exception.

I met my Ted in 1977, when I was working as a governess at Durham Downs, a Kidman cattle property in south-west Queensland. Ted was the head stockman, very handsome, with a smart handlebar moustache and an Akubra hat to match. I had arrived at Durham Downs in January of that year to supervise correspondence lessons for the manager's three young children. I think I failed as a governess—I just didn't have what it takes. In the end, I only lasted nine months, but I loved the station life. Ted and I became very good friends during this time, and when he decided to make an honest woman out of me, I didn't hesitate for a second. We wed on 17 March 1978, at the Broken Hill Cathedral.

Ted has been working for Kidman and Co since he was fourteen. In fact, he was practically weaned on Kidman stations as his parents, Bill and Beryl Brown, worked as managers for the company. Kidman and Co is a large pastoral company with its head office in North Adelaide. The company was established by Sir Sidney Kidman, the 'Cattle King', in the late 1800s. Today, the company has sixteen properties scattered over Queensland, South Australia, New South Wales and Western Australia.

I am so proud of my Ted! In the thirty years he has been with Kidman and Co, he has successfully managed two large cattle properties and is probably the hardest working manager I know. Our two teenage sons, William and Bernie, will, without a doubt, follow in their dad's and grandad's footsteps and work for the company. After all, they are true-blue Brown boys!

I am no stranger to the outback. I was born in Broken Hill on 9 July 1959. My parents, Barney and Joss Davie, were managing The Selection, a station north of Broken Hill. When I was four, we moved to Tibooburra, about 336 kilometres north of Broken Hill. My parents bought The Family Hotel, a popular pub in town. The name seemed appropriate as there are seven children in our family. Mum and Dad managed the 'Family' for twenty-five years. The hotel is famous for its

The Brown girls—I'm second on the right.

murals in the bar which were painted by artists such as Clifton Pugh, Russell Drysdale and Eric Mitchin. Mum and Dad were good mates with these artists. Clifton Pugh would come back each year and stay at our hotel and paint landscapes around the area.

I didn't like growing up in the hotel environment. The patrons who came in for a drink were boisterous and the bar stank of stale cigarettes and beer. My parents were always busy attending to the bar and cooking for guests. They never seemed to have much time for us kids. I didn't like having to share our family life with so many people—our time was never our own. These days, whenever I go back to Tibooburra, I don't have any sentimental feelings for the hotel at all.

Tibooburra is surrounded by hills of large granite boulders. As a little girl, I would play for hours in these rocks with my sisters and friends. We had no fear of snakes or spiders! We would build cubby houses and sometimes take a scrap of wire netting, a box of matches and a handful of snags to cook for our tea. There was no television in Tibooburra but the P&C committee sent movies up from Broken Hill once a week and showed them at our local school. Everyone looked forward to this big night out and we used to get dressed up to the nines.

I went to primary school in Tibooburra. At the time it was only a two-teacher school with about fifty pupils. When I turned twelve, like my older brother and sisters before me, I was sent away to St Joseph's College, a boarding school in Broken Hill. Broken Hill seemed a million miles away. It was dirt road all the way and it would take at least five hours to get there. I always spent the first half of the trip in tears, missing Tibooburra, my family and my friends already. For this reason, I never really liked school and, as a result, I didn't do very well except in sports.

By the end of my third year at St Joseph's, I won a battle with my mother to stay home and do my fourth year by correspondence. This too, I think, was a waste of time—in any case, I didn't learn a thing. By the end of my fourth year, I decided to give school the flick once and for all, and began working as a domestic and waitress for Mum at the hotel. I enjoyed the work and felt like a real grown-up. It certainly taught me to be more responsible and independent. I stayed at the Family for a year before I applied for the position of governess at Durham Downs. The prospect of living on a distant station in far south-west Queensland was very exciting for a seventeen-year-old—at any rate, it seemed more inspiring than laundering sheets and making beds!

When I met my Ted, he had been working at Durham Downs Station for eight years. His mum and dad came to Durham in 1969 to manage the property. After Ted and I married, he decided that it was high time to move on. He was offered, and accepted, a job as manager of Morney Plains Station, another Kidman property in the Channel Country. This meant droving a hundred horses across country and travelling more than 300 kilometres on horseback! I guess you could call it our honeymoon— Ted certainly thought it was, because we never got to have a real holiday together after our wedding.

Ted, along with a close friend, Max Gorringe, and my older sister Joanne, set off from Durham Downs on horseback. I was left to drive the Toyota with the cattle dog for company—I couldn't ride a horse and someone had to drive the tucker wagon!

It took five days and nights to reach Morney Plains. I loved sleeping in a swag in the open bush. The night sky was clear and full of stars. Joanne and I would go ahead of the men in the late afternoon to set up camp for the evening. We would choose somewhere close to a bore or a dam, preferably with some kind of a makeshift yard or enclosure, so we could water and hobble the horses for the night ahead. Joanne and I would have a dip in the dam or a shower under the overflow of the bores before getting the tea ready. The tinkling of hobble chains and the ringing of the horses' bells would lull us to sleep. When we eventually arrived at Morney Plains we were a little tired and the worse for wear from the travelling, but it was an unforgettable trip. What a beaut introduction to married life in the bush!

In our first months as managers at Morney, Ted briskly set about looking after the land and the stock while I remained at the homestead. Joanne kindly decided to stay with me for an extra month to teach me how to cook. I think she did a pretty good job because I haven't had too many complaints. Ted's mum also came to stay with us for a spell. Nan, as we called her, had lived on stations practically all her married life, and she too was a competent teacher and an excellent cook. She taught me how to run a homestead efficiently and was wonderful company.

When I look back to that first year of married life at Morney Plains, I realise that for Ted and me it was really a matter of 'make or break' the relationship. We were both very young—I was nineteen, and Ted twenty-five—and absolutely determined to make a go of managing our first property together. What I had not bargained on, however, was that Ted would be spending long periods out at mustering camp. His day would start well before sun-up and he wouldn't get to bed until long after dark. I remained at the homestead without any possibility of communicating with him since the camp did not have a radio. Mrs Gorringe, Max's mother, came to stay with me while the camp was out. Together, we worked in the kitchen, looked after the garden, and went for long walks down by Morney Creek.

When Mrs Gorringe couldn't come out, Ted would leave the camp cook behind to keep me company. On one occasion, I had gone to bed early because I was feeling a bit on edge. The house was large, and there were always strange noises at night. Around midnight, a loud bang woke me up. It came from the kitchen, which was in a separate building detached from the main house. I climbed out of bed, and with my heart pounding, crept around the verandah. From my hiding place, I could see the camp cook fossicking about in the kitchen cupboards. Minutes later, he stumbled out cursing to himself, and headed up to the main house. I was too frightened to make any sound. As it was very dark, he didn't see me. He moved right past me, went inside our house, took a bottle of whisky from a cabinet, and then swaggered off. I don't think I slept a wink that night— I was too terrified! The next morning I called a neighbour on the HF radio who came to stay with me until I could get a message to Ted. When Ted came home from camp, he sent the cook to town. It appeared that the cook had gotten 'dry' and was long overdue for a bender! After a week in town on the grog, he dutifully returned to the station on the mail truck, sheepish and sober.

After a year managing Morney Plains, Ted and I were transferred to Naryilco, a much larger cattle station between Cooper Creek and the New South Wales border. We arrived at the property in January 1979, to a bloody heat and a sorry mess. The station's 7,057 square kilometres had seen better days. Not one vehicle was roadworthy, most of the bores and windmills were broken down, the coldroom was out of order, and all I had in my kitchen was an old gas fridge with a large bullet hole in one side! There had been no improvements on the run—no fences, and worse still, cattle running amuck everywhere. The pace of station work picked up as Ted immediately set about retrieving cattle from neighbouring properties and getting Naryilco back into shape. When we checked the books, we discovered that there had been a large net financial loss in 1978. In fact, no profit had been recorded for some years. This was mostly caused by the drought, low cattle prices, and the Tuberculosis Eradication Campaign which involved clearing diseased cattle from the herds. However, after just one year managing Naryilco—and for the very first time in years—my Ted succeeded in achieving a net profit. To his credit, there hasn't been a loss since. It took twelve long years before things returned completely to normal. These days, in a good season, he will run roughly 10,000 head of Shorthorn Santa cattle. In 1990, the highest ever branding was recorded—5,958 calves. What an achievement!

My Ted

I am so proud of my Ted! He has so much energy and such devotion to this property and to the company. However, along with all the successes, there have been many sacrifices. The time my husband has had to spend away from his home and his family still does not seem to me to be quality time, which is something that I have missed and needed. Yet I know his work is very important to him, and I would never attempt to stand in his way. I guess I just have to learn to accept it.

Our first child, a boy, was born on 15 October 1980, in Broken Hill. What a little champ! Ted came to fetch us from the hospital in our truck. Driving home, he suddenly announced that he had to do the 'bore run' which meant stopping at all the bores to make sure the water was still being pumped up from the subartesian basin below. How typical of my Ted! He was running a lot of pump jacks which pump water, when there is no wind to turn the windmills, for the stock. After checking the final pump jack, it suddenly dawned upon Ted that this was what he should call our son—'Pump Jack Bill'! I couldn't believe it! Eventually we agreed to a compromise and called our first son William.

When William was a little fellow, he idolised John Wayne. There was a giant poster of John Wayne mounted over a bullock hide on his bedroom wall and I once overheard him tell a tourist, who had accidentally strayed onto our property that, actually, his name was John Wayne! William spent his primary school years at the station doing School of the Air. We employed a governess to supervise his lessons but from day one, 'William-John-Wayne' hated school. He made it very clear to his governess and to myself that he would much rather be outside tearing around with a gun and holster on his hip, and his cowboy hat pulled so hard down on his head that I was sure that his ears would stick out for the rest of his life. When the time came to send him to boarding school, Ted and I chose Downlands in Toowoomba—1,145 kilometres away—because we had two aunts living in town who could keep an eye on him.

For the first six months, William was on cloud nine. He found this new life exciting and wonderful. He loved being with all the other kids and playing sports. Whenever he called home he would tell us how big the place was. What he didn't like, however, was the schoolwork. His four years at Downlands were a constant struggle, but we made it. In 1996 we agreed to let him finish school after Year Ten and enrolled him in the agricultural college in Emerald, near Longreach. I have never heard my son sound so happy. Emerald is the land of jeans, riding boots, hats, and a rodeo every weekend—William's idea of heaven!

Our second child, Bernard George, was born in Broken Hill on 4 May 1983. Like his older brother, he loves the outdoors and wide-open spaces. He was a real little torment—something he inherited from his 'pop', my dad. He was also a very inquisitive little boy. I remember when he was seven, and the governess, William and myself were sitting down to our tea, when Bernie suddenly piped up and asked, 'What's a homosexual?'

The governess nearly choked. I just sat there for a minute wondering how to answer this, when William, who was ten at the time, turned to his brother and scoffed, 'Don't you know what a homosexual is, Bernie? Golly, everyone knows that!'

I asked William to explain to the whole table what he thought it was.

'A homosexual,' he said, 'is a person who only has sex at home.' The governess and I were doubled up with laughter. I'm always amazed at how the young mind works!

Bernie dreaded going away to boarding school. All he ever wanted was to be with his dad and work at Naryilco. He absolutely hates being away from home. He detests his school. 'Too many brick buildings and concrete everywhere, Mum,' he is forever telling me. 'It's like a prison.'

He has found it very difficult to settle in. At home, he basically had the run of the schoolroom with just the governess and himself. Now he has to share one teacher with about thirty other boys. Bernie and I have shed many tears over the last twelve months but I do believe that, together, we shall slowly get there.

Sending a child away to school at the tender age of twelve is one of the hardest things I have ever had to do. I don't think any bush mum likes the idea of placing her kid in the hands of strangers—strangers who end up spending more time with the child than mum herself ever does! You feel that you lose control of your child's life and, therefore, you can only hope and pray that the teachers will encourage and guide him along the very same lines that you had been following for so many years. Bernie still has a long way to go, but I know he will be all right in the end, because he is 'Brown-built'.

Five years after Bernie was born, a most wonderful thing happened—I gave birth to a little girl, Emily Rose. For Ted and myself she is the most precious thing in our lives. From the beginning, it has been an absolute delight to watch her grow into a little lady. Like her brothers before her, little Em studies at home with the Tibooburra outback School of the Air. She loves it and finds the schoolwork easy. She always grows very attached to her governesses, whom she regards as her big sisters.

In my opinion, the School of Distance Education is a remarkable way to educate children. At the end of each term, a 'mini-school' is held in Tibooburra where all the children gather from the bush to attend 'real' classes for a week. Once a year, all the kids get together in Broken Hill for Education Week, which ends with a big contest where they sing the songs that they have been rehearsing with their teachers over the airwaves for many weeks before.

Ted and I have always tried to manage Naryilco as if it were our own, but we still have to answer to somebody if anything goes wrong. As it is a large property with two out-stations, there are a lot more people involved in the day-to-day work. Apart from a mustering camp of about eight men, there is a camp cook, a governess, a grader driver, a pilot, a station hand and his wife, and an Aboriginal cowboy, Archie. Before Archie arrived, we had 'Old Baldy'. Old Baldy was an elderly pensioner who was at Naryilco when we arrived. He lived here until he had a stroke in 1988 and was moved to a nursing home.

Whenever Ted went away to camp, I would call on Old Baldy to help me. He and I had more fights than feeds, but he was always around like a shot if I needed him. I can remember Old Baldy and me trying to start the motor in the mornings. Baldy would be on the crank handle as I pulled the compression levers. If he didn't have a big enough swing up, and I pulled the levers over, I would stop him dead in his tracks and we would have to start all over again. Old Baldy always called me 'Missus', and when the boys were babies he would come down to the kitchen block before tea and either nurse one of the babies or take them for long walks around the homestead. This gave me the chance to finish preparing tea. As much as we would fight, I really miss having Old Baldy around.

Life is hectic on a large company station—there is hardly any time for relaxing. We have a constant stream of visitors passing through Naryilco— truck drivers, dam sinkers, Kidman employees, contract workers, itinerant teachers, even stranded tourists. I work as the station cook and usually have to prepare three full meals and smoko for the staff every day. We need to radio the Kidman head office twice a day and this is also my responsibility. We run various courses for our staff and other Kidman employees, such as bull fertility testing and colt starting courses—where horses are first handled and broken in. There are so many people coming and going that at times, it becomes quite a strain. I love to go for walks because it is the only time I have to myself. The only other welcome break occurs when the blokes are out at camp, but even then I still need to be on call seven days a week, twenty-four hours a day. I am 'Mother Brown' to all.

The telephone has not stopped ringing since the day we had it installed in 1991. I think there must be a little bird out there that tells everyone when Ted is home from camp, because the phone will start ringing for him as soon as he walks in the door and won't stop until late evening. Before the telephone was installed we used the radio to make all our calls. We also sent telegrams. The flying doctor base would sound a whistle on the radio every hour and read out the list of telegrams which had arrived. When the operators received your call sign, they would broadcast the message back to you. The static on the radio, or the interference from bad weather, sometimes made it impossible to hear clearly and created a lot of confusion. The radio phone was an improvement, though it was not very convenient for making outgoing calls. You would have to call in and wait for your turn, hoping that the people ahead did not have too many calls—otherwise, it could turn into a very long wait indeed.

Rural power was connected only one year ago. To be able to switch on a light at any time of the day or night, or to use electrical appliances whenever we want, is a real treat. Before this, we relied on a 240 volt lighting plant. It was my job to check the motor's oil before I started it in the morning and there was a remote control button for turning off the motor at night. The engine shed was a long walk away from the main house and, as the remote control was dead most of the time, I often had to go all the way, with a flashlight, to stop the motor manually. Once it was switched off, everything turned pitch black. I have had some scary trips at night to stop the motor.

Occasionally, I would hear the dingoes howling. I couldn't get back into the house quick enough! We also had a grumpy bull that used to hang around the homestead and I was always on the lookout for him. Once when I was carefully making my way back to the homestead, I came across fresh tracks. I swung my flashlight around to see where the bull was and saw him staring at me from a few metres away by the horse yards. I made a mad dash to the car shed and ended up driving to the homestead.

Before marrying Ted, I had no training in first aid. The knowledge I have today is the result of years of living in the bush. During this time, I have had to treat quite a few medical emergencies. There have been stockmen with broken arms, legs and collarbones, and one with a fractured skull. I have also treated a two-year-old child who was gnawed by a feral pig, a station hand with badly burned legs, and my dad, after a moving vehicle ran over his leg, which peeled the skin off his hand like you would peel a banana. There have also been lots of minor accidents such as welding flashes, cuts and abrasions. When my Ted came down with appendicitis, he had to be flown out in an emergency evacuation, but not until I'd stuck a needle in his backside to help relieve the pain!

The Flying Doctor

Honestly, I would not feel as safe living here if we didn't have the flying doctor on call twenty-four hours a day.

Ted and I take a very active part in the fundraising for the RFDS. All the gymkhanas, race meetings and bronco brandings are to support our flying doctor. Every year, we hold a 'ride-a-thon' from our station to the Noccundra Hotel, 150 kilometres away, to raise money. It is a three-day ride on horseback, camping out in a swag under the stars. We also have the Coopers Cup down at the Moomba gasfields. This is a friendly cricket match between the Moomba workers and the station hands. As the blokes get underway with serious cricket, the ladies make their acquaintance with each other. It's a fun day and all for a good cause.

Ted and I run a 'dry' station—no alcohol on the premises—so the staff have to travel to Tibooburra if they want to have a few drinks. We enjoy a pretty close relationship with all our staff. We share our table and our lives with everyone at Naryilco. Sometimes I wish we could just lead a normal family life and do all those simple things such as having a meal on our own, and not necessarily with the whole mustering camp. To be honest, there hasn't been much chance for the family to enjoy our privacy and this is what I miss.

Since March 1989, we have had a new addition to our 'extended family'—

Anne Maree and William.

Sister Anne Maree. Over the years she has become a wonderful friend. She has so much to give the families in the outback and, as we live on the very edge of her territory, we feel very privileged to have just qualified to be included on her flight path!

Father Terry first flew in one day in 1984, and for many years after that we enjoyed his monthly visits to Naryilco. When Terry decided to retire, we were so pleased to learn that Anne Maree, who had been his offsider for a while, was taking over the controls of the little Cessna. Anne Maree has prepared all our children for their sacraments. She has watched them growing up and has been a part of our family life. The kids love her, especially Em. I admire Anne Maree's energy. The time she puts into her work, travelling the vast outback and listening to everyone, simply amazes me. My Ted loves chatting with her. He says it's a relief to be able to get things off his chest. She always has good, sound advice, but mostly she is there to listen to you. Often the men, if they have a concern or a worry, will get on their horse or their bike and ride it out of their system. There have been times when I have felt pretty low, especially when there has been a crisis with the boys at boarding school. I guess I just save those concerns up for Anne Maree because I can't dump my worries on the staff. God Bless you, Sister Anne Maree!

Over the last ten years, Ted and I have become really good mates. We have grown much closer and understand each other so much better. I think our love and support of one another helped us get through these many years of life in the outback. He is my best friend.

Ted and I have a little farm twenty minutes out of Toowoomba. One day, we plan to retire on this land, and build ourselves a house sheltered under plenty of beautiful native trees. We may not have a lot of the things that city people have, but I don't think we have missed out on much. My Ted is content—this is the only life he knows. As for myself, if I had to choose all over again, I would not wish for a different life.

CIRCUIT ONE

MAREE MORTON—
INNAMINCKA STATION

Like Dale, Maree Morton married at nineteen and went on to help her husband manage a large company station. When I met Maree in 1989, she was a young mum trying to juggle the day-to-day running of a family property as well as teaching her two young children, Catherine and Stewart, at home.

Over the years, I have been close to Maree at several crucial moments in her life, such as her time of heartbreak at having to send her children to boarding school. The worst time was after Stewart left and she was home alone. She felt so lost, and I shared her distress. I was also with the family when their home, Karmona Station, was placed on the market for sale. It was a difficult time—a time of great uncertainty for the entire family.

Fortunately I was able to follow the Mortons across to their new residence at Innamincka Station, a large Kidman property in South Australia. Graham, her husband, is the one who gave me the nickname the 'Sundowner'—because I always seem to touch down at their property just as the sun is setting.

I was only nineteen and a newlywed when I came to the outback. My husband of just two weeks, Graham Morton, had brought me out to Durham Downs, a cattle station in far south-west Queensland which was bigger than most of the towns we drove through on our way to the property. I kept reminding myself that to be a good bushman's wife I had to accept the bush as my new home. But with Graham out most weeks at stock camp, and separated by more than 1,000 kilometres from my friends and family, isolation suddenly took on a whole new meaning.

I never gave much thought to spending the rest of my life in the bush until after we wed—I suppose there never was much of a choice for me if I wanted to be with Graham because the bush was his livelihood and his passion. I certainly found the experience of living in the bush very different from visiting it as a young girl during school holidays. Back then, country life seemed like great fun. I went horse riding, fishing, swimming in the river and enjoyed singalongs in the pubs with some real bush characters. But when I began my married life in the outback, the bush seemed strange and frightening. My new home was a basic three-room cottage on 8,000 square kilometres of open country with flat and stony gibber plains stretching as far as the eye could see. There were a few people around, Graham, and several thousand head of cattle to keep me company. This was not what I dreamt bush life would be like.

In the bush, you seem to hear about people from far and wide. I heard of Graham Morton when my family first moved to live out west, but wasn't officially introduced to him until years later when I went to a race dance in Betoota. Travelling long distances to attend a dance was not uncommon, although crammed in the back of a dusty utility trying to keep one's ball gown from being crushed or soiled was always tricky. People turned out in droves for these events, where you met most folk and often future husbands. Unfortunately for me, the majority of dances were held when I was away at boarding school.

Graham and I at a bush dance.

My big romance began when I was sixteen. Like most bushies, Graham was rather shy. He worked as a station hand at Pandi Pandi Station, thirty kilometres from Birdsville, across the South Australian border. I was home for the holidays and Graham invited me to his sister's twenty-first birthday party. It was to be held the week after I was due to return to school. I asked my parents if I could stay home the extra week to attend the party. As I suspected, this was out of the question. Education was very important in my parents' eyes and there was no way they would allow me to miss even one day of school. To my good fortune, there was a downpour of rain when I was supposed to catch the plane in Birdsville. The road to town became flooded and impassable, so I made the party after all. Graham and my courtship was sealed from that day onwards, all thanks to the floods.

I was born on 3 September 1955 in Augathella, a small country town north of Charleville in Queensland. In 1962, my parents, Mick and June Brunckhorst, drove us from Augathella to the big smoke—in our spanking new Holden wagon—to what they thought would be a better life. Coopers Plains, a suburb of Brisbane, was where we eventually settled. We lived there for several years, but when Dad couldn't find work he was forced to make the long journey back to Augathella during the week to shear on a station, returning to Brisbane on the weekends. This solution didn't work out, so my parents decided to move to Milbong.

Milbong was a small farming area south of Ipswich where my grand-

Mum, Dad and me.

parents, Eric and Josephine Condren, owned a dairy farm. During the week, Mum worked at the small Milbong post office while Dad helped my grandfather manage the farm. A dairy farm demands constant work but it has its rewards. If I wasn't riding my beloved horse Claude, I'd be keeping an eye on the cows in the sorghum patch with my older sister Narelle, or helping my grandfather on the tractor with the ploughing and seeding. As a child, one of my greatest joys was going into town with my grandfather. He would take Narelle and I along for the drive, letting us ride up in front of his old truck and spoiling us with lollies. When my grandfather took ill and passed away in 1966, everything changed. The family decided to lease the farm out and Granny moved to Brisbane. Mum and Dad were going to the bush to work on Cluny Station, a cattle property near Bedourie. Tears and tantrums could not sway my parents into letting me go with them to Cluny. Instead, I was packed off—at the age of eleven—to a Catholic convent school 1,500 kilometres away in Ipswich.

My first year at boarding school, with the Sisters of Mercy, was a difficult experience. Some of the sisters were friendly, while others were not so pleasant. Apart from the less friendly nuns, not having my family around was what affected me the most. It was my first real separation from them, and when you have such emptiness in your heart and cry at the drop of a hat, there is nothing you can ever really enjoy. This feeling did eventually pass, but it took three years before I finally settled into my small boarding school. I travelled home to Cluny several times a year by plane for the term holidays.

Cluny Station was managed by my uncle and aunt. It wasn't hard to keep myself occupied at the station during the holidays. I loved the freedom of the open country, which was a welcome change from the stifling boarding school environment. At Christmas, for their annual holidays, Mum and Dad would take Narelle and me to the South Coast and then on to visit Granny in Brisbane. They would drive me back to boarding school before returning to Cluny. This was to be our routine for the next six years, with Mum and Dad moving successively to Morney Plains Station near Windorah, and later to Durrie Station north-east of Birdsville.

Everywhere station life is always the same. Mum worked as the station cook while Dad was the 'cowboy', or station handyman. As I grew older, I developed various interests to occupy myself during term breaks. It didn't bother me that I was practically the only teenager around for miles. I enjoyed the solitude and divided my time between reading Mills and Boon novels in the cool of the verandah, playing cards with residents at the property, and helping Mum around the homestead. When I was old enough, Mr Bill Brook, the owner of the Birdsville general store, let me work with him in his shop, which was great fun. The store was like any other country shop and carried just about everything you could think of.

Birdsville was a quiet town then, with few tourists travelling through—nothing like what it is today.

After I graduated from high school, my parents returned to Coopers Plains. Mum's health wasn't good and Dad wanted her to be closer to doctors. Graham and I were corresponding regularly and whenever he could get to a phone he would call. I missed him terribly. It is very hard to keep a relationship alive when separated by almost 2,000 kilometres. So when Graham finally popped the question, I accepted.

Durham Downs Station was our first home. Graham continued to work as a stockman while I took up a position for a short time as governess. Looking back, I don't think I was prepared for bush life. Not only was I very young, but I was frightened—how was I going to endure living out here? Graham was away at camp for weeks at a time and, as I was very sociable by nature, I felt lonely. I repeatedly told myself that I would soon be starting my own family, but this did little to ease my solitude. Instead, I busied myself with cleaning and painting our small cottage in an effort to make it a real home for the two of us. As Graham predicted, with the passing of time I became more settled and less worried about being alone.

I only dared venture out once on my own during my first year at Durham Downs. Still not the world's most accomplished bushie, I was reluctant to stray too far from the station. In June 1976, I was delighted to discover I was pregnant. Around this time, my mother fell seriously ill and had to be hospitalised in Brisbane. I decided to go and see her. I had never driven very far by myself, and was nervous about the long journey. I set out from Durham in Graham's Ford utility at dawn and drove to Quilpie, our closest town, in just under nine hours. It's a miracle to think that I even made it that far, as I was not the world's best driver on bitumen, let alone on unsealed roads choked with bulldust. Brimming with newly found confidence, I travelled on to Charleville, two hours east of Quilpie, then continued the journey to Brisbane by bus.

It was great to be with Mum, but sadly this was to be the last time I saw her, as she passed away three months later. On the drive home to Durham Downs, I stalled the ute in a bad patch of bulldust near Kihee Station, eighty kilometres south-west of Eromanga. A mob of cattle surrounded the ute and, feeling scared, I locked myself inside, praying that someone would eventually come to my rescue. I was very relieved when, several hours later, the manager's wife from a nearby property passed by and offered to tow me back to her station. I was offered a bed for the night and the next morning a kindly jackaroo jump-started the ute and sent me on my way. I was so glad when I saw the homestead again. I had a new battery delivered on the next mail run.

Towards the end of 1976, Graham became manager of Orientos Station, a privately owned cattle station 600 kilometres south-west of Quilpie. I was eight months pregnant at the time, and the doctors advised me to go to Brisbane to await the birth. Our daughter, Catherine, arrived two weeks early at the Mater Hospital in Brisbane on 25 February 1977. It was awful being away from Graham. Heavy rains and severe flooding kept Catherine and me away an extra week but luckily, a friend who was a pilot offered to fly us home.

Like most new mums I was anxious, but I was never too worried about caring for a newborn baby on my own in the bush. Somehow instinct takes over. Occasionally I spoke to my sister on the radio to ask for her advice—she is a trained nurse—but it was more to get confirmation that I was doing the right things.

Six months later we were on the move again. This was to be our last move for sixteen and a half years. We went to Karmona, a privately owned cattle property fifty-five kilometres south of Durham Downs. Optimism quickly turned into despair once I set foot on the property.

'Chin up,' chirped Graham. 'It's not as bad as it looks.'

I was doubtful. The homestead was very old and had seen better days. From the outside, it looked as if it was in two minds about staying upright. Inside, it was even worse. The cobwebbed walls were cracked and large chunks of plaster and rubble were scattered in every room. The floor-boards had almost rotted away. A flimsy roof made out of sheets of corrugated iron leaked and threatened to fly right off at the first blow in a dust storm. Worse still, there was

Graham

hardly any furniture. Having only lived on company stations until then, I was used to fully furnished accommodation. I'd never thought about buying any furniture. Vegetable-packing crates were used as drawers for our clothes—cauliflower for mine, and lettuce for Graham. The power supply was thirty-two volts only, and there was no hot water whatsoever. Graham eventually installed a 'donkey'—an old forty-four gallon drum encased in cement with water pipes and enough room underneath to light a fire—so at least I could have hot running water in the house. There was no telephone—I ordered food or supplies via a two-way radio and the orders had to be large enough to last for several months. No-one can imagine the actual problems of ordering huge quantities of dried and canned food from far away and for long ahead. My shopping list was frequently misunderstood, which resulted in some very odd deliveries. For example, a request for three boxes of Cornflakes somehow became thirty!

Things did not look very bright during those first few months at Karmona but, as always, I had little choice in the matter and just got on with it. Whenever I felt like having a grumble about my lack of mod cons, I would spare a thought for the pioneering women before me who had to put up with a lot worse when they followed their husbands out west. If they could stick it out, so could I! Life out here was becoming very dear to me. Graham already had bush life in his blood and slowly taught me to love it as well.

In the next few years, as oil exploration began to open up the country and new roads were being laid, visitors started to call in. Barbecues were arranged at a nearby camp and social evenings were held at Nappa Merrie Station, 145 kilometres west of Karmona. A weekly mail plane brought goods and supplies from Port Augusta in South Australia, and a road mail service travelled to nearby Durham Downs each fortnight. Some years, floods would cut us off, leaving us stranded for three months at a time. But they also brought flourishing pastures for the stock. Whenever I could, I helped Graham muster and draft cattle. Naturally, Graham had been doing this since he was a boy but as I was new to this, tempers would fly when there were just the two of us working the cattle in the yards to get them ready for market. Driving cattle along the road in the station Land-rover was fine, but with Graham in the drafting yard, and me hopping from rail to rail swinging the gates for a mob of stirred-up bullocks, it was a different matter altogether. Working together under the hot sun, we'd shout at each other until finally I would curse him and head back to the house in tears. It would take some time for me to cool down and return to the yards to finish that afternoon's drafting.

Our second child, a boy whom we named Stewart, was born on 11 May 1979. I flew to Birdsville on the mail plane and then on to Brisbane, leaving Catherine in the care of Graham's mum at Pandi Pandi Station. I missed Graham and Catherine terribly while I was in hospital, but there was no other alternative—I just had to be patient until our baby arrived.

Several months after Stewart's birth, our new house—forty-six squares in all—arrived on two semitrailers along with the builders to construct it. It was thrilling to have a real home. At long last I was going to have 240 volt power, better cupboards for our clothes and a decent kitchen. The builders proved to be good company, and I enjoyed cooking for them in exchange for their babysitting Catherine. With the 240 volt power came an 8 kva lighting plant with a remote control switch. Previously, the rule was that the last one to bed had to turn off the generator. I didn't mind in the least—but I did after the switch packed it in. This wasn't much fun when it was raining and I had to race back from the engine room, across the flat, in a soaking nightdress.

When Catherine started walking I had to have eyes in the back of my head. There was a dam close to the house, and Cooper Creek was only metres away. My biggest fears were that she might drown or be bitten by a snake. One day she went walkabout and was missing for several hours. We had no septic toilets, only an outhouse with a very large hole—this was the first place I looked for her, and the second was the dam. Hunting high and low, Graham and I eventually found her curled up asleep behind the gas freezer. She had placed a chair in front of the refrigerator so she could reach a box of chocolates on top. She had slipped and the gas from the freezer had caused her to doze off. In a panic, I radioed the flying doctor for help. Karmona's airstrip wasn't very serviceable and we were worried that the doctor would not be able to land. Luckily Catherine was not too seriously affected by the gas so there was no need on this occasion for an emergency evacuation.

I've been fortunate to have had only two emergency evacuations in my family. The most recent one involved Graham. Late one afternoon I heard shouting and loud knocking on the front door. I found a very sweaty, red-faced stockman on the verandah who mumbled something about Graham being hurt at the cattle yard. I rushed out and found Graham lying half conscious in the dirt. The stockman told me that they were in the middle of drafting cattle when a mob of bullocks suddenly came crashing through an iron gate, crushing Graham behind it. I bundled Graham into the truck and drove at breakneck speed to the homestead and called the flying doctor. Meanwhile a group of station hands went down to the airstrip to light the emergency flares so the plane could land safely. Graham was flown out to Broken Hill later that night and spent the next few days in hospital with several bruised ribs and severe bruising to his hips and thighs. Bushmen are never any good in hospital and Graham was soon protesting that he was well enough to go home to finish the drafting. Without the Royal Flying Doctor Service, I don't think I would enjoy the same peace of mind. So many of us bushies owe our health, and indeed our lives, to this small team of dedicated doctors and nurses.

As soon as Catherine and Stewart were old enough, they went out mustering and branding with their dad. They were a welcome extra pair of hands around Karmona. Catherine learnt to drive the Toyota when she was eleven. Stewart was only seven, and had to stand up, leaning against the seat, to look through the steering wheel. By 1982, the education of the children had become a pressing issue. I thought about getting a governess—but what young, single girl would want to live out the back o' beyond? Nonetheless, I employed four great girls for four years running. The last girl we employed eloped, after only a year at the station, with a fellow who worked on the oilfields. At this point, I decided to teach the kids myself. It seemed the most sensible solution, especially since having an outsider living under the family roof puts a strain on everyone. At first I was worried that I was not a qualified teacher—for starters, it was such a long time since I last did any studying! It was not easy for me to reopen old textbooks. Besides, I also had to cook, keep the books, clean the house, feed the animals and attend to all sorts of other chores. Still, they were my kids, and I wanted them to have a good education, so into the schoolroom I went and did the best I could.

At first Catherine and Stewart didn't like the idea of having Mum as their teacher, but they quickly got used to the new routine and buckled down. With the help of the School of the Air teachers our lessons worked out smoothly. However, when Catherine was sent away to boarding school, Stewart became unsettled in the schoolroom. All he wanted to do was go out and work with Dad.

Boarding school was tough on the entire family. When the children were old enough to understand, I began preparing them as well as I could for the moment when they would have to leave Karmona for school. They accepted this but still found it very hard when the time actually did come. I had been so concerned with preparing *them* that I never realised how it would affect *me*. I missed their company so much. It was also extremely costly, and money was scarce.

When Catherine first went away, in 1989, there was no telephone. If she had something important to tell me she would call on the radio phone, and then I would travel to Jackson—roughly an hour and a half drive—to call her back from a pay telephone. This was the only way for us to have a private conversation. But it could also be very frustrating because I was not always able to get away on that very day, and sometimes had to wait for a couple of days before I could return her call. While in Year 8, on her way back to school, she was left alone on a bus that had broken down. It was a traumatic experience for her. When I found out, I was horrified. I couldn't understand how a bus driver could abandon one of his passengers, let alone a twelve-year-old. When the police called to say they had found my young girl stranded on a broken-down bus on the outskirts of a small town, so many 'what ifs' raced through my mind! Speaking to a teary Catherine on the telephone I felt miserable as, from such a distance, I was powerless to comfort her. How I wished I could have given her a hug! As a mother, I often felt guilty for not being by my children's side to protect them. I remembered my own lonely days at boarding school, and how homesick I had felt, so far away from my parents. Still, I had to keep reminding myself that it would be unfair to keep the kids at home. Boarding school gives children from the outback the chance to mix with their peers, play sport and join in other social activities which cannot be provided in the bush. Neither Catherine nor Stewart ever complained of loneliness when they were growing up. They had each other, and the fact that there were no other children around for miles never seemed to bother them. They are both naturally independent and, like their dad, have such a love for the outback that I don't think they will ever want to leave.

As a practising Catholic, I felt it was my duty to give my kids a sound basis in religious instruction. Before I came out to live in the bush, religion was an important part of my life, but I guess because I was so young when I came out here it became less of a priority. Also, it is practically impossible to keep one's faith alive without outside support. No priests ever came out our way. As time went on, however, all that my mother had taught me and what I had learnt at the convent school progressively came back to me. I applied for a correspondence course in religion for the kids but as this became a chore, I discontinued the sessions. I was delighted when the Aerial Ministry began in 1984—it suddenly brought the Church to the bush and to families like ours living in isolation.

The ministry came to me out of the blue—quite literally—when Father Terry Loth touched down at Karmona one day in his small Cessna. The last person we ever expected to meet out here was a Catholic priest! Graham was sceptical, whereas I thought it was a wonderful idea to have mass celebrated in our lounge room. Father Terry began flying into Karmona once a month and would spend the night at home with us. He helped with the teaching of the children and prepared them for their sacraments. Father Terry was a very learnt man who could talk at length on nearly any topic. Graham discovered that Father Terry shared his love of footy so, in due course, he opened up to him.

For me, what made the Aerial Ministry so special was that it gave me the chance to meet a priest in a completely different context—after my experience at Catholic school, I'd forgotten that priests can be human too! But as much as I enjoyed Father Terry's company, communication with him was still a little awkward for me because he was a man. I would have preferred a woman's presence, and I think many other women felt the same way. When Father Loth retired, he called to tell us that one of the Presentation Sisters would be taking over from him. I was surprised and impressed that a woman would be continuing the work of the Aerial Ministry. I certainly couldn't imagine any of the nuns I knew as a girl piloting a plane!

When Anne Maree landed at Karmona I wasn't sure what to expect, but I know I was longing to spend time with another woman. Anne Maree was a little shy at first, and so was I, but the awkwardness disappeared when we sat down to a cuppa in the kitchen. That's Anne Maree for you. She makes it so easy to be friends.

Anne Maree arrived at a time in my life when things were not very rosy. I was worried about Catherine going away to boarding school, but more importantly, life at Karmona was entering a difficult phase. The owners had gone into liquidation towards the end of 1989 and the property was to be sold at auction. Graham and I were uncertain about our future after the sale. Suddenly our lives were turned upside down. Karmona was eventually tacked onto Durham Downs as an out-station. Graham was forced to step down from his position of station manager to become the out-station manager and overseer at Karmona. Throughout all this upheaval, Anne Maree was there to lend her support. I was home alone a great deal at this time. The sweetest sound to my ears back then was the humming of her Cessna as it circled over the homestead heralding her arrival.

Anne Maree's visits are always perfectly timed—whenever I need her, in she flies. She must have a sixth sense! I don't rely on her to solve my problems for me, but it always helps to have someone with whom to talk things through—someone who listens without judging and who can put things into perspective. Her schedule is as hectic as ever as she flies from one property to another, from one town to the next. But she never makes anyone feel she doesn't have enough time for them. She gives me advice when she thinks it appropriate and is always ready to lend a hand inside the house, or out on the station. Every year at Karmona, severe flooding left us stranded at the homestead. On more than one occasion, Anne Maree came to our aid, flying us across the Cooper to buy supplies.

Most mishaps leave her unfazed—she just takes it all in her stride. Graham has a lot of respect for her and gave her the nickname of the 'Sundowner', which I think she secretly loves, because she always manages to fly in just as the last light is fading.

It must be an exhausting life for Anne Maree. She is always on the move, sleeps in a different bed every night and rarely has a moment to herself. Graham admires her energy. 'She's one helluva tough old bird,' he says.

She never complains or talks about her own problems but I know from what she has told me that it is only when she is in her plane that she can at last let go and relax.

Wherever I go in the bush, everyone has heard of the Flying Nun and speaks highly of her. Anne Maree wins the respect of all the people she meets. There are a variety of religious denominations out here, but even non-Catholics still feel comfortable confiding in her. People in the bush, no matter what their religion is, practise what I would describe as 'good living'. We are kind to our neighbours, we open our homes to strangers and we look after our own. This is our religion.

When a close friend of mine was tragically killed in a car crash, I desperately wanted to attend the funeral, which was being held in Adelaide. I immediately thought of Anne Maree and phoned around to find her. When I told her what had happened, she modified her schedule, flew me to Broken Hill and then caught the bus to Adelaide with me. If it wasn't for her generosity I wouldn't have been able to pay my last respects. The list is endless. 'Keep the Flying Doctors flying' is the message of many outback fundraising campaigns for the RFDS. There should be one for Anne Maree as well, because like the flying doctor, she relies on the charity and goodwill of people in the outback to keep her ministry going. We all try to help out whenever we can, with fuel and maintenance for her Cessna—anything to help her stay up in the air!

After the sale of Karmona to Kidman and Co, better opportunities came our way. Graham and I accepted an offer to manage Innamincka, a large cattle station in South Australia. The kids and us were sad to leave our old house—after all, sixteen and a half years in the same place is a long time. We will always retain a soft spot in our hearts for Karmona.

Innamincka was purchased by Kidman and Co at the turn of the century. It is a 13,818 square kilometre property located in one of the most arid and desolate areas in Australia. The land is quite similar to Karmona's, with its open plains, sand dunes and spinifex, but there are also rocky, flat-topped hills and gibber slopes with a wide range of grasses, trees and plants. Cooper Creek forms on its flood plains, so we are never short of water. Just five kilometres away from the station, there is a small historic township with its own pub, a general store and four private homes, but apart from these buildings, there's nothing else out here. We are exactly 1,100 kilometres from Adelaide and about the same distance from Toowoomba—as far away from the city as you can possibly get.

I was daunted by the size of Innamincka, with its large homestead and numerous outbuildings. Not only do we now have separate quarters for married couples and single men, but a meat house, saddle shed, store, and a hangar to house the company plane.

Innamincka homestead

A company-owned property and a privately owned property are basically operated along the same lines, the only difference being that on a privately owned property, money and lack of employees can be a problem, especially if you experience a bad season or two. Working for a large company like Kidman means that our income does not necessarily fluctuate with the cattle prices. We have wage security as well as financial help for the children's education. It is Kidman policy to make you feel a part of the company. They invite and appreciate your initiatives and they give you some freedom running the property. Usually the position of manager on a Kidman station is a job for life. They like to keep the same manager on a property to generate a sense of personal commitment. Sometimes we find it stressful to have to deal with staff disputes or other personal problems, but with so many different individuals living and working together, you learn not to interfere in people's lives.

It's Kidman policy that the men retire at about sixty. Graham is still a long way from retirement, but one thing is certain—he will never move to the city. At best, he'd move to a small farm with a few head of cattle, somewhere outside of Toowoomba perhaps. Nowadays, whenever we have to go into town, we have had enough of it after about a week and all we want to do is pack up and come home.

When I look back, it's funny to think how isolated and lonely I felt when I first moved to the bush. Now if I am asked about solitude, I readily admit that I am geographically isolated, but I would never say I feel any personal loneliness. I may be hundreds of kilometres away from town, but I no longer dread being alone as I once did in those early years of station life. Life in the west is very rewarding. Time is not measured by the clock but by the sun in the sky. The people I meet are genuine. Perhaps because there are so few of us out here, we take the time to say 'g'day'. Family life is what matters most. Husband and wife will do everything together. The bush forces you to work out your differences and get on with the business of marriage.

Since finishing high school, Catherine decided not to stay on in town and is working at Innamincka as the station cook—her mother taught her well! Stewart will soon graduate and is looking forward to following in his dad's footsteps. I think both my children always thought the city kids were the unlucky ones. They love the bush and see their future here working on the land. Things may change as they find their own direction in life.

Life in the bush is as you choose to make it. Mine is happy, and I thank God every day for it. Living in the west has opened my eyes. I never imagined it would be so fulfilling. I couldn't have asked for a better life than the one I took on when I married Graham.

CIRCUIT ONE

CATHERINE MORTON—
INNAMINCKA STATION

Maree's daughter, Catherine, has given me better insight into the young people of the west. It seems they grow up faster out here, taking responsibilities in their stride, just like their parents before them.

Catherine was twelve years old when I met her. She was being taught at home by her mum, and struck me as a very independent girl with a strong personality. Then she was off to boarding school in Toowoomba and we only caught up with each other during her school holidays.

Catherine and her younger brother, Stewart, always make me feel part of the family when I touch down at their station. I especially remember one enjoyable Christmas holiday when they took me crayfishing down at their favourite waterhole. I hadn't fished for many years but luckily I didn't fare too badly.

It's been wonderful watching Catherine grow up. It's not easy for a teenage girl out here, but she loves the bush and says this is where she intends to stay. Now that she has graduated from high school, she is happily working as the station cook at Innamincka and she certainly isn't one to take any nonsense from the blokes!

I'm the only teenager living here at Innamincka Station. In fact, there are hardly any teenagers around these parts, let alone girls. I've always got on better with the men so it's never been a problem for me. The fact that I've grown up on outback stations all my life, mostly among blokes, must have something to do with it, I guess.

Apart from the governesses and cooks employed on neighbouring stations, or the girls working up at the Innamincka pub, I rarely see another female face. At any rate, I'm definitely not one of those 'girlie' girls. I'm quite happy hanging around with the ringers who work for Dad at the station. When I was younger, I was always out in the stockyards or mustering with my dad. I was a regular tomboy back then, and loved riding motorbikes and horses.

I was born at the Mater Hospital in Brisbane on 25 February 1977. I was just six months old when our family moved to Karmona Station, on Cooper Creek. When I was two, I remember Mum mysteriously disappearing to Brisbane and Dad sending me to live with Grandma at Pandi Pandi Station near Birdsville. I  was flown home to Karmona six weeks later and lo and behold, much to my surprise, I found that during my absence, Mum had brought back a baby brother. We named him Stewart.

Stewart and I at Karmona.

At Karmona, Stewart and I did everything together because we only had each other for company. There were no other kids living on the station, but I don't think we ever really cared, because we had too much fun exploring the bush. One day when we were playing outside, things must have got a little rough as Stewart fell over and split his lip. Mum radioed the flying doctor, then drove us to the dirt landing strip. It was all very dramatic as the doctor's plane roared in with a huge cloud of dust. Poor Stewart was stitched up on the spot without any anaesthetic whatsoever. All I remember was a lot of screaming and crying coming out of a very big aeroplane!

Saturdays were always special for Stewart and me because that was the day we would go with Dad to Durham Downs Station, our closest neighbour fifty-five kilometres away, to collect our mail for the week and play with the children who lived there. Once a fortnight, all our perishables and frozen goods would also arrive at Durham. It always felt like an adventure. If we were lucky enough, Dad would let one of us drive his Toyota. Stewart and I had our fair share of brother–sister fights but we were always, and still are, very good mates. After all, we were the only ones around, so we had to learn to get along!

There was no real power at Karmona. Instead we had to make do with a 240 volt motor which ran for about twelve hours every day. We didn't have a television until I was much older, so Stewart and I were always outside getting up to mischief. If we weren't fishing for yabbies or swimming in the Cooper, we would be out with Dad on the bore runs and generally lending a hand around the property. Both Stewart and I learnt to ride a motorbike before we were nine and to drive Dad's Toyota before we were twelve, so we could help out with the mustering. In 1989, when Karmona was put up for sale, Dad, along with Stewart, myself and another fellow, Ray, mustered the entire property by ourselves. We also branded and counted the cattle. It was a hard slog and it took us two weeks. I was twelve at the time, and Stewart only ten, but we were expected to pitch in. I suppose that is one of the real differences about growing up in the bush—it teaches you to be more responsible and independent. Out here, you grow up faster.

The School of the Air.

Since Karmona was only a small property—630 square kilometres—Dad managed it by himself. If he needed help, it was usually Mum, Stewart and myself who would be called upon to lend a hand. It wasn't always easy for him, and sometimes Mum would allow Stewart and me to leave the schoolroom and help Dad in the cattle yards, but she always made sure that we caught up with our schoolwork on the weekends. If cattle needed to be trucked out, the owner of Karmona would bring his semi and a family member to help out for a few weeks.

For my primary school education I was enrolled with the School of the Air. I loved doing my lessons with a teacher over the radio. I learnt spelling and my multiplication tables over the airwaves! Cooking and art classes, where we made things following the teacher's instructions, were also great fun. All the schoolwork came from the School of Distance Education in Brisbane and then later from Charleville. I had three papers—English, maths and social science—which I had to complete every two weeks. I had different governesses teaching me from Year 1 to halfway through Year 6, until Mum decided to take over the teaching herself. Our schoolroom was a stuffy little room tacked onto the back of the homestead.

Once Mum became our teacher, there was not much of a chance to play up, although I used to help Stewart with his work when she wasn't looking. Stewart sometimes acted up. He couldn't see the sense in sitting in the boring schoolroom for hours when he could have been outside working with Dad or riding his motorbike. He would always try and put one over Mum and worm his way out. I, on the other hand, figured that the smartest way to get back outside was by concentrating hard and finishing my assigned work quickly. That way I could leave the schoolroom a lot faster.

From Year 4 to Year 7, Mum and Dad sent Stewart and me away to camps organised by the School of the Air. They said it would give us a chance to meet other kids who were studying by correspondence. It was interesting putting a face to kids who we only knew by their voices on the radio. Twice a year, itinerant teachers would come from Charleville to visit us at Karmona. They travelled to different stations and properties in the area to help children like ourselves. They came to check on the progress of our studies and usually spent several nights with us at the homestead. It was great fun having them come to stay because they brought a computer and games to play. As always, any visitors to Karmona were most welcome.

A fortnight before my thirteenth birthday, Mum and Dad sent me away to boarding school at St Ursula's in Toowoomba. It was a twenty-six-hour round trip by car and exactly 1,152 kilometres from Karmona's front door. Although Mum had tried to prepare me for the separation, I don't think I was ready for the shock of being so far away from home. I had never lived with sixty-three strangers under the same roof before, let alone sixty-three girls! For the first two years, I felt numbed by the whole experience. I was homesick most of the time and felt lost. I didn't know a soul apart from two cousins from Birdsville. I missed the freedom of Karmona.

Initially I hated boarding school because of the different attitudes and the clash of personalities—there were constant fights between girls, teachers and dorm mistresses. I was used to being around adults and found it hard to relate to other girls my age—they all seemed so different. I also missed the freedom of home. Back at Karmona, I'd finish my lessons and then hop on my motorbike or go for a swim down at the Cooper. At school, we only had about two hours of free time in the evening after classes, which never seemed enough. Fortunately I got on well with my dorm mistress and could talk freely to her, so I did not feel too lonely. Basically I kept to myself a lot in those first few years and tried to do my best academically, counting the days until term holidays when I could at long last return to Karmona.

The hardest thing about being so far away from home was that I could not share any of my problems with Mum or Dad. For many years, there wasn't a telephone at Karmona, a radio telephone—so if I needed to talk to Mum, we could never have long conversations or talk about personal things because being on a network, people from miles around could hear our conversations. Poor Mum! If I wanted to talk privately to her, she would have to get into the Toyota and drive for an hour and a half to the nearest pay phone and call me back. I remember once receiving a phone call from Mum telling me that Dad had been involved in a plane crash out at Durham Downs. It was hours

until she could call again and tell me he was okay. The queue at our school phone was always long, so conversations had to be brief. Halfway through Year 9, a telephone was finally connected at Karmona so I could call Mum at any time of the day.

I spent five years away at school, which meant that Mum and Dad missed out on a vital part of my growing up. However, I am very grateful to them for sending me away to school. As all parents say, 'school is the best part of your life'. I believe there is some truth to this saying. When you live in the outback, sending children to boarding school is the only way to give them a chance to study and to experience a different way of life.

When I went home to Karmona for the holidays, I would help Mum around the homestead. If there were any race meets or rodeos on in the district, Dad would drive the whole family out and make it a real social occasion. I never found Karmona lonely or dull because I was always glad to have a break from the girls at St Ursula's. I much preferred the quietness and solitude of the bush to the hustle and bustle of Toowoomba.

When I was sixteen and in my second-last year of high school Mum and Dad were offered a fantastic job managing Innamincka Station in South Australia. Stewart and I were very sad when they broke the news to us that we would be leaving Karmona—still, a 3.4 million acre station didn't sound half bad!

It was exciting arriving at our new home for the holidays and meeting the dozen or so staff who were employed by Kidman and Co to work with us. The place was enormous compared to Karmona. Not only was there a very roomy homestead for our family, but also numerous guest and staff quarters, stores, sheds—even a kitchen with recreation room. Dad was impressed with how well maintained the property was despite several years of drought which had forced 'destocking'. Innamincka is magical. I don't think anyone in our family ever regretted moving here.

Certainly, there isn't much to occupy a teenager on an isolated station but since I have always lived in the bush, I am well used to it. I never really enjoyed going to parties, shopping, and the other things most girls like to do. I prefer being on my own. The isolation has never bothered me, nor the heat. Although it gets very hot out here in the summer, with temperatures well above the forties, it doesn't affect me so much because I've grown accustomed to it. Anyway, there's always the Cooper, which is only a short walk away from the homestead, if I want to cool off.

The flying doctor is on call around the clock for medical emergencies and there is a clinic on the station every six weeks. An eye specialist and a dentist fly in once a year. We set up the dentist's chair in the shade of a gum with a view out to the hills. It's funny watching all the ringers lining up nervously when the dentist is visiting, all jostling each other and pretending they aren't scared!

I guess the only real worry I have out here is during times of drought. It's tough for anyone in the bush to suffer months or years without rain. One of the main difficulties is to find water for the cattle. Without rain, you don't get feed to fatten the cattle, which in turn leaves you without money. At Karmona, every time after it rained there would be the most wondrous carpet of wild flowers springing up all over the paddocks. I haven't seen wild flowers out this way for a long time. For the most part, it's hard country—very rocky and arid. Fortunately Innamincka has managed to survive its dry spells quite well. There was a very bad drought for several years just as Dad took over the management. The lease, which previously carried some 14,000 cattle, dropped to 4,000 in just three years. Since then, there have been plenty of good seasons and cattle numbers have picked up.

I have been out of high school for just over a year. Mum was keen for me to stay on in town and continue studying but I wanted to come back to the bush. I've always loved the outback—it's been a part of me for so long that I don't ever want to leave. Stewart feels the same way. Once he graduates, he'll be back in a flash. I love this lifestyle too much to want to give it up and move down to the city. What for? I simply can't see the attraction. Too fast, too polluted, and too many people. There is no freedom to do as you like—nowhere to roam. Had I stayed away, I know Mum and Dad would have been happy for me, but I don't think I could ever stand living in a town again. I'd feel too cooped up.

I'd like to find a nice country bloke who loves the bush as much as I do. I've found that town blokes aren't my type.

There are several governesses and cooks on neighbouring stations, so I do meet other women from time to time.

Sister Anne Maree flies in occasionally and keeps Mum company. She met Mum while we were still living at Karmona. I met her briefly when I was twelve but didn't meet her properly until my first school holidays. As I was used to seeing Father Loth, I was surprised when Mum introduced her as the new pilot of the Aerial Ministry. I never thought nuns knew how to fly planes!

At St Ursula's there were quite a few sisters teaching us. I can't say that I liked all of them, but I certainly realised Anne Maree was different. She didn't have a pious air. It's only in the last couple of years that I have come to know her better and now that I have finished school, I have been able to see more of her. Religion isn't that important to me, but that does not mean that I can't talk to Anne Maree.

Every year at our local ride-a-thon, which raises money for the flying doctor, she is out there in the thick of it, lending a hand. She may feel more comfortable in her Cessna than in the saddle, but you would never know. She never complains. She is important to the many women who, like me, live in isolation and rarely get a chance to see many other people. The ringers all

With Pop and Sister Anne Maree at Innamincka.

love her down here! Mum tells me how much Anne Maree supported her when we were living at Karmona. I know that when the property was put on the market and I was about to be sent away to school for the first time, it was a worrying time for Mum. Anne Maree seemed to arrive at just the right moment in our lives. When we moved to Innamincka, she altered her flight plan to include us in her outback parish. Dad is very fond of her and loves to give her a hard time whenever she comes to visit. He's always teasing her. He's the one who gave her the nickname the 'Sundowner' because for some strange reason she has this knack of always landing at Innamincka just as the sun is setting. Mum used to worry about her arriving late, because there are no lights on our strip—only emergency flares for the flying doctor. But since Anne Maree obtained her night licence, we don't have to worry as much.

I'm now officially employed as the station cook here at Innamincka. I cook for a dozen people—three main meals and two smokos—every day. Not your elegant restaurant food, just the regular meat and two veg. No-one has died yet from my cooking! On Saturdays I only work for half a day and then have the rest of the weekend off, unless the men are working. The blokes all seem to like my cooking. They will always respect the cook!

Although I can get grumpy at times because I'm up at five and on my feet all day till past seven at night, I love my job. It's well paid and I have been able to buy my first car—a fantastic four-wheel drive—with the money I've saved. I've decided that I will eventually enrol in a nanny's course which I can do by correspondence. This may come in handy if I decide to stop cooking one day. Many families in the outback are on the lookout for good nannies.

I've noticed that the men have a much better chance of finding work on stations than the women, mainly because they are better suited physically. There aren't too many jobs going for women, because there is still that macho notion that a woman may not be tough enough to handle the work. I don't think this is necessarily true. But if a woman thinks she can do it, she will still have to prove herself to the blokes. It's difficult sometimes to let women go out to work in the stock camps. The camps, which usually last for a week, or even for a month, are hard going for them. As you can well imagine, there could be plenty of problems with women bunking out there with the blokes!

Last year, Kidman and Co conducted a survey to find out why there weren't enough women employees on their stations. The survey showed that the men thought women were put to better use in the homestead kitchens as station cooks, than out in the yards or camps. They believed that the women were not mentally strong enough, let alone physically, to handle the work. There is some truth to it. The kind of life we lead out here can be difficult and lonely, and the men's attitudes are chauvinistic at times. Still, you can't generalise. In this respect, some blokes are worse than others. But the boys working at Innamincka are just great. I can vouch for that! I've never had problems with any of them. We are all best mates and they don't treat me any differently. And I really don't think it's because I'm the boss's daughter!

Right now, I am saving up all my money from my cook's job so that, one day, and this is my dream—I will be able to travel Australia and overseas, like the tourists out at the Innamincka township. We get plenty of travellers in the summer and winter months, who come out to visit the famous Dig Tree where Burke and Wills died. I may as well put my cooking skills to good use and make some money for myself. That way I can stay out here forever.

CONVENT LIFE

As Catherine talked about her early days at boarding school I was reminded of my own experiences when I first entered the convent. Although I was much older than her when I left my family to live in a community of women, the sense of isolation and homesickness was great at times.

Before entering the convent, well-meaning friends and relatives invited me out and fed me nearly every night of the week to celebrate—or perhaps because they thought I'd be deprived of meals when I entered. I wasn't quite sure, but all those three-course meals resulted in my gaining at least two stone!

I resigned from the Commonwealth Bank at the end of January 1974 and my parents took me to Singapore for a holiday. Dad wanted to return to the place where he had lived as a prisoner of war. We visited the house which he had shared with his army mates. Amazingly enough, it was the only one still standing and was in exactly the same state as Dad remembered it from thirty-one years before. He walked around the bare room, identifying every corner saying, 'So-and-so slept here, so-and-so slept there . . .' It brought back many mixed emotions for him, but I think it was good for him to confront the horrors of the past.

Soon after we returned to Australia, it was time for Mum and Dad to meet some of the sisters living at the convent in the Brisbane bayside suburb of Manly. This was home to the postulants—young women who are given the opportunity to experience religious life in a congregation. Mum and Dad had just retired to their holiday unit on the Gold Coast and I was put in charge of driving them to Brisbane. By some miracle I found the way to the convent, but on the trip home became hopelessly lost. Fortunately, I stumbled on a back route to the Coast. Dad had been dreading the drive to Manly for the monthly Sunday visits, and the discovery of a short cut put an end to his fears.

The sisters sent a list of items I was required to bring with me. Once Mum saw me packing pyjamas, underwear, sheets and towels she was greatly relieved. I don't quite know what she thought the sisters had in mind, but to see me taking 'normal' things was a sign that all was going to be okay. After that, she took my entry in her stride. She confessed to me that she was glad to know that I wouldn't be wearing shorts again!

On 10 March 1974, I awoke with butterflies in my stomach. Anxious and nervous, I slowly dressed, putting on the new outfit I had bought especially for the occasion of my entry day into the convent. I carefully packed the small tape recorder which had been presented to me at a farewell lunch (yet another!) at St Anthony's parish the day before. For my nineteenth birthday, three months earlier, my parents gave me a new Holden car. It was a very generous gift but, to this day, I'm puzzled as to why they decided to give it to me then. My brother Tony joked that maybe it would come in handy for a fast getaway if things didn't work out at the convent!

We planned to leave Toowoomba at noon. This left me with plenty of time to prepare myself and make some last-minute goodbyes. My younger sister, Bernadette, had left home the week before to start her nursing training at the Toowoomba General Hospital. It was compulsory for her to board at the nurses' quarters. I think Mum was beginning to feel a great sense of loss, with her two daughters leaving home in the same week. I vividly remember, as she came down the corridor and passed our empty bedrooms, she burst into tears and fled into the kitchen. Nobody felt very cheerful that morning. Just before noon, we heard on the wireless that it was raining heavily in Brisbane and roads might be cut so we decided to leave early for the convent.

The day of entering religious life is, I am sure, etched forever on each sister's memory. My day of entry was unforgettable for the very simple reason that it coincided with the great Brisbane floods of '74. As we cautiously navigated our way through torrential rain, we discovered that most of the roads were already flooded and impassable. I remember fretting that we would be late for the introduction ceremony while Mum, who was sitting up front, cried all the way from our front door to the convent. There was as much water flowing inside the car as there was outside!

In the end, we arrived at Manly Convent early. Although the sisters were not ready to receive us, they graciously invited us in. We had lunch down in the convent catacombs, which didn't help anyone's nerves much. I was introduced to two other girls who were entering with me. They were even younger than me—fresh out of high school. Both were Queenslanders—Sue was from Emerald and Mary from Brisbane. We chatted nervously, not

The Brides of Christ, 1960.

daring to admit to each other how terrified we actually were about going to tea with all the sisters.

An hour before the ceremony, the three of us were taken to the novitiate building to change into the plain white habits which symbolised our new life. For me, donning the habit also represented forsaking the family life that had been mine for the last nineteen years. This ritual is no longer practised by the Presentation Sisters, as over the years we have come to realise that our style of dress has very little to do with our spiritual commitment. I'm amazed that as recently as the 1950s and 1960s, our sisters were required to don those full-length white wedding gowns when they entered the novitiate. Hence the nickname 'Brides of Christ'. By the early seventies, this ritual was obsolete, thanks to the Second Vatican Council. I was immensely relieved that I only had to wear a simple cotton habit and veil.

At three o'clock, in front of the Leader of the Congregation, Mother Gabriel, the other sisters and our families, I took part in the introduction ceremony based on the Word of God. It involved Mother Gabriel asking each of us what we expected from the congregation, who in turn declared their willingness to accept us for the period of our preparation. It was a moving ceremony. The rest of the afternoon passed in a blur and before I knew it, it was early evening and time to see my parents off.

I said goodbye to Mum and Dad with mixed feelings—I was excited by my new life but also apprehensive about what lay ahead. The parting was made all the more difficult as it was the Lenten season—a six-week period during which we were not allowed to write home or have any contact with our relatives. This was my first real separation from my family for any length of time. Watching them drive out of the convent gates, I remembered Tony's joke about the Holden Mum and Dad had given me. Suddenly a getaway car did not seem such a bad idea!

Two weeks after entering the convent, I felt strongly tempted to run away. A big party had been organised at Manly to celebrate the eightieth birthday of Sister Evangelist Murtagh, the oldest sister in the order. Sisters came from Presentation convents far and wide to join in the festivity and, naturally, they were curious to meet the new postulants. It terrified me that I hardly knew a soul and was painfully shy, but here I was joining them for life. It didn't make any sense.

The 1890s two-storey timber house was barely large enough to accommodate its thirty-five residents. As well as the two other postulants and myself, there were first- and second-year novices, sisters studying or already involved with community teaching, and a small group of older, retired sisters. My room was on the top floor of the convent with only enough space for a single bed, a dresser and a small desk. It was spartan and functional, but I was fortunate enough to have a view over the sprawling tropical lawns which rolled from the convent down towards the blue of Moreton Bay.

Learning to live harmoniously with the other sisters was demanding. I had never had the experience of living with so many women under one roof before. In my first week, I was placed on kitchen duty. Preparing forty boiled eggs for the sisters' breakfast was a nightmare—some liked two-minute eggs, while others preferred them to simmer for three or four minutes. Fishing eggs out of industrial-size vats of boiling water was no mean feat—at best, it was a disastrous affair which served as my first real introduction to community living. The next time I was rostered on kitchen duty I decided to do a trade with a second-year novice. I would do her garden duty if she did the cooking. I also agreed to become the chief dishwasher—anything, as long as I did not have to get near a stove.

I was homesick during most of my nine months of postulancy and many a night would find myself in tears hiding out on the top balcony at Manly. One particular incident really unsettled me just weeks after entering. Sister Joan Cusack, my novice mistress, summoned all the postulants and novices together for a meeting and explained in a hushed tone that Rosemary, a second-year novice, was going home.

'Gee,' I thought, 'that's wonderful news.' But I didn't realise that 'going home' implied leaving the convent for good. I was devastated. It was like a death. The congregation fostered a strong family spirit and encouraged us to live and work closely together. The other sisters and I made a promise between ourselves that if anyone else contemplated leaving we would tell each other beforehand. It wasn't too long until another novice announced she was going. I think knowing two weeks beforehand was actually worse. The 1970s was a turbulent period in religious life with many sisters leaving the congregation and renouncing their vows. It certainly was not a good time, I thought, for one wondering why she was staying.

Daily life at the convent was regulated by a noisy clanging of bells—a bell to wake us in the morning, a bell calling us to chapel and a bell to end meditation. Breakfast was always eaten in silence. I used to love it when the superior of the house would push her chair back from the breakfast table, stand up and utter the magic words, 'Praised be Jesus and

The Brides of Christ following the sisters and novices.

Mary, now and forever, amen.' This meant we were allowed to talk.

In my first year as a postulant, I was introduced to prayer, the Bible, and taught how to meditate. Most mornings I would sit through the hour's meditation and wonder what on earth I was doing there. I passed the time by watching the elderly sisters nod off to sleep, their heavy black veils drooping into their laps. The other postulants and I would often get the giggles if some unfortunate sister's stomach rumbled.

Our days were filled with studying Vatican II documents, the vows of Poverty, Chastity and Obedience—which means to depend on God, to trust God and to share in God's constant love—and the history of our congregation and its foundress, Nano Nagle.

One of my friends from home entered religious life in the same year as I did, but in a different congregation. Its founder was still living which made me deeply envious. I constantly complained to her that she never had to experience the difficulties of deciphering 200-year-old documents and letters. It seemed unfair that Nano Nagle had been born over a century earlier.

I had difficulty with group singing, depending on whom I stood beside, but with regular practice I eventually found I could hold a note on my own. The dread of my life was public speaking. I hated it and at times felt as if my whole life centred around this fear. It would take two weeks for me to prepare my one-minute speech and I was jealous of the other sisters who would write their speech the night before.

Every evening after tea, there was compulsory recreation during which we were expected to learn a handicraft. Being more of an active, outdoor type of person, it was misery for me to sit quietly and darn. For the first time in my life, I learnt to knit and crochet! As a result, for every birthday, Mother's Day and Christmas, Mum was presented with a doily or prayer book cover. I finally got the hint that enough was enough when she suggested that there might be some other people I would like to give these to.

My first year of postulancy at Manly Convent, Brisbane.

During the three years at the novitiate, Mum and Dad visited me on the first Sunday of every month. Visiting hours were from three to five in the afternoon, but on Christmas Day and Easter Sunday they were extended for an extra two hours. What a strain it was preparing for visiting day. The sisters supplied the afternoon tea and we used to have to match up about one hundred different cups and saucers, as well as starch and iron dozens of white tablecloths. In the beginning I must have seemed somewhat distraught to my poor parents when they came to visit. I was always wary of not letting them find out that I was having problems settling into convent life. I did not want to worry them, especially Mum. But I am sure they must have departed after the tea and scones wondering what was the matter with me.

At one stage I seriously contemplated leaving the convent, convinced that the superior general would ask me to go because I could not, for the life of me, get along with one particular sister. I disliked her and the feeling was mutual. I recall discussing this problem with my novice mistress. How could I possibly live a religious life if I hated someone? I was living in the clouds! I felt every inch a hypocrite, but in truth I was merely naive and spiritually immature.

I guess I had some very funny notions about religious life and what was expected of me. I grew up in a very conservative and sheltered environment and was, in some ways, unprepared for these changes and challenges of real life. It took quite some time before I felt at ease with myself and my faith.

What I missed most was my sport. I was prepared to give up tennis when I entered religious life, but I did not realise how much I had depended on it to release tensions within me. I discovered new emotions—frustration and anger—that I did not know how to handle. In those first few months, I had more sick days than I had ever had before because I was so emotionally confused. Luckily my novice mistress, Sister Joan, was very understanding and patient. She helped me through this difficult period of adjustment and I owe her a lot of gratitude.

Gradually I came to lose the two stone I'd put on before entering the convent and returned to my normal size. To counter the lack of physical exercise, I volunteered to be the chief lawn mower. I borrowed the parish Victa ride-on mower and had hours of fun mowing the convent lawns. The other sisters soon became familiar with the sight of me, in my white habit and veil, whizzing back and forth at full throttle. Visitors to the convent were somewhat startled. 'Don't mind Anne Maree,' they were advised, 'she's just practising her three-point turns.'

We all looked forward to occasions, such as meetings or conferences in town, when the superiors of the house would leave Manly for the day. As soon as we heard the crunching of gravel under tyres, off went our veils and nylon stockings and the kitchen was raided. What a sense of freedom!

At the end of 1974, after twelve months as a postulant, I was allowed to make a more formal entrance into the life of the Presentation Sisters. This was celebrated in a ceremony called 'Reception into the Congregation'. Once again, a change of dress symbolised this new step in our journey. I was presented with the white veil of the Presentation novice. Thankfully, it was the seventies and the influence of the miniskirt had somehow filtered through the convent walls, which meant our habits' hems had also retreated upwards—to a few inches below the knee.

For the novice, the emphasis was placed on the significance of taking her First and Final Vows, and not on her dress. The first year of novitiate was an intense time of preparation. Our major focus was on developing an intimate relationship with God. This demanded a 'journey of truth' and asking myself, 'What is the vision of God for humanity and the contribution that I, as a member of the Presentation Sisters, can make to the Christian life in my own time and place?'

Me (right) with Sister Sue, Mother Gabriel and Sister Mary.

The discovery of God in other people is never ending and I committed myself to it then, and such remains my commitment today. The novitiate experience was based upon prayer and study. We also spent part of our days teaching catechism (a summary of the principles of Catholicism) in the local State primary school and occasionally helping Meals-on-Wheels in the area.

Once a week we joined other novices from around Brisbane in combined lectures. As it was difficult shuttling large groups of sisters back and forth, the convent purchased a minibus. Thanks to my prowess on the ride-on mower, I was elected to sit for a bus licence. The minibus was a great boon as it enabled us to go on the occasional picnic and outing. I always found it amusing that whenever we arrived at a picnic spot dressed in our 'regular' (habit and veil), other picnickers would suddenly pack up, get in their cars and scurry away. I guess a group of sisters in habits was an intimidating sight, but at least we were assured of a prime picnic spot!

Towards the end of my novitiate year, I went on a 'decisive retreat' to ascertain the Lord's calling for me. On my return, I entered into a mutual agreement with the Presentation Sisters to continue on for a three-year period and, on 6 January 1977, took my First Vows in front of my family and congregation.

Again, this occasion, known as the 'First Profession', was steeped in ritual. It involved making temporary vows to commit my life to Jesus and included the three vows of Chastity, Poverty and Obedience. I renewed this commitment at the end of my three years as a junior professed sister, and then each year after that for a further two years. From First Profession to 'Finals' can take up to ten years.

At the end of five years of Temporary Profession I was at long last ready to commit myself for life, taking the Final Vows in my home parish in Toowoomba on 3 January 1982. Both Sue and Mary, the two girls who had entered the convent on the same day as me back in 1974, also made their Final Profession. Sue is still a Presentation Sister but has changed her ministry and is now a social worker, while after fourteen years in religious life, Mary has left the congregation.

Without a doubt, religious life has undergone many changes. This is nothing new, although in recent years it has meant for most congregations, including ours, a decline in numbers. Of the thirty-five sisters from the Manly convent, only nine remain today. Personally, I see it as a decisive time and a holy one—I like to think that I am living between the respected old and the emerging new. My task is to live this present moment, and to live it in such a way that a future model can evolve with confidence and courage from our current condition. There is only one place that is sacred, and that place is the here and now.

CIRCUIT TWO

BEV MAUNSELL—JUNDAH

The most painful time for anyone—and not just for those in the bush—is coping with the loss of a loved one. It's a time when people need plenty of support. It can be very hard to retain their faith at such a time. Thus, each time I take off from Longreach and head south-west towards the tiny bush town of Jundah to visit Bev Maunsell, I thank God that I was able to be with Bev just after her husband died.

Bev was working as a teacher's aide at the Jundah State School when I met her in early 1989. We hit it off instantly and have been good friends ever since.

In March 1993, she was injured in a boating accident and had to endure long months of painful treatment, flying in and out of hospitals. I never heard her complain. I am so impressed by her incredible inner strength and the courage she has shown over the years when faced with difficult situations. Little did we realise back then, that before long she would be calling on that same strength to nurse her husband on his deathbed.

My husband passed away peacefully at home on 19 January 1996. We'd been married for thirty years. I tried in earnest to contact a priest. Sister Anne Maree was on holidays with her parents. She had provided us with a contact number, but I was reluctant to interrupt her precious time of relaxation. Twenty-four hours later I frantically called her and, as always, she took complete control. The relief of hearing her voice, her genuine grief and reassurance that she would contact a priest was of heartfelt comfort to me. I depended on Anne Maree to get things back on track. She gave me the emotional support which carried me through one of the darkest and bleakest times of my life.

Graham arrived home from council camp late one afternoon suffering acute back pain and severe headaches. At midnight he suffered a stroke. We were home alone—220 kilometres from our nearest town. Graham had insisted on waiting for the flying doctor's arrival the following morning for emergency evacuation to the hospital in Toowoomba. After an emotionally exhausting week, the jury finally came in with the verdict. A life sentence.

'One to six weeks,' the doctor told me. Massive malignant tumours had formed in Graham's brain. The cancer was well advanced and inoperable. Amid shock, disbelief and tears we brought Graham back home to Jundah. All we could do was wait and pray.

Graham was stronger than I. We discussed all aspects of life before and after his impending death, yet still I couldn't accept it. Anne Maree helped me cope spiritually, but mostly she was there for me emotionally. I didn't feel the least bit afraid confiding in her about my roller coaster emotions during Graham's illness. The feelings of anger and helplessness were sometimes overwhelming. Anne Maree reassured me that it was acceptable to have these emotions.

I made every effort to ensure that Graham didn't become a patient in his own home and purchased bed linen in his favourite colour (blue) and other bits and pieces to brighten up his bedroom. He lived in overdrive, trying to stretch out each day and making the most of what little time was left to him, all the while witnessing the support and friendship that we, his family, would later discover to be ongoing after his departure. The freezer was near bursting with cakes and prepared meals delivered by friends showing their care and concern. The children's impending grief lay heavily upon our shoulders as we tried to cope with the enormity of this situation that we could not change.

Graham was a racehorse jockey. When I met him, he was working on a property outside the township of Windorah training horses for a fellow called Percy McPhellamy. I was working on various cattle properties in the area and as a telephonist on the Windorah telephone exchange. Graham was a quiet, reserved man, a jockey dedicated to the world of horseracing, while I was outgoing, enjoyed dancing, and had no knowledge whatsoever of horseracing. But as they say, opposites attract, and we married at Our Lady of Lourdes in Toowoomba on 1 January 1966 and started our life together in the outback.

Mum, Loretta, Dad, me and the twins Monty and Evelyn.

I was born in Pittsworth in 1947, the third child for Flora and Vince Barr. They had six children, including two sets of twins. Reared on small properties for most of my childhood, I was already comfortable with the freedom and serenity of the bush. My father had been a station owner who operated his own earthmoving equipment business. In the early 1960s, he bought a house and a garage in the small town of Windorah. As there were no high schools in the district, I was sent away to board at Concordia College in Toowoomba. The experience was so awful I made a promise—unkept—never to send a child of mine away to boarding school. With my first visit home from school came the shocking realisation that I'd previously only 'brinked' on the edge of being a bush kid. Now we were *really* living in the bush.

The little town of Windorah seemed too remote and primitive for my liking. My first impressions of the place were not favourable to say the least—there was no 240 volt electricity or bitumen roads and very few houses. Our home lacked all the modern conveniences. My father installed a thirty-two volt lighting plant in an engine room at the rear of the house. Before this, kerosene lanterns, gas lights and carbide lights were used. A kerosene fridge provided little ice, but plenty of black soot, and like most of our neighbours we had a wash house, a small, unlined corrugated iron building behind the house with an old copper for boiling up the clothes. A clothes line, propped up with long fork-like sticks, stretched along the width of our backyard regularly depositing the washing in the dirt and burrs. There was much excitement the day Dad brought home a thirty-two volt wringer washing machine for Mum—she'd been hand-washing for seven! Some wringer washing machines were petrol-operated. They conked out as often as the power plant at the town hall. Little wonder we are a patient lot out here!

The flying doctor held a monthly clinic in a small wooden cottage. Dr Timothy Leary, with his dry sense of humour and taste for a 'wee whisky', was to become a legend in the outback and a good friend. As I soon discovered on my visits home from school, the town was occupied by genuine people, whose friendship I continue to enjoy today.

The countryside out west was like nothing I'd seen or experienced before. The magnificent red-orange sand dunes amazed me. The twins built sandcastles in the dunes, as they once had on the seashore, except we were miles away from the coast. Cooper Creek, with its grand old gum trees, provided venues for barbecues, record hops on the river banks, and watersports. It was down by the creek that I had my first accident which required medical assistance. I fell from a tree, tearing my leg open above the knee, and now wear a six-inch scar—the legacy of my father's attempt at stitching the wound because floodwaters barred access to medical help.

Cricket, tennis and football were played in dusty paddocks. Perhaps the least credible 'sport' I participated in was to catch weakened, drought-stricken emus, adorn their necks with a bell or bow and anxiously wait for a roo shooter to ask whose 'pet' he had accidentally shot! Record hops were always a popular social event. Sometimes we used the aerodrome flares to light up the claypan parties and then frantically refilled and replaced them before getting caught. I shudder now at our irresponsibility because of the possibility of a flying doctor evacuation which would have required use of these emergency flares. On Sunday nights, movies were shown in the paddock beside the post office. We watched the movies from our cars. As there were no sound boxes, the projector volume was turned up as high as possible, so parents certainly knew what time the movies finished at our makeshift drive-in. In later years, my brother and I played at being projectionists for the pictures screened in the shire hall. This was perhaps the best meeting place for young people. Courtships were surmised by who escorted whom to the Sunday night flicks.

Graham was a true Windorahite, and although the population of Windorah was less than a hundred, we barely knew each other for many years. He and Percy McPhellamy spent most of the year on Paragua Station or travelling with racehorses to as far away as Oakey and Roma. It wasn't until my older brother invited Graham to attend a Bachelors and Spinsters ball in Yaraka, along with myself and some friends, that we were officially introduced. Our attraction grew from that night on. My family taught him to dance—in our lounge room to records on an old player which cost us

Playing the drums at a bush dance.

a small fortune in new batteries and needles! We were a musical family and had open house on Sundays when locals sang and danced with my brother playing the drums, my father the button accordion, and myself the mouth organ. I also played the drums for local district dances for many years, but with Graham learning to dance it wasn't long before I forfeited the drums for a quick twostep with him. When Graham came calling, we would often sit in front of the wood stove making toast on the coals and sipping tea. I can't recall much of our courtship without the company of my six-year-old twin brothers, Kevin and Trevor, my older brother Monty, and my younger sister, Loretta, keeping a watchful eye on Graham and me. Family bonds were extremely close during the years before television, and the closeness formed lasted a lifetime. As a family, we did everything together.

Graham's life revolved around racehorses, so naturally it was inevitable that I too became educated in this area once we were married. Graham's employment as a strapper (horse groomer) took us to Brisbane. Very quickly, babies and racehorses dominated my life. Although the abundance and novelty of clean water, 240 volt electricity and no dust storms kept me happy for a while, my loathing for city life never ceased during those five years we spent in Brisbane. Feelings of homesickness for the west were frequent, so any visitors from out Windorah way were always welcomed throughout those years. When I was seven months pregnant with our second child, Graham suffered a severe kick to the back of his head by a racehorse. He underwent major brain surgery and was hospitalised for many weeks, but fortunately there was no permanent damage—or so we thought. This injury was later to cost him his life.

Preferring a bush environment for our children, Jeffrey, Tanya and Toni, we moved back to Windorah. Flying over the Channel Country, I realised how much I'd missed the bush. From several thousand feet in the air, I could see how the countryside was in a constant and dramatic state of change. With the Cooper in flood, the channels looked like tiny veins as they wound their way through the claypans. Once-parched flats were transformed into carpets of spectacular wild flowers in shades of brilliant yellow, blue and white spreading as far as the eye could see.

Home in Windorah, I missed daily newspapers, fresh bread, fruit and vegetables, and the conveniences the city provided. It was back to dirty river water from the Cooper, smelly kerosene fridges, no rural power and dust storms. But watching our kids playing happily in the red dirt soon made me feel grateful and I settled happily back into our old lifestyle.

Graham resumed his career as a jockey, riding the Western Racing Circuit while being employed at Macs Roadworks. His circuits from Birdsville to Quilpie covered eight race meetings within ten weeks. The children and I travelled with him, trekking around the country in a convoy of trucks, cars and horse floats. Many a muffler and discarded tyre line the table drains as mementos of these trips.

Graham

In 1972, we moved to Currawilla Station. A sizable cattle station owned by the Beltanna Pastoral Company, it was some hundred kilometres from Windorah, on the road to Birdsville. Graham was employed as the head stockman. The years spent on Currawilla were blissful. The men went to camp for long periods leaving the women behind to hold the fort. Weekends were spent camping and fishing at the numerous waterholes. The children learnt to drive our cars on the claypans while the men tested the art of 'land-skiing', which involved towing a car bonnet around the claypans and giving anyone a ride who dared to test their balance and courage.

Supplies to Currawilla were trucked in from Quilpie and delivered by Des Andrews, who also doubled as the mailman and 'Avon Lady'. The children believed Des was the provider of all things as he played Santa Claus at Christmas, ferrying their presents across the flooded channels by boat. Neighbouring properties with fruit trees and additional vegetables shared them around, but fresh meat was provided by the station. On 'killer nights', a barbecue was held with neighbours from Morney Station attending.

There was no telephone at Currawilla, only a Flying Doctor Service radio for transmitting and receiving telegrams. Many minor injuries were patched up following instructions from the doctor via the radio. During the absence of the manager's wife, I manned the wireless and I tended to men's accidents on a regular basis. On one occasion, a friend lost a finger on a windmill. He was pasty-white, as was I, but kept insisting my brother go back and find his finger before the crows did. My brother, Kevin, assured him that the crows would have already swooped down so there was no point trying to retrieve the finger. To top it all off, the doctor on the radio had a thick Irish accent which didn't make things any easier.

Many property ladies, like myself, didn't have a washing machine so raw knuckles from scrubbing rough work clothes were common. We had a gas iron, but it was often cast aside for an old pot iron because the handle was often hotter than the iron. Interest in the daily newspapers was long forgotten, but not in 240 volt electricity. Snakes regularly haunted the homesteads, especially in the long, hot summer months. Having once been bitten by a snake, my fear of them was real and I wouldn't be consoled by the mere shooting of one. A total mutilation had to be performed before I was pacified, much to Graham's embarrassment if his workmates were around. He reached a better understanding after a king brown wound itself around his leg to resemble a corkscrew. Fortunately, in true bronco style he flung it free and avoided being bitten. The snake appeared as shocked as my husband.

Sadly in mid-1975, we lost a baby due to a miscarriage. Following four bedridden days on the station during heavy rain, I was transported thirty kilometres in a four-wheel drive to the nearest dry airstrip. Evacuation by the flying doctor from a short airstrip was a hair-raising and frightening experience. I was flown to Charleville Hospital where I had to endure my first medical separation from the children.

I thank God for the flying doctors and the life-saving service they provide. Recently a fellow from Sydney complained of an ambulance taking twenty minutes to reach his friend who had been hurt in an accident. But could he survive our isolation? During my pregnancies and Graham's hospitalisation I was forced to endure long waiting periods for medical consultations and treatment, which serve as reminders of how effective our flying doctor service is, performing these functions in half the time. Although availability of specialists is minimal throughout the west, I do not think for an instant that we are as medically disadvantaged as some people may think.

Tanya, Toni and friend Gerry powdered for heat rash at Currawilla Station.

After five contented years at Currawilla, another pregnancy determined our move. Graham was concerned that my workload had become too strenuous—I was cooking for the station as well as teaching the children. The doctor had already cautioned me about overdoing things following my miscarriage. Another consideration was the children's education, and the lack of interaction with other children their age. We sent them to board at the Quilpie convent while Graham and I fulfilled a contract with Main Roads, 128 kilometres west of Windorah. We agonised long and hard over this decision but it was the best alternative for the children. They travelled home for the weekends and holidays on a friend's road train which we christened the 'school bus'.

Three months before the birth of our fourth and last child, Raelene, we moved to Jundah in the Barcoo Shire. Like Windorah, Jundah is only a tiny town with a population of less than a hundred. A post office, hotel and store provide service to locals, and a mail truck delivers other provisions and mail to town twice a week. In the last twenty years, the road to Longreach has been upgraded and STD telephones connected. The most important improvement came last year with the connection of a water treatment plant. Crystal-clear water has replaced the muddy river water. Local women celebrated this improvement with a dinner at the Jundah hotel.

Western women confront problems head-on. We are, I feel, more independent and less fazed by things than our city cousins. We are undaunted by floods, bushfires, droughts and most physical tasks which come our way. We are used to travelling long distances alone, and as there are no mechanics, RACQ or NRMA to call, tales of changing tyres, getting out of bogholes or breaking down bring many laughs to the dinner table. I would rather be bogged than conked out at traffic lights with a dozen horns honking, or race a storm to town than a hundred other cars any day!

Life in the outback makes you resilient. We just 'swear and bear'! Dust storms, heat, flies and no access to proper shopping facilities would daunt any city woman. It's a 426 kilometre round journey to my nearest shopping centre. I feel like a real bushwhacker in city supermarkets. There should be lanes so you can walk safely up the centre for all the heavy traffic. I couldn't live in a city again. I love the freedom of the western life. We don't realise just how lucky we are here until we spend some time in the big smoke.

While Graham continued working for the local council, I returned to the work force as a teacher's aide at the Jundah State School, with the company of my children. I was at school when our flying priest, Father Loth, arrived with a nun whom he wished to introduce to the teaching staff. Her name was Anne Maree.

Father Terry Loth had been our flying priest since the early 1980s. Loth, or 'Lofty' as he was nicknamed, was unlike other priests—he didn't drive, he flew! He was a competent pilot, but I recall one occasion when he had trouble starting his plane. He asked the nun travelling with him at the time, Sister Marie Carroll, to man the controls while he turned the propeller. When the plane started, so did Father Loth! As the plane careered towards a fence, Father Loth clung to the wing for dear life. Thankfully the fence pulled them up and one very relieved priest fell to the ground.

Graham was a practising Catholic. I, on the other hand, was raised by parents who were strict Presbyterians, but I became a Catholic later in life. In Jundah, Graham and I both took a fairly active role in the Church community. Graham assisted the local police sergeant whenever the church needed painting, while I cleaned the church and provided meals and transport for 'Lofty' when he was in town. One Sunday, after spending hours bogged in blacksoil country on what turned out to be an eight-hour journey from Longreach to Jundah, Father Loth insisted on visiting me. Graham suggested that he refrain from dropping by as I was tired, muddy and had too much to do before school the next day. The subsequent falling-out between Graham and Father Loth put an end to our attending the monthly mass for several years, and it wasn't until Anne Maree took over the Aerial Ministry that we returned to church.

As a child, I remember my brothers and sisters and I spying on two convent sisters walking along a footpath in town. Large ladies, they were dressed in the obligatory black and white habits. I couldn't get in the car quick enough! They terrified me, and we children spent many nights frightening each other with 'spook' stories about them.

It wasn't until our one-year-old granddaughter nearly drowned in an esky of water that I really came to know Anne Maree. She visited our home full of concern for us and supported our granddaughter's parents even though they are not practising Catholics. This was the turning point for me, and we became fast friends.

Anne Maree shows love and care to people of all denominations. She is truly unique. There can't be too many nuns who have a pilot's licence! It amuses me no end that she joins forces as a volunteer worker at all of the western race meetings and can be found at the food canteen, serving at the bar, or collecting for the RFDS. She does this as easily as she performs her spiritual duties. However, I do worry about her. She is only human, and I'm conscious of the fact that after dealing with our problems she has to get back in her plane and switch off emotionally. How she handles this workload remains a mystery. I think it has something to do with her strong faith. Many of us depend on her for moral support and it doesn't seem very fair on her having to constantly take on all our problems. I'm concerned that she may exhaust herself, yet I am selfish enough to despair at any thought that she may one day leave the west. She's as essential to us out here as the flying doctor.

During Graham's long illness, Anne Maree consistently reassured me of my competency with his medical and emotional care. She understood and discussed our physical and mental exhaustion and my feelings of apathy. When I felt I had no emotional reserves left and true depression threatened me, she assured me that we would cope with whatever confronted us; that God-given strength would see us through.

On Christmas Eve 1995, I was at home with Graham. Taking care of my terminally ill husband was an around-the-clock job. Home care took on a totally different meaning as I read all the available documentation from the Queensland Cancer Fund, trying to stay ahead of symptoms and the inevitable course wreaked by this destructive disease. I found myself entering into robot mode while coping with daily demands yet never accepting the doctor's predictions. Christmas and New Year flew by with friends avoiding the usual Happy New Year wishes. On 1 January, the children hosted our thirtieth wedding anniversary party. On the surface, our lives took on a false sense of normality and I carried on with the pretence.

Graham was a patient in his own home. All his medication was regulated and monitored by me. Although I listened carefully as he expressed his personal wishes and concerns about our children and me coping with his death, I felt guilty because I wasn't the one inflicted with the cancer. Even though we had many such intense conversations, a part of me withdrew mentally as I rejected any admission of his cancer being terminal.

Graham lived his seven weeks at home to the fullest. Surrounded by our children and seven grandchildren, Graham's positive attitude was an inspiration to us all and to the Jundah community. For the children and I to have witnessed this outside love and care—an indication of his popularity—was a comfort during those last weeks of his life.

I am a sentimentalist, a real softie at heart, though I have been judged to be strong. I've gained strength through the sadness which has touched my life. I've emerged more educated but nothing ever dims the heartache and pain. I wonder whether the loneliness and grief will ever subside. I miss my husband very much.

When Graham died, he did it with dignity. That very same evening I called Sister Anne Maree.

CIRCUIT TWO

NELL BROOK—BIRDSVILLE

When I consider the changes in religious life over the years, I wonder what the sisters of old would think of a sister in shorts barracking at the Birdsville Races!

For the last five years, I have been a regular at the Spring Carnival race meetings. It was a fellow pilot, Nell Brook, who was responsible for introducing me to the Birdsville Races. I had never set foot on a racecourse before that, let alone such a dusty one. Nell taught me that the second the horses gallop past, I had to turn around swiftly so as not to get dust in my eyes! Now, each year, I'm a regular at the famous races and fly to Birdsville to help Nell prepare for the busiest weekend of their social calendar. It's a nightmare time with plenty to do, but with an extra pair of hands it's amazing what we can achieve.

I first met Nell when she and her husband, David, invited Father Terry and me to stay the night in their Birdsville home in 1989. I was still waiting to finalise my unrestricted pilot's licence and Nell was most encouraging and helpful. On 26 April 1996, I received a phone call during a meeting of the Australian Women's Pilot Association in Longreach. It was a friend of the Brooks, who said that David and Nell's eldest son, Deon, had been killed in a helicopter accident. I was stunned. I flew to Birdsville immediately. It was the longest three-hour flight of my life. I landed half an hour after David and Nell returned from the crash site. To see my close friends in such pain was hard to bear. That same evening, Deon's body was flown home to Birdsville from the desert where he had crashed his helicopter.

Five hundred people attended Deon's funeral. It was a remarkable tribute to the family and a great display of solidarity. The funeral was one of the most moving I have ever attended. There was so much grief, and yet even greater hope. It was an unforgettable spiritual experience.

'*Y*ou *haven't turned your head and looked out across my valley yet,' he said. 'When you do you'll see the place where I'll build my homestead. There'll be horse paddocks and bullock paddocks and I'd like to dream of a girl with chestnut hair waiting for me by the sliprails at sundown. What are you going to do, Joan?' She had not yet turned her head. 'I'm going to marry a moonshiner,' she said shyly. 'You're quite sure, Joan?' She looked into his eyes. 'I've never been so sure of anything in my life. I've loved him very much for a long time. One whole week.'*

The Moonshiner by Lucy Walker

Lucy Walker wrote sentimental novels set in the outback. I guess you'd call her the 1960s' pioneer of Australian romances. Her stories almost always involve a stockman, or a property owner, falling in love with a young girl—a governess, a nurse or a visitor from overseas—and they live happily ever after. As a teenager growing up in South Africa, I hungrily devoured every Lucy Walker novel I could get my hands on. I loved her writing. Now, more than thirty years later, I look back and am amazed that I actually ended up marrying someone who resembled one of the fictional heroes out of her books. Who would have thought that I would have a similar tale to tell?

I met David Brook in Rome in 1965. I was on a school trip, touring Europe, and David, who was from Birdsville, was on a similar journey. Our two school groups met quite by accident in a restaurant. That same evening, both groups went on a night tour of Rome, and I found myself sitting behind him on the bus. At the end of our stay, we exchanged addresses and, back home in South Africa, I began to correspond with David. When I started working as an air hostess for South African Airways, I wrote to him explaining that I might be flying out to Australia and asked naively for directions from Perth to Birdsville. I had no idea of the distance involved.

We didn't meet again until eight years later when David came to South Africa—to see lions and elephants, he said—but Cupid had other ideas. Something clicked between us and our friendship quickly blossomed into a romance. After David returned to Australia, I managed to arrange a few trips to visit him in Perth and Adelaide. Our relationship was largely

As an Air Hostess for South African Airways.

helped along by South African Airways and the Royal Flying Doctor Telegraph Service. David wanted me to visit his home town. I couldn't find Birdsville on any map, but it didn't matter. I was going to be with this handsome young stockman and that was what counted.

I flew from Broken Hill to Birdsville in David's small aeroplane. I was over-awed by this huge expanse of country with its never-ending sandhills separated only by a little creek or rocky hill! At that stage I could not understand how one could fly for hundreds of miles and still be over the one property. I quickly learnt not to call properties farms—'stations', David kept reminding me. Throughout the flight, I was more excited than nervous because I was on my way to see the place where David had grown up. I had seen many photos of Birdsville and from what David had already told me, I knew that it was only a small town. He told me it was named last century, by a local identity as a compliment to the birdlife in the area. It was amazing seeing the wedge-tailed eagles, brown falcons, hawks and crows circling over the town. I had never seen so many birds before in my life, even though as a young girl I had spent most of my winter holidays in the South African bushland—the Bushveldt—and was fairly accustomed to a natural environment. One thing that did strike me, however, was the lack of wild animals, which we would so readily see on South African farms—springboks, impalas, kudus (antelopes) and wart-hogs. I somehow expected them to be roaming the Australian outback whenever we crossed sandhills. 'Not a hope,' declared David.

David was born and bred in Birdsville. He was an only child. His mother passed away when he was nine and he lived with his father behind the town's only general store. The Brook family have strong roots in Birds-ville. David's great-grandparents had married here in 1885 and his grand-mother used to own the famous Birdsville Hotel. David's father worked on nearby Cordillo Downs Station as a stockman. Years later he bought the place. Not bad going for a stockman, I thought.

David worked on his father's other large cattle property, Adria Downs. He loved Birdsville and taught me to love it as well. I felt strangely at home within my new surroundings. Corny as it may sound, I knew this was to be my destiny. David was smart enough to wait three days during my first visit to Birdsville before discussing marriage. Just in case!

Since both David and his father had a strong relationship with the Birdsville community and were very well respected, the prospect of David bringing a lady home to meet the family was certainly of interest to all the locals. David introduced me to most of the townsfolk at the Birdsville Races. Somehow I must have passed muster because we announced our engagement shortly thereafter.

We married in 1974, in my home town of Pretoria in South Africa. Many of my friends thought I was either mad or very brave to leave my family and my country and move to another continent—and all for a man I'd only met briefly when I was a schoolgirl! Yet, I have always believed that one can be married and live next door to one's parents and still be miserable, or one can live on the other side of the world and be happy. I knew my parents could visit me often and vice versa. Although I am now an Australian citizen, I still harbour strong ties with South Africa. I'm proud of my heritage, but I'm also proud of my new citizenship. I firmly believe that my South African background has prepared me well for my present environment.

I was born Margareta Ellen Schulenburg in Pretoria in 1949, in the Republic of South Africa. My father, Richard, was a well-respected doctor who had married a nurse called Ellen, but whom everyone affectionately called Nell. I was the youngest of four children and grew up in a rambling, typically Dutch, gabled house in the centre of Pretoria, a home filled with love and laughter. My father was often away overseas, attending medical conferences, but when he was at home, I remember how he would always read to us. He encouraged us to have inquiring minds. I've continued with that avid yearning for knowledge, and try to read as much as possible. Sadly I don't have much time for that now, but it's on my program for retirement!

After leaving high school, I studied economics at the University of Pretoria. After graduating, I decided to spread my wings and become an air hostess. For as long as I can remember, I have loved flying. Flying is what brought me to Australia in the first place. I guess I should thank South

African Airways as well as Lucy Walker for bringing me closer to David and to Birdsville!

I am a believer in fate. Marrying David marked a new chapter in my life. I was ready to take the plunge and not at all frightened by the challenges of living in a remote 'town' in the Australian outback. This was David's life, and if I was to share it, then I had to learn to love the outback as much as he did.

Birdsville, twelve kilometres north of the South Australian border, is as far away from any major city as you can get—1,200 kilometres north of Adelaide and 1,600 kilometres west of Brisbane. It has a population of only one hundred, and because it is so remote, it makes an ideal stopover for travellers. The airstrip ends where the main road begins, so many visitors simply park their plane then walk across the road straight into the bar at the Birdsville Hotel!

Little has changed since David brought me out here twenty-two years ago. After we returned from our honeymoon, we settled into the family home in town. David's father moved into another residence behind the family store. The Brook family had been operating the store since 1963, and for many years it provided a source of employment for young girls in Birdsville. I continued the family practice, which proved to be an ideal way for me to meet the locals. David's father was very proud of his shop and always made sure that it was well stocked with a good selection of clothing, shoes, pharmaceuticals and groceries. For many years it was the only fuel outlet in town, selling both diesel and petrol. The store has been a part of my life ever since.

With the support of some very wise women during my first year in Birdsville, I was steered in the right direction whilst finding my bearings— even to the extent of naively accepting the position of caterer for the local gymkhana. Having close friends, as I quickly discovered, is invaluable out here. The community made me feel very welcome and despite some minor cultural differences, I had no great difficulty in adapting to my new environment. Finding a freshly slaughtered bullock hanging in the coldroom in my first week was a bit of a shock, especially after being used to serving delicate cuts of steak to passengers in first class jetting over the Atlantic. There was also the problem of the bush lingo, but it did not take too long to understand that 'smoko' could be morning or afternoon tea; 'dinner' was lunch, 'tea' was the evening meal, and 'supper' a late-night snack. In South Africa, 'lunch' was lunch and 'dinner' the evening meal. A 'pub' was the bar of a hotel! The frequent dust storms and sand blows, which would instantly fill the house with dust and dirt, took some getting used to, and the hot northerly winds were depressing. But I just learnt to adapt and get on with things. Complaining will not get one anywhere.

There was only one 'proper' telephone when I arrived, and that was in Bedourie, 180 kilometres to the north! Anything that was newsworthy—market reports, cattle sales figures, orders for produce and clothing for the store and hotel—were sent by telegram. When I discovered I was pregnant with twins, everyone knew it—via a telegram sent from Adelaide—before the news reached David! The connection of the radio telephone into the Roma exchange in 1976 completely transformed our lives. Although restricted to only one line, we were able to conduct our business more effectively, and in private. No more worrying about eavesdroppers on the party line. This limited access to communication often caused me great anxiety and frustration.

Once, David was out aerial mustering on our station, Adria Downs, and he had not returned by nightfall. I was at home with our baby twins, Deon and Dalene, frantic with worry. He finally walked in much later that night and calmly told me that he had crashed the plane. Since he was not injured he had decided to continue mustering and yarding the cattle with the other stockmen before returning home to Birdsville. Needless to say, it wasn't long after this incident that I had my own radio installed in the kitchen. I never wanted to have to sit alone in the dark and worry where he was again. It wasn't until nine years ago that we finally had telephones installed in town. It took months of negotiating with Telecom (now Telstra) but we eventually arrived at a deal—if the Birdsville community would raise ten per cent of the total cost of the installation, then Telecom would provide a satellite phone service for the town.

David and I have six children. The twins, Deon and Dalene, were the first 'cabs off the rank' in 1975, followed closely by Anthony in 1977, Gary in 1980, Karen in 1985 and Jenna in 1987. Our children were born in Calvary Hospital in Adelaide, which involved a 1,200 kilometre trip from Birdsville. My parents made the journey from South Africa to Adelaide for the birth of each child.

It has always been our policy to teach our children to be independent. By the age of twelve, Dalene could drive a car and often worked by herself in the general store. Children learn independence and self-reliance very quickly out here. There is simply no choice. If something should happen to mum or dad, or should any other emergency occur, the children must know what to do. It's a question of survival.

Roughly 40,000 tourists pass through our town each year. As a result, we now have better roads, a bitumen airstrip, and improved mechanical and fuel facilities. Birdsville also has a policeman, and a small one-teacher school which runs classes from kindergarten to Grade 7. In the past, only male teachers were sent to Birdsville. An inspector also visited once a year. Now our fondly called 'Sir', Ms or 'schoolie' has become a multi-skilled principal who balances the books, as well as teaches the children.

Although our family lives in the centre of town, we manage three large cattle properties in the Birdsville area: Adria Downs Station to the west of Birdsville is approximately 8,690 square kilometres and extends well into the Simpson Desert; 200 kilometres to the north is Kamaran Downs Station comprising 4,640 square kilometres; while Cordillo Downs in the north-eastern corner of South Australia—once the largest sheep station in Australia—is approximately 7,873 square kilometres in size. We run roughly 22,000 head of cattle in total, mainly Poll Herefords because we have found them to be a good breed for this type of country. Because we live in town, the daily routine of so-called 'station life' is different. Whereas most company stations have their head office in major cities and employ managers to run the stations for them, we operate in a way that enables us to get more involved with the day-to-day running of each of our stations and maintain a closer working relationship with our employees. There are families living on Kamaran Downs and Cordillo Downs who manage operations for us, but our Adria Downs employees have their homes here in town like ourselves. Our Birdsville home is thus the hub of operations for all our stations. A fax machine and computer help to keep us up to date with our stock management. We can monitor cattle and weather reports, and are able to respond quickly to market changes. I am not directly involved with the physical aspects of station management, although I do love to go out and help whenever I can.

I gained my pilot's licence in 1984, ten years after we were married. It was one of the best things I have ever done. I would like to do more flying but David uses the plane almost daily for station work. He flies out to the mustering camps. He has always used an aircraft for mustering, helping those on the ground in trucks and on motorbikes to herd and yard the cattle for branding or drafting. We look upon our plane, now a Cessna 210, in much the same way, I suppose, as people living in the city would view their cars—just as a practical means of transport. There is nothing grand about owning a plane. It is a basic tool of our business and provides the only fast, efficient way to manage our properties. I do the long-distance flying which has given me a lot of freedom. It means that I can reach other towns quickly, attend functions and conferences, and collect the children from boarding school in Adelaide. It also leaves David free to do other things, and I am glad I can relieve him from this particular chore.

My love of flying was what brought me close to Anne Maree when she first came to Birdsville in 1989. We could compare notes! She has since clocked up many more flying hours than I have and is, without a doubt, a far more experienced pilot! Whereas David has always been a practising Catholic, I originally belonged to the Protestant Dutch Reformed Church of South Africa. When I fell in love with David, we considered our religious differences but we knew that since we were travelling down the same path together, they should never become an issue. Eventually I became a Catholic. It was a personal decision, which marked a process of spiritual growth within me and I feel it cemented my relationship with my God.

Our home has always been open to visiting clergy, although in our remote community such visits were, until recently, few and far between. The Catholic priest who baptised Anthony in 1977 came all the way from Quilpie, 600 kilometres to the east. The poor man had to drive for half a day over hazardous roads in a ute! In April 1983, we welcomed our first flying priest when the Rockhampton Diocese launched its Aerial Ministry. It seemed that the Catholic Church had finally recognised the need for closer contact with its parishioners living in the bush. Although Birdsville is actually part of the Toowoomba Diocese, we were included in the Aerial Ministry thanks to the wisdom of our bishops. Father Tom Martin was the first pilot priest to touch down in Birdsville. He was a delightful man, but obviously not a born flier.

In fact, I suspect he secretly disliked flying. Father Tom was eventually replaced by Father Terry Loth. Terry conducted services in our home and instructed the older children in their catechism. When he told us he was retiring from the Aerial Ministry, we were naturally disappointed and sad to see him go. Furthermore, David and I were concerned that we would be deprived of regular access to religious services and contact with the wider parish. From what Father Terry had told us, we realised it would not be easy for him to find a suitable replacement. Running the Aerial Ministry was a physically demanding job and there were few priests game enough to take on the venture.

Sometimes Father Terry brought one of the Missionary Sisters of Service on his flying circuits. We were accustomed to seeing a nun with Terry, so we were not surprised when he introduced us to Sister Anne Maree—until he explained that she was going to be the new pilot of the plane! I thought it was fabulous, and it made perfect sense. We were so used to having pilot priests that I don't think anyone had ever considered asking a sister to take over the Aerial Ministry. The whole family thought it was a lark having a flying nun. And so Anne Maree was welcomed into our home. She has become intimately involved with our lives. We think of her as a member of the family and always look forward to her staying overnight in our home. David enjoys talking with her about spiritual matters and we've all enjoyed interesting round-table discussions with her. She's great at finding relevant quotes in the Bible! When she brings Father Jeff Scully from Quilpie with her, we always put pressure on them to pray for some rain! She is a well-known identity around town and participates in all the social functions of the area.

My first Birdsville Races!

Every September the Birdsville Races attract huge crowds. The first horseraces were held back in 1882 and since then have grown in popularity to become a major Australian sporting event—perhaps the most important social occasion in the outback. Two hundred people gathered here in 1973, but more than 5,000 attended last year. David was secretary of the racing club before we married, and still holds the position today. The entire family enjoys the races and we like to race as many of our own horses as possible. We bring them up from our small horse stud near Mount Barker in the Adelaide Hills especially for the event.

The first year Anne Maree flew down for the races, she was overwhelmed. This mostly peaceful community had suddenly erupted into a mad frenzy. Our household was turned literally upside down. We usually provide accommodation for many of the race officials and major sponsors. It is also an ideal time for friends to come and stay. Heaven knows where we all fit, but we do! Dear Anne Maree helps me around the house—we make an excellent team.

Anne Maree must be the only nun who attends a race meeting on a regular basis and I know she secretly looks forward to it now. She will discuss a horse's form with my son Gary, have a punt, and loves to socialise with the locals. On race day, you can see her smiling face as she is working at one of the catering stalls. Not even the 96,000 beers consumed at the last races put her off! I guess this is because in small bush communities like Birdsville, we are much more informal about our faith. All the various denominations find a common harmony and religion is not a matter of conventional organisation. Christmas and Easter services are celebrated by whichever member of the clergy happens to be in the area at the time. When Anne Maree flies into town, we can have a service no matter what day of the week it is. We may celebrate Easter two weeks before the actual weekend to fit in with her schedule. In the bush, it is the person of faith whom we will turn to.

When Anne Maree took over the Aerial Ministry from Father Terry, I know she had a great deal of trouble trying to find a priest to fly with her. There was, and still is, a shortage of priests, and therefore she has had to manage more or less on her own. Personally, I prefer to have her with us. I think it would be strange to call upon a priest who does not know me or my family to conduct religious ceremonies because Anne Maree is not able to. I know how frustrating it can be for her after she has personally prepared children for the Holy Sacraments, to have to find a priest in order to perform the actual ceremony. But she has learnt to live with this predicament.

Over the years, Anne Maree has become a spokesperson for the quiet achievers of the outback—men, women and children who, by going about their daily lives, contribute to the wealth and wellbeing of all Australians. We were all so proud of her when she was awarded the 1995 Australian Achiever of the Year award for her dedication and service to outback communities. I can't think of anyone more deserving than Anne Maree. She is one of the most unselfish people I know. Together we can share our many flying experiences and compare notes, but I always like to tease her about getting preferential treatment in the sky because she has a 'direct line to God'.

Recently, I have had to turn to Anne Maree more than ever before. Our oldest son Deon—Dalene's twin—was killed when his helicopter crashed. It was late in the afternoon on Anzac Day. He died a few months before his twenty-first birthday.

Flying was Deon's passion and he regularly flew helicopters in the area for an aerial mustering company. He left home the day before to fly his helicopter to Windorah, 180 nautical miles east of Birdsville, for a regular 100-hourly maintenance overhaul. When he called the next afternoon to confirm that he was leaving Windorah for Cordillo Downs, I clearly remember asking him if he was satisfied with the service. He was happy and I wished him a safe flight. He was travelling to Mickerie Waterhole via Cadelga out-station and was to land where the other men were camped. They were to begin mustering cattle there the following morning. About sunset, his employer attempted to contact him via company radio frequency. Unable to reach him, they called me at home to say that Deon had not cancelled his SAR (search and rescue time) and could not be reached via radio. David, Gary and a group of stockmen began a ground search in different directions, looking for any campfires and listening out for radio signals. I remained at home, close to the radio and phone, ever hopeful throughout the long night, as I still believed there were no reasons to worry about his safety. As surprising as it may seem, no-one was overly concerned at first. Bush logic prevails in such times—a helicopter can land nearly anywhere and radio problems are not unusual. We assumed he had simply landed somewhere and set up camp for the evening. He had his swag with him. At first light the following morning, a full-scale air search was initiated by Air Services Australia Search and Rescue. Ten aircraft and three helicopters were dispatched to retrace Deon's flight path. Our aeroplane was also used in the search, with David as pilot, myself, a friend and our two sons as spotters. When we finally found the wreckage, I immediately felt a profound change in my life

David

and in our life as a family. The sight of Deon's swag still rolled up by the helicopter sent a shiver down everyone's spine. Gary said afterwards that he had kept praying that Deon would walk out from under the trees a few hundred metres away.

We were all trying to keep our emotions under control for David's sake as he had the task of flying the plane. We circled above and watched a rescue helicopter land at the site. After what seemed like hours but was perhaps just minutes, a paramedic confirmed officially via radio that the pilot was deceased. We flew to a nearby station, Mt Leonard, in total silence. We had no words for our feelings.

Anne Maree flew to Birdsville as soon as she heard the news. She dropped everything to be with us. Her presence provided amazing support to the entire family. In the days that followed, she assited our household while we began the funeral preparations. The family went to the Birdsville cemetery to choose the place where Deon would be buried. The cemetery lies between two sandhills on the outskirts of town. The choice was easy— we simply selected the spot with the best view of the pub—his favourite watering hole. In the bush, it's at times like this that you realise what it means to belong to a community. Our family had always been part of the local life, and although it was heartbreaking to dig a grave for our son, we felt we could share this with the entire community.

Deon's body was flown home from Mt Isa after an autopsy, arrving just two hours before the funeral. We rested his coffin on a bullock hide on our verandah and spent a few last, precious moments with him. Coolibah leaves were tied with blue ribbons and a cross was fashioned out of metal and welded onto a forty-four gallon water drum to serve as an altar.

Deon's swag and his coffin were placed on a camp stretcher. The great support and community spirit of the district was evident when 120 cars joined the procession to the cemetery. Throughout the service, we remembered Deon's spirited life and asked God to watch over him and guide us through the times ahead. Father Jeff Scully blessed water from the Diamantina River and sprinkled it over Deon's coffin. As we buried Deon, the wind was blowing, a wedge-tailed eagle soared overhead and music from an African lullaby, 'Tula Tula' (sleep my baby), broke the silence.

Deon

Anne Maree has accompanied me in my journey through pain. With her support, I have learnt to establish a new relationship with my son—through my thoughts, heart and prayer since I can no longer do it face to face. Sometimes I have to take time out when the heartache and longing become too intense. With Anne Maree's help, the wound left by my oldest son's death heals a little each day.

A new life is emerging in our family—we love each other more deeply, and our faith is growing. I wish I could protect my children from the pain they continue to experience but they are progressively learning to cope. Deon is never far away from our thoughts—his memory enters into our conversation often, leaving us with a tear or smile at the end. Only recently I changed ownership of his mobile telephone but up till then, no-one in the family wanted to erase his recorded message—we liked to hear his voice. Fond memories.

Despite all that has recently happened, I can honestly say that I have never felt isolated in my grief. I am often alone, but I am never lonely. People often ask me how I can stand living in the middle of nowhere. But I have all I need. Right now, I would not wish to be anywhere else. We can visit the place where Deon's helicopter crashed. Walking across the stony gibber plains to the crash site has become a sort of pilgrimage. It is so beautiful and peaceful out there. We sit in a creek bed, not far from a cross erected in his memory, and have billy tea. Dalene sometimes wonders what it would have been like for Deon's spirit to spend the night out here after he crashed his helicopter. As she says, he was not alone, but shared these beautiful surroundings with the Aborigines, early explorers and pioneers who have passed here before him.

We come alone into this world, and alone we shall leave it. Meanwhile, we should cherish this one life that has been given to us.

CIRCUIT TWO

LIZ DEBNEY—

GLENORMISTON STATION

There is no grief counselling when you live in the bush. Many of the women I meet out here who have lost a child have had to go through it more or less alone. It is at times like this when you really feel the isolation.

I first called in on Liz Debney at Glenormiston Station in February 1992, but I didn't catch up with her again until the following year after the death of her twelve-year-old son Matthew.

The Debneys are a close family and, at the time of Matt's death, were fortunate to have each other and a small community of friends to help them come to terms with their loss.

I always enjoy spending time with Liz and count her as one of my dear friends. I especially value our early-morning walks on the bank of Lake Idmea at sunrise. I also enjoy swapping flying stories with her husband Mal, who manages Glenormiston and is a keen pilot. Liz is still trying to reform my taste in music by introducing me to country and western music. Slowly, I am learning to appreciate Garth Brooks so I guess there is hope for me yet!

Glenormiston has brolgas and big reds.
Land turns red as the sunset spreads.
Early morning rises in the cattle season.
Never say die when the weather is freezin'.
On the hot plain the cattle fight for shade.
River runs long in the channels it has made.
Monstrous bullocks we sell each year.
Infected cattle we find none here.
Sizzling steak on the barby at night.
Toko Ranges are a wonderful sight.
On the big flat we see a drover.
NAPCO has stations like this all over.

Matthew Debney, aged twelve

I have had to develop a philosophical outlook on life. It would be so easy to just cave in. Accidents aren't things that happen to other people, they happen to my family. At times I would dearly love to have a husband who sits at a desk all day instead of mustering from an aeroplane several hundred feet above the ground, or a daughter who doesn't spend her days in the cattle yards and on a motorbike, but then they wouldn't be who they are and neither would I. I guess we could have used the tragedies in our lives to turn our backs on this way of life, but that would seem like a betrayal. Although my children Anna and Matthew are no longer with us, their spirits live on in the outback. Anna was too young to have really understood the bush, but Matthew loved it with a passion. When they died, the outback lost a part of its future.

I spent my childhood in the city and adult life in the outback. I grew up in Brisbane, not really in suburbia, but what we called 'in the bush'. We lived on a two and a half acre block, on a dirt road with a little over a kilometre to walk to the shops, school and the bus. My father and brother still live there, but it looks very different now that the area has been built up.

I wanted to study agricultural science at university—even then I wasn't interested in city life—but my Year 12 results weren't good enough. I did matriculate, however, which was a help many years later when I decided to apply for university entrance as a mature age student.

After leaving school I worked at the University of Queensland as a lab assistant and enrolled in a part-time laboratory technology course. That year was a blur of work, night lectures and illness. I abandoned the course and found a job in an office. I hated the job, was sacked several months later to make way for a returned Vietnam veteran, found another office job and hated that too. Finally, a friend of my brother's, whose family had moved out west to manage a station, called in to see us. His mother wasn't well and needed someone to give her a hand at the station. Two weeks later, I was on a bus to somewhere called Boulia, and although I didn't know it then, I was never to return to the city to live. I was eighteen years old.

It was dark when I arrived at Coorabulka Station. My first impression of the place was of the noise the generator made. I thought the outback was supposed to be quiet! The next morning I received my second lasting impression—where were the trees? If you stand on the flat at Coorabulka and do a 360 degree circle you won't see many trees. I still hate the sound of generators but soon learnt to love the open, rolling downs with its Flinders grass and saltbush.

The old homestead was built out of timber and, at one stage, plagued by rats. The jackaroos rigged up traps using forty-four gallon drums and would catch the vermin at night. Coorabulka was where I learnt to do housework—something I have a deep and abiding dislike of and will avoid whenever possible. I also learnt some basic cooking skills, but more importantly, Coorabulka is where I met my husband.

There were quite a few jackaroos working on the station and Mal was one of them. He was nineteen and adored Slim Dusty. We were chalk and cheese, from two different worlds. Mal grew up on Arrabury Station, on the Queensland-South Australian border. He was a country boy through and through. I, on the other hand, was city born and bred. Yet looking back, I think we were mates right from the start, and being mates has seen us through some pretty tough times.

In early 1973, Mal had found work as a station hand at Islay Plains, a large North Australian Pastoral Company station near Alpha in the Central Highlands of Queensland. I secured a job as a governess on a nearby property. We were engaged some time that year—August I think—and married in Brisbane the following January, six weeks short of my twentieth birthday. We started our married life at Islay Plains living in a quaint but spartan cottage which adjoined the station homestead. Islay was managed by 'Long John' and Wendy Ohlsen who were to become our very dear friends. The station was not as isolated as other NAPCO properties and we were lucky to have a mail service twice a week as well as a telephone connection to Alpha.

Station life was hard work, but Mal and I loved it. I took up governessing again until I fell pregnant in the middle of 1975. I caught the bus to Brisbane a couple of weeks before the baby was due. Unfortunately, my baby, Anna, was late so I was away for over a month, which felt like eternity.

Being out bush with a new baby can often make mums uneasy, but it never really worried me. Anna was a colicky baby so Mal and I shared the floor walking her back and forth. She was a beautiful baby who looked just like her dad.

Anna, aged four weeks, March 1976.

The year after Anna's birth, Mal was transferred to Monkira, a 3,730 square kilometre NAPCO cattle station in the Channel Country, to work as the head stockman. We lived in the station's guest quarters for several months while a two-room cottage was being extended for us. Mal was out in the camp most days. I missed him terribly, but I wasn't lonely. I had an active toddler to care for. Anna and I used to go for a long walk every afternoon. We had a special rock where we would sit and eat an orange. At night I would read for hours. I remember reading Xavier Herbert's *Poor Fellow My Country* then.

By the end of 1977, I was pregnant again. Six months later, Mal was asked to manage Cordillo Downs, an offer too good to refuse, although it meant leaving NAPCO. Cordillo was next door to Arrabury, the station where Mal had grown up. Mal was excited by the move because he was 'going home', so to speak. I reluctantly set off for Brisbane to wait out the arrival of baby number two leaving Mal behind to do the packing. My baby daughter Megan was only fourteen days late. Mal had been with me when Anna was born, but this time he was out at stock camp. Fortunately he was able to come down to Brisbane a few weeks later and drive us to our new home at Cordillo.

Cordillo is isolated by anyone's standards. It is roughly a four-hour drive from Birdsville and a similar distance from the town of Windorah, yet to me it was the centre of the world. I was busy with my two kids, and after a few months I was even doing the cooking too. In May 1979, I drove to Brisbane to attend my brother's wedding. Mal was too busy to come with me, but his cousin Rosslyn who was working at Cordillo as a jillaroo agreed to keep me, Anna and Megan company. Just outside the town of Roma we collided with a truck. Rosslyn, Megan and I were only slightly injured, but Anna was killed. Within a month we were back at Cordillo trying to pick up the pieces of our shattered lives. Six months later we decided to leave. As much as Mal and I both loved Cordillo, and despite my fear of leaving what had been Anna's home, it was time to move on.

Gleeson, north of Cloncurry, was new country and a fresh start for our family. Straightaway we knew we'd made a mistake. Even the dog hated the place and turned savage. We only stayed until the end of the year. By then we had a new baby. Matthew was born in July 1980. He could not replace Anna, but between him and two-year-old Megan, I was kept busy.

Towards the end of 1980, we rejoined NAPCO, accepting a job with them at Alexandria, one of its larger stations in the Northern Territory. 'Alex' was a sprawling 16,359 square kilometres and ran, in a good season, some 60,000 head of cattle. But the drought had set in which made working conditions difficult. Dry times are depressing, yet experience tells me that there is always a certain acceptance of whatever conditions prevail at the time. You learn to get on with the job.

Alex had its own streets and houses, and a small mobile school. Megan and Matt loved it there. One thing they weren't lacking at Alex was the company of other kids. Mal's job kept him very busy. It was the tail end of the Brucellosis and Tuberculosis Eradication Campaign and he had two stock camps on the go. At times I resented the fact that we didn't see a lot of him. But it couldn't be helped.

In our first year at Alex, Wendy Ohlsen and I started the Barkly branch of the Isolated Children's and Parents Association (ICPA). In 1982, a State

Council of the ICPA was formed in the Northern Territory and I was a member of the council for the next four years. This gave me an outside interest, and certainly provided me with some much needed intellectual stimulation. I attended meetings and conferences in Darwin, Katherine, Alice Springs and Tennant Creek.

We left Alex in September 1986 when Mal was transferred to manage Glenormiston, another NAPCO station. We were sad to leave Alex but pleased about Mal's new job and returning to the Boulia district where we first met. The kids were heartbroken at the thought of leaving all their friends at Alex. It was the only home either of them remembered.

Glenormiston is a magic place. Set on the edge of a large waterhole called Lake Idamea and bordered on the west by the Toko Ranges, the place is steeped in history. Our present homestead of stone and mortar was built in 1898, and there are ruins on the southern end of the property which are thought to be the remains of dwellings left by early Afghan traders. We are much more involved with station work at Glenormiston than we were at Alex. Mal musters by plane and gets around the property in a four-wheel drive. I started cooking a couple of weeks after we arrived and ten years later I'm still the station cook.

I was determined that my kids would get a good education and that they would not grow up believing they were somehow inferior because they didn't attend 'normal' schools. The kids were enrolled in the Brisbane Primary Correspondence School and with the Mount Isa School of the Air. I had some typical urban preconceptions initially—'real' school was a classroom with teachers. When Megan was in first grade, we travelled to Alice Springs and I arranged for her to have a day in a real schoolroom. She hated it, and from that day onward my ideas about education changed. Correspondence lessons, on-air lessons and a home tutor—mum or the governess—who works as part of a team with the teacher at the School of Distance Education provide for the educational needs of isolated children very efficiently, particularly in the primary school years. In fact, I believe that kids who study by distance education have advantages that city kids don't.

Employing a governess is a real hit-and-miss business. You can never really know how someone is going to cope with living out here until they are on the job. A girl we employed in 1986 stayed on an extra year and was fantastic with the children. Her replacement, on the other hand, only lasted six months. After her sudden departure I found myself back in the schoolroom. I still had to feed the men but decided I would have to sacrifice the housework if I was going to continue teaching Megan and Matt. I developed a theory which I still hand out as free advice to new teaching mums—as long as the kids are taught and the men are fed, everything else just falls in place. It certainly wasn't easy, and by the end of a school week I would be a total wreck. My kids knew to give me a wide berth on Fridays. Teaching my kids was a privilege. I've learnt that I'll sacrifice a lot for the sake of my children's education.

In due course Megan was bundled off to boarding school. We had been brainwashing the kids and ourselves for years that boarding school was the best solution. It was a 'necessary evil' in our lives. If Megan said she didn't like her school I would never stick up for the school, I just agreed with her. I didn't like her being there either, but I learnt to swallow my fears.

I remained very involved with the ICPA for many years because of my continuing interest in the problems faced by both children and parents living in isolation. In 1988 I was elected to the Queensland State Council. I spent five years on the council—three of them as treasurer. This involved trips away from home, something I have always had mixed feelings about. I hated the thought of going, but ultimately enjoyed myself once I arrived. I loved meeting other people and the intellectual stimulation these conferences provided. I have made some very good friends through the ICPA. Although I resigned from the Queensland ICPA Council in 1993, I am still president of our local Georgina branch and will continue to have an interest in future projects and developments.

On New Year's Eve 1992, four weeks before Matthew was due to leave for boarding school, he was out riding his motorbike and crashed into a fence. He died instantly. The crazy thing is that Matt had been on and off motorbikes since the age of eight and in four years he'd never once had a serious prang, no injury any worse than a bruise.

When Anna died, Mal and I coped more or less alone for two reasons— we were socially and geographically isolated and we were young, only in our mid-twenties, and did not have a network of friends to support us. At the time of Anna's death, Mal and I relied solely on each other. When

Matt was killed we received incredible support from the Georgina community, support which is still there many years later. I really believe that living where we do has helped me deal with the loss of my son and daughter, especially after Matt died. I was surrounded by a group of friends to whom Matt was important and who felt his loss very deeply. I have always felt comfortable in the company of these friends, but for a long time after Matt's death I found being with

The last photo of Matt taken several weeks before he died.

strangers awkward. On what would have been Matt's thirteenth birthday, six months after he died, four families came and spent the day with us. We have never had to spend the anniversary of his death alone.

After Matt died, Anne Maree became a regular visitor to Glenormiston and is one of those friends who have helped me cope. I met her a short time before Matt's death. When she first called on us at Glenormiston, I was rather sceptical. Glenormiston is on the very edge of her territory and I was not sure why she wanted to meet us. I was brought up in a strict Protestant family and grew up thinking Catholics had two heads. I had a Catholic boyfriend when I was fifteen, much to my mother's dismay. Anne Maree was the first Catholic sister I'd ever had anything to do with.

My life is very busy but when Anne Maree flies in I can pull up for a while, linger over a cup of coffee, and have a yarn about all sorts of things. Together we've sorted out the Catholic Church! She is deeply committed to her ministry and to the women and the families she visits. Mal doesn't get involved with 'that religion business' but always enjoys catching up with Anne Maree. They share a common interest in flying. I've noticed that whenever pilots get together they seem to disappear into a world and language of their own. Mal and Anne Maree can chat for hours about their respective Cessnas.

Even though we live in isolation, we have had the opportunity to discover different religions and faiths, but one thing I've learnt out here is that you do not have to belong to one particular Church to discover spirituality. As we live so much closer to nature, we tend to develop our own ideas of God. There is no feeling of segregation out here as visits from various clergies help us to develop our faith. Anne Maree has helped me explore my own spirituality. She has changed my perceptions of Catholics, the Church and the clergy. She has occasionally brought priests out with her and I have to say that they are the most loving and compassionate men I have ever met.

Anne Maree never shoves religion down anyone's throat—it's simply not on her agenda. She is different things to different people but if you need a shoulder to lean on, she will always be there. It's important for us to have her here because she helps lessen the burden of isolation on our lives. Just because we are geographically isolated does not mean we have to be socially or spiritually isolated. She adds a dimension to our lives that simply would not be there without her.

After Matt's death, I began to rethink life. I had often thought about doing some sort of distance education myself and was worried about no longer having an excuse for not doing the dreaded housework. I applied for a Bachelor of Arts course as an external student and found studying to be almost therapeutic in those first dreadful months after Matt's death. It gave me something to focus my mind on. I have always wanted some sort of a career and not limit myself to being just the station cook. Another drawback that living in the outback presents to women is that it tends to heavily favour men and their work. I have known families to leave the bush because the woman wanted to pursue a career of her own. That is why studying is so important to me. I guess I am lucky that I didn't have a career to give up. But I think this searching for something interesting and stimulating to do with my life is more to do with my age and the empty nest syndrome than with living in the outback. I just have to be more creative about how I deal with my life than a woman in the city would.

Soon we will be celebrating a decade of living at Glenormiston. Managing a cattle station is really a way of life as well as a job. We, especially Mal, are on duty twenty-four hours a day and the only way to get time off is to leave the property. I can't imagine what it would be like being married to someone with a regular nine-to-five job. I have my own station work to get through as I am closely involved with all aspects of the day-to-day running of Glenormiston. There are times when I think it would be great to get up in the morning and not have to cook breakfast for a mob of people. I've just come to accept this as part of the routine of station life.

The last ten years have seen a lot of changes, not just in our lives but in the outback. In 1988 we got satellite television. For a long time we only had one commercial channel and the ABC, but thanks to satellite TV we now have SBS as well. As exciting as it was

Mal

getting TV, the really big event which revolutionised our lives was the telephone. I've heard it said often that telephones have ruined outback life because people no longer communicate the way they did back in the days of the old HF radio. That is simply not true. If people no longer communicate with their neighbours, well that is their fault and not the telephone's. Phones and faxes have really helped lessen the barriers that isolation can create.

I am always amazed by the prejudices that city people have of our way of life. The standard questions I'm always asked are: 'What do you do all day? Don't you ever get bored?'

My days are varied, and no, I'm far from being bored. There is always something to do in the next five minutes . . . or the next hour, or tomorrow. As the station cook I will spend the best part of my day in the kitchen, especially if the stock camp is in. I have breakfast, smoko, lunch and tea to prepare for a dozen staff. Lunch, we call dinner, and dinner we call tea, just to confuse city people. I also like to go out with Mal and see the rest of Glenormiston whenever the chance arises. The housework is always there, as well as the station office work, ICPA and Landcare business to attend to. No, I can't say I am 'bored'.

It's funny. I know to many city people we are perceived as being backward and ignorant, and yet I think I am just as well informed about the things that interest me as the average city person is. I watch the news every night and read a wide range of magazines. I know that there is life beyond the Great Divide, which is more than I can say for plenty of city people, but I get cross when they are surprised that we are not ignorant and backward. It also annoys me when they think that I am somehow deprived and to be pitied for living 'out in the sticks'. I'm very much aware of the physical isolation of my lifestyle but it isn't an issue most of the time. It only becomes an issue when my hair is in desperate need of a cut and colour, or the last half of the bag of spuds is rotten and no-one is going to town for days. 'Town' for us is usually Mount Isa which is 360 kilometres away, or it can be Boulia which is 140 kilometres down the track. And as for all those things we are supposed to be missing out on or lacking in our lives, well I wish someone would just tell me what they are! I don't feel the least bit deprived, socially or culturally.

Megan working as a jillaroo at Glenormiston.

And so this is where I find myself today. I have a comfortable home which I dearly love, plenty to keep me busy, and books and music for the rare quiet moments. I have known, and still experience, extreme sadness with the loss of my two children, but I have also known love and friendship. When the kids were little we would often spend Christmas away, but since 1987 we have spent every Christmas here at Glenormiston and that time has become very important to us. Of course it's not been the same since Matt died, and our memories of that last Christmas spent with him are very special. One day I will have to face Christmas somewhere else, but not for a while I hope. I believe I am who I am because I live in the outback, not in spite of it. Holidays spent each year on the coast mean we can visit family and friends and experience city life for a while. A while is about all Mal and I can handle. When I turned my back on city life twenty-four years ago, I had no idea what lay in store for me. Now I couldn't imagine living anywhere else.

I've always argued that we are just ordinary people living ordinary lives, but perhaps there is some element in living out here that is out of the ordinary. Everything requires that little extra bit of effort—nothing just happens. Every aspect of our lives involves commitment and effort. Perhaps that is what makes it so satisfying. You have to work hard, but there is a sense of pride and achievement, and then, as a bonus, there are the wide open spaces, the beautiful sunsets, and a feeling of belonging in a world that only a few people really understand and can appreciate.

CIRCUIT THREE

LEONIE NUNN—
SUNNYSIDE STATION

S unnyside Station is my first destination on the third and final circuit each month. The privately owned sheep property near Longreach is managed by a husband-and-wife team, Jim and Leonie Nunn.

Father Terry introduced me to Leonie and her three boys in April 1989 when we flew to Sunnyside to celebrate mass at the homestead. I've been flying in every month since then to spend a couple of days with the family who have become my dear friends.

Many people I visit are battling against drought, and the Nunns are no exception. Jim virtually manages Sunnyside on his own. The running of these smaller, private properties can crush families with worries and anxieties, but Leonie is one of the strongest women I know. She remains optimistic, even in the face of adversity. Faith is very important to her and keeps her going during this time of drought. When I first took over the Aerial Ministry, I quickly discovered that I had much to learn about the bush. I certainly did not fully realise the importance of rain, particularly for those running a private station. Usually when I land at Sunnyside, we hold a simple prayer service around the kitchen table and pray for rain.

I am sitting on a bush verandah watching the first storm of the season. The night is still, the only sounds are insects thump-thumping on the screens, and the lightning turns the earth an indigo blue. The rain creeps in gently and soon begins to drum on the roof like a rapturous crowd in a grandstand. We turn off the lights and listen in silence ... The night is sweet. I am remembering simple pleasures that the people of the bush have not forgotten—like how the difference between despair and optimism is only two inches of rain ...

Heather Brown

I think living on the land almost demands a belief in God. The only thing that will end this drought is rain, and this is something totally out of the control of human hands. There is little or nothing we can do to make it rain except pray to God. As we watch every change in the weather, without getting any beneficial rain, our spirits tend to sink lower and lower. Jim doesn't like to talk about it. His theory is that because he is out in it most of the time, he doesn't want to come home to a wife bemoaning their fate if it doesn't rain. I cope with the drought by busying myself with my boys' schoolwork, the housework, or talking to friends like Sister Anne Maree.

I prefer not to read rural journals which speak only of doom and gloom. I try not to listen to radio and television programs which dwell on the negative. It's soul-destroying to turn on the radio these days and hear some eminent climatologist say that we are in a twenty-year drought cycle and that it has only just begun. Then the market report comes on and we hear how the wool market took a nosedive and cattle prices were depressed at a recent sale, Japan doesn't want our beef, Australia didn't win the latest Korean tender, and the USA has too many cattle. Rain is the linchpin of our existence out here. If, and when it does rain in the bush, people still like to ring each other up and talk about it. The phone will not stop ringing if there is decent rain around. It's disheartening when someone calls the house to report that two inches of rain fell on their place while you've only received twenty points. You are delighted for their sake, but all the same you feel like kicking in the wall.

Jim and I came out here to south-west Queensland in 1983. Sunnyside is a 32,000 hectare sheep and cattle property a couple of hours from

Longreach. We had only one son at the time, Luke, with another on the way. Prior to moving to Sunnyside, we'd lived on a large cattle property, south of Oodnadatta in South Australia, where Jim was the station manager.

Jim has worked on cattle stations practically all his life. I am no stranger to the bush having grown up in Marree, in South Australia. My father, Bill Gwydir, was a well-known drover. He was the last drover to take cattle down the Birdsville Track. I think I must have inherited my love for the land from him.

Moving to Sunnyside was a very exciting time for Jim and me. It was a dream come true. We bought the property with the help of partners and a lending institution. Initially we had very few sheep and cattle, and hardly

Sunnyside

any equipment as our monetary reserves were quickly drained in those first few months of setting-up. However, nothing daunted us because we believed we were going to be successful graziers. Little did we realise that we were to face the highest interest rates ever, the collapse of the wool industry with the lowest wool prices on record, and the worst and longest drought, which has sent cattle prices plummeting to an all-time low. Today, thirteen years later, we are still here, with only one partner—the bank—three more children, low stock numbers, and a firm and burning desire to remain on the land! I know plenty of people think we're mad, but Jim and I can honestly look back on our thirteen years here and know that if it wasn't for the drought we would be well on the way to achieving our goals. We could have withstood the low commodity prices if only it had rained . . .

I love the bush. I have no desire whatsoever to live in the city or on the coast. Besides, it would literally kill Jim. He's grown up here and this is where he'll stay. As we live less than a two hour drive from Longreach, I could never say that I feel isolated. Longreach is a good service town where we can purchase most of our requirements. Any other items come via mail order catalogues. As for loneliness, it's not an issue—I'm too preoccupied to think about it.

When Jim and I first moved to Sunnyside, the house took a low priority on our agenda. An old corrugated iron cottage, set high up on stumps on an ironstone ridge, it looks very much like a lopsided tree house. It was run-down, and for a long time it had been occupied mainly by men. One day I'd like to lower the house, re-clad it, and make it more respectable. But right now, our priorities lie elsewhere.

Rural power was already connected when we arrived. Having come from a property where a generator was the only source of power, Jim and I were thrilled to have the luxury of 'real' power. Unfortunately there was no telephone, only a party line. The telephone line limped from tree to tree across miles of scrub, connecting anything from two to six properties, across creeks and in our case, the Thomson River. Consequently, I didn't have a telephone for several years until a neighbour kindly let us join his line which worked better than ours. Thankfully, those days are now gone and we have an excellent telephone system called the DRCS, which is linked by a series of towers. We have a ninety-foot tower outside our house with a dish-like structure perched on top—a remarkable piece of technology which is our lifeline to the outside world. The only downside is that we use it too much. Our telephone bills are astronomical because we have to use the phone for conducting business and placing orders for goods and provisions as well as keeping in touch with family and friends. We don't have a local call to anywhere, so I'm always amused when the threat of timed local calls is mooted. I would find life very difficult and lonely out here without a reliable telephone service.

Another small yet important improvement is that I am now the proud owner of an electric stove! The first couple of years I cooked for the family on an antiquated wood-burning stove which resulted in plenty of failed meals and blackened walls from the smoking chimney. As anyone who has ever cooked on a bush stove knows, the major discomfort is the intense heat. It billows out with such force that in minutes your face and body feel as seared as the steaks you're frying. The heat is obviously worse in the summer.

Looking at the improvements over the years from Jim's perspective, he has had a bore sunk from which we pipe water to various paddocks, repaired the original shearers' quarters, built quite a lot of internal fences and undertaken numerous other general repairs and maintenance on the property. Several years ago Jim started to build a new shearing shed. This was before the collapse of the wool floor price system, so whenever time and finances permit, he adds a little more to the shed. It's his pet project and I suppose it stands as a reminder of more optimistic times.

In the late 1980s, we were lucky enough to receive satellite television with the purchase of a dish and a decoder. It was expensive at the time, but there is no such thing as free-to-air surface reception. I have mixed feelings about television. It keeps us up to date with what is happening in the world but at the same time I believe it detracts from family life. Fortunately we are only able to receive three channels so my boys are not indoors glued to a small screen all the time.

The education of our sons takes up most of my time. I decided to teach them myself rather than employ a governess. I'm now a great admirer of bush mothers who've taken on the task of teaching their own children. Many of these women have had no formal training and they do a wonderful job. I am fortunate enough to be a trained teacher, but I never have enough hours in my day and must juggle teaching with the running of a busy household and property chores. We have a schoolroom next to the kitchen which I've set up with desks and books. Daily half-hour radio lessons with a teacher from the Distance Education Centre in Longreach are followed by working on the set papers. However, my dilemma is not the work itself, but battling with my boys who refuse to stay in the schoolroom because life outside is infinitely more interesting, particularly if Dad is home. Cameron is only at preschool age so he is easier to handle than the others. During shearing season, the two older boys are often required to help Jim draft the sheep before school starts, a job they dearly love. After a couple of hours with Jim and the shearers, they tramp into the schoolroom covered head to toe in dirt and dust from the sheep yards. An hour later, they are at me to let them go back to the shearing yard for smoko because the shearers have a far better one than what Mum has prepared. The boys have barely settled back in the schoolroom when it's time for the shearers' lunchbreak and they are sure that Dad needs help again in the yards. After an extended lunch hour they slowly make their way back to school and keep an eye on the time until three o'clock—the shearers' afternoon smoko, which they simply must attend. Consequently, school during shearing season and at other times of increased activity at Sunnyside is often a non-event.

It is imperative that our four boys go to boarding school to complete their education. Just because Jim and I love our life in the bush does not mean that our boys should follow suit. I want them to have every available opportunity to follow a different career path and should this be something other than working on the land then both Jim and I would support their decision. As with any occupation or business enterprise, there is a down side and ours, at the moment, is drought. This drought has affected us for the last five years. We've had some rain during this time but never a good season. We've lost over half our sheep numbers and we've just barely managed to keep the nucleus of our cattle herd.

Our youngest son, Cameron.

There is little you can do during an ongoing drought. Our income is about a third of what it was five years ago and our costs have increased in that time. In this current situation, we have fewer sheep cutting less wool, and of course the cattle are faring badly as well. In a dry time, we have to give our cattle supplementary feed so that they get enough nourishment to stay alive. Sunnyside has edible trees such as mulga, and our cattle can survive with the aid of lick blocks (nutritional and mineral supplements) and another concoction of salt and phosphorous which Jim has found works well in our type of country. But what has made this drought such a strain for Jim and me are the low commodity prices—once again something entirely out of our control. We are price takers—we can't pass our increased production costs down the production chain as we are at the bottom of the chain. As primary producers—all we have is our wool, sheep and cattle—there are limited outlets where we can sell our products. When commodity prices go down and costs rise, our profit margin narrows considerably.

If, one day, it does rain, that will be only the beginning. We will still have to wait for the sheep to grow wool and the cattle to fatten and breed up. There is much emphasis now on being a 'viable producer' and managing the land in a 'sustainable' fashion. With the seasons against you and depressed commodity prices, I can't start and wonder *who* is viable and *what* is sustainable. The powers that be, either the government or a lending institution, do not really understand the connection between our livelihood and our lifestyle. They are so closely interwoven that it is almost impossible to differentiate between the two. I try not to dwell on the drought and low prices, preferring to focus instead on the positive aspects of our life. There are days where I could cry at how unfair it all is, but Jim and I are happy, in good health, and refuse to lose hope that it will one day rain.

There are many women on small, privately owned properties who work outside with their husbands as well as running a household and doing all the wifely chores. Since the rural downturn and drought, some men have been forced to leave their properties and look for work elsewhere while their wives stay at home to hold the fort. I don't take an active part in the day-to-day running of Sunnyside. This is left to Jim and the boys. When we came to Sunnyside, I occasionally helped Jim with drafting sheep or branding cattle, leaving the baby in his pram covered with a fly veil in the shade of a tree. Eventually Jim decided it was easier to do it on his own rather than put up with me and several babies in his way. He was used to working on much larger properties with a full staff of men and couldn't get used to having a woman around, especially when I pestered him with what he thought were silly, useless questions. He's battled more or less on his own, occasionally employing contract staff until our boys were old enough to help out. Jim has had plenty of dramas trying to teach them to do the right thing, however. On one occasion when Peter was about seven, Jim asked him to help shift the cattle. As soon as the cattle were let out of the yard they headed straight for Peter. A large Brahman bull led the herd which was all too much for him who turned tail on his small motorbike and raced through the scrub, yellow helmet flashing through the trees. Needless to say Jim was not impressed. His biggest lament is that just when the boys are becoming useful, I want them in the schoolroom, or they are sent off to boarding school.

Sunnyside is in a very quiet corner of south-west Queensland. It was difficult moving to a new area. When Luke started school it gave me an opportunity to meet people and to get to know others in a similar situation, but it was also through the Aerial Ministry that I received much needed support and friendship.

We first became aware of the ministry when Jim and I had only been at Sunnyside for five months. I had just returned home from a long stay in Longreach waiting to give birth to Matthew. The house was a mess and with baby's bottles and nappies when a car pulled up at the back gate—not the grandest of entrances—which proved that the visitor was a stranger to the property. The man introduced himself as Father Terry Loth, a Catholic priest who was travelling through the bush assessing the needs of families in our area. I can't recall exactly when I first met Sister Anne Maree, although she tells me that it was back in April 1989. I never dreamed that I would become so close to Anne Maree and that she would become one of my best friends. After my experience of Catholic boarding school in Adelaide I seriously doubted if I could ever call a nun a best friend. Back in those days, nuns were strict, humourless women and easily feared. It's been wonderful that my boys are able to grow up and see a religious person like Anne Maree as a 'normal' person who's become a part of our family life. They even consider the bishop, Brian Heenan, a personal friend because he has visited our home on several occasions. They have no qualms talking openly to him, whereas I grew up in a time where children would never have felt comfortable about doing such a thing.

Anne Maree puts her Christianity into practice. When she flies down to Sunnyside she holds religious services—simple, relevant ceremonies accentuated by her creativity in relating them to the seasons of the Church, feast days and the Christian calendar in general. She has helped out with the shearing, catering for rodeos, and on one occasion helped Jim and me pull down and re-erect a portable cattle yard.

I can talk to Anne Maree about my problems. She makes me look at things from a different perspective and keeps me in touch with myself. She is the one person I know outside my family who cares deeply for me and worries about how I am coping, especially with this drought on. But most of all, she reassures me that I am not alone. If I did not have her coming around on a regular basis, it would be a struggle. I'm not saying I would give up my faith, because it is very important to me, but it would be all the more difficult to keep alive.

Sister Anne Maree and her godson, Cameron.

Anne Maree was present at our youngest son's birth. She drove me to Longreach Hospital at dawn and stayed by my side for the duration of the labour, and the birth. It's not every day a Catholic nun is there with you in the delivery room urging you to stay calm! After Cameron was born, she went to find Jim to announce the good news. Jim later asked me what had I done to poor Sister as she looked decidedly unwell and ghostly white!

I do not envy Sister's job or lifestyle. The pressures placed on her are enormous—adapting to a different situation on an almost daily basis and having to listen to everyone's problems and grievances. The ministry is her life and she does a wonderful job. She's one of my best friends. I would feel lost without her.

I live in a very male-dominated household, in fact the dog and I are the only females at Sunnyside. Generally speaking, life in this part of the country is somewhat chauvinistic, and my husband would have to be one of the worst offenders. I am sure he thinks that woman's work—cooking, cleaning, washing and teaching the kids—are all trivial pursuits.

Being intimately involved with our sons' education, spending each day with them and going everywhere together as a family reinforces family values which I believe to be one of the most positive aspects of our lifestyle. I do not know what it is like to leave a child in day care, or even see one off to school every day. The downside of this is that Jim and I have very little time alone as a couple. It's a rare occasion when we go somewhere together without the children. However, I am convinced that life in our situation would be intolerable if both Jim and I did not get on well. Both partners must endeavour to maintain a good, strong relationship, otherwise it would be hell. Jim is my mate and despite having very different outlooks and ideas, we are lucky to have each other.

Community spirit is also important in the bush. Not long ago, Jim had been working on his shearing shed when the ladder slipped and he fell to the ground smashing his elbow. He was flown to Brisbane for treatment.

At the time, we were carting water because our house dam had gone dry, as well as pumping water from a bore for the stock. The assistance given by our neighbours in this time of need touched me deeply and was greatly appreciated. After Jim came home from hospital people were still forth-coming with offers of help. Friends helped us muster cattle to send them away on agistment as well as helping the boys and me with the other chores around the property. Jim's accident heralded a new phase in our lives. He had to rely on the boys and me to do most things which was a situation he'd not known before. He found the whole affair very frustrat-ing to say the least. He didn't like his wife meddling with his work. The arm got better as soon as I announced that I was going to take a more active role in the running of the property. Jim couldn't bear the thought of this happening, so he worked furiously at a speedy recovery.

I fear that sometimes people living outside of the bush will exclaim, 'Not another whingeing cocky!' With all that we've had to endure out here with this drought, I've become very aware of this whingeing cocky tag and don't want people to think that we stay on the land just to complain about it. Because we have been in a drought situation for so long, our physical and mental reserves are low. We run a privately owned station and are first-generation graziers. Therefore

Jim

we don't have much in the way of financial resources. We have to be careful and think long and hard about decisions concerning the prop-erty. Once a decision is made, it's final. It's of no use to be wise in hindsight.

In a drought situation we tighten the belt—the fence doesn't get built, we don't purchase equipment and we don't embark on new projects because we don't know when it's going to rain. After a while things start to run down, especially mechanical equipment such as bikes and engines. Things are repaired in a patch-up, band-aid fashion, our attitude being 'hold it together until it rains and things improve'.

To help stay sane during this drought I have tried to establish a small garden. The green, cool atmosphere that can be created by a garden does wonders for one's morale. To look out on a hot day and see something green is uplifting, particularly when further afield everything is grey, parched and denuded of all vegetation. Yes, the situation is not a pleasant one, but we don't live in a state of pessimism. What sustains me through all this is my belief in God, the love and support of my husband, my four delightful sons and the unswerving friendship of people such as Sister Anne Maree.

I don't want people to think of me as a poor thing living in the back of beyond trying to eke out an existence. Unless you live our lifestyle it's difficult understanding the whys and wherefores of living on the land. At the moment some of our cattle are away on agistment and some at home living on mulga and memories. The woolshed Jim started building many years ago before the drought kicked in is still standing. It's a constant reminder of more prosperous times in the wool industry long past and why we've decided to stay on the land and wait for the rain to come in.

CIRCUIT THREE

DOREEN ROGERS— BELMORE STATION

For an elderly woman, to manage a large sheep and cattle property is no easy task. I have immense admiration for the stamina and courage of Doreen Rogers, who battled on her own after the death of her husband Alan.

I was introduced to Doreen on 17 April 1990, at a mass held at nearby Sunnyside Station. As sole manager of Belmore Station, a 24,500 acre property south-west of Longreach, Doreen had to make all kinds of decisions—from what sort of Toyota to buy, to when to sell her sheep. She told me she had so much to learn after her husband's death.

Against the advice from family and friends, she refused to leave Belmore. During the drought, I would go out into the paddocks with Doreen to look for feed for her sheep. Together we cleared scrub, mended fences, mustered and pulled bogged sheep out of dams.

Recently, Doreen was diagnosed with cancer. She joked with me that she's been through worse, particularly with the drought. I thank God for the strength of her spirit and of her faith.

Belmore came into the hands of the Rogers family in 1911. My husband, Alan Rogers, and I managed this 24,500 acre sheep and cattle property together until he got sick and passed away. Because we both loved this place so dearly, I decided to stay on. I have been looking after Belmore on my own for the last twelve years.

One never expects life to change, until suddenly it does. Alan was hale and hearty, but then our world was turned upside down, and in just a few months, at the age of sixty-one, I found myself alone. In such times, nature seems to take over and shock makes you numb, which is a protection of sorts. Alan and I had no children. We filled our time with each other and our work. When he died I did not know what I was going to do. Friends and family suggested that I sell up and leave, but I chose to stay, and so I have continued on—month by month, year by year—trying to keep all the things that were dear to my husband and me from changing.

Although I would often help Alan around Belmore, I quickly discovered that I had plenty to learn about the wool industry and the management of a large sheep and cattle property. Alan used to come home weary after a day out mending fences and would say to me, 'Doreen, those fences in the river make my feet hurt.'

I never had an inkling of what he was talking about until it was my turn to walk the empty river channels and mend all the fences. It was hard going and rocky. Some channels stretched for miles, going from one paddock into the next. There was no way of guessing where they ended and which fences Alan would have worked on. Sometimes I would go and stay out the entire day, just walking the dry beds. In those few early months, it helped me somehow to come to grips with my loneliness. Loneliness can wear you down. I don't think you can ever really come to terms with it, especially if by nature you are a person who likes company. My aim has been to keep things going as well as they did when my husband was alive. This is not always easy because a grazier's workload seems to get heavier and heavier.

I do not really worry about being out here on my own. This does not mean that given the chance I would do it all over again, but I am glad I have stayed on at Belmore. Now that I am in my seventies, I feel that I will not be able to continue much longer. I think that when the moment comes, I will have to sell. I won't like to leave, but then who would wish to leave a place where they have been for a long time? I will just retire and do a few other things.

I was born in Blackall, a small country town, in 1923, to a young, pretty mother and an older stockman father fourteen years her senior. Dad was a stockman through and through, who roamed the bush. Yet at the end of the First World War, he suddenly decided he would try an occupation that would keep him closer to my mother and me, and he became a mailman! It was Dad who brought the first Hudson car to the town of Blackall. He was also responsible for running the mail from Ilfracombe to Isisford.

My mother hailed from Isisford. Dad had clapped eyes on her when she was only a wee girl. He was droving sheep through Isisford, and when she ran barefoot out into the paddock where he was working and got burrs on her feet, he gallantly carried her back to the house in his arms. They wed twelve years later. My mother loved pretty clothes and trinkets and treated me to the same. Because she had married so young—she was seventeen—and as I was often the only one around, she confided in me as a friend and an equal. This resulted in my being a very precocious child and often what I would say was not childish or childlike.

I cannot ever recall Dad drinking, but apparently in the early days of his married life he had what we used to call 'one or two'. On occasion I would go across to the house next door and play with the neighbour's little girl, but she was never allowed to come to our house. My mother would tell her parents that Dad was sick, and tell me the same. Pearlie, my little friend, would cry to her grandmother asking why she could not come to play in the cubby house at our place. 'No, Pearlie,' her nanna chided her. 'Doreen's father is sick.'

'Is your father really sick, Doreen?' Pearlie asked me. When I said nothing, she kept up the wail. 'Is your father dead, Doreen?' she finally asked.

'No,' says me, 'but he's dead bloody drunk at our place!'

Pearlie's nanna thought it funny enough to tell my mother, who did not think it funny at all.

I was the only child until I was four so I had plenty of time to become spoilt. My mother loved to dress me up and I always had a handbag, long gloves and a felt hat. When I was five, Dad moved the whole family to Isisford where my grandparents lived. Isisford, forty miles to the south of Ilfracombe, on the banks of the Barcoo River, was roughly the same size as Ilfracombe with a population of a little over a hundred. There was a general store, a school and several hotels, as well as saddlery and black-smith shops. The Oma Waterhole, which was close by, was a popular spot for picnics, swimming and fishing. As in most bush towns, folk helped one another through the rough patches of life and lived like one big extended family. Nowadays, little has changed. In fact the town is still much as it was almost seventy years ago, except that

At age three.

new families have arrived and older ones have gone. Dad went back to his stockman's work of droving and was out on the road for many months of the year. But he was at home long enough to give me three more sisters and one brother.

When I was old enough, I was enrolled at the Isisford State School. On my first day I was sent home for drinking the ink! In those days—the late twenties—there were little china bottles of ink fitted into our desks. I was given the biggest hiding ever! I loved the little three-room school and played in the mouth organ band. Each morning we played to file the small group of children from the playground into the classroom—the full bit, vamping and all. I do not know what has become of most of my little schoolmates from that tiny school but I learnt that some became doctors, bank managers—one even a brain surgeon! Perhaps many more did very well for themselves too.

After five years at the Isisford State School I was sent to a convent boarding school in far-off Townsville. I felt very grown-up travelling by myself but it was a long, tiring journey by steam train with an overnight stay in a hotel and then another train ride on to Townsville. Boarding school was not as wonderful as I had originally imagined. I was never so homesick in all my life! At first I didn't like the nuns very much at all. They were very strict and constantly told us to be 'ladies'. We were for-bidden to pull up our stockings in public because a 'young lady' never did such a thing. Since we wore the thick, woollen variety of stockings, which always snaked their way down our ankles, we were forever scuttling off to secluded spots and behind bushes so we could pull them up, out of the sisters' sight.

Each Saturday we were given sixpence if we had not collected any black marks against ourselves during the week. A 'lolly man' accompanied by a Chinese gardener would come into the schoolyard on the weekend and we would buy sweets and vegetables from them. I would always choose several Cowboy Chews and a fat onion which I would cut up and eat with my bread and butter for tea. When I started boarding school, I decided that when grown up, I would either be a nun or an actress. I took part in all the school plays and did 'art of speech' to the Australian College of Music standard and was very honoured to receive my cap and gown. But by graduation, I abandoned the idea of a career in the Church or on the stage. Instead, I trained as a nurse at the Maryborough Base Hospital. The idea of attending to the sick appealed to me but best of all, I could not wait to get out into the wide world and become independent.

Life at the hospital was very regimented, and the pay small. The house rules were far worse than at the convent school. We were only allowed to leave the hospital grounds three times a week and the punishment for being caught outside without permission from the matron was severe. Even when off duty, we still had to be dressed in our full uniform and report in every evening at nine o'clock sharp. However, this never prevented us from sneaking in and out of the dormitories whenever possible and many a time we would be lying in bed, fully clothed under the sheets, pretending to be asleep as the night sister shone her torch into our numbered rooms. The worst thing was that she would start her rounds fifteen minutes before midnight and return every twenty minutes, and not always on time. Therefore it was very tricky to make the break, and return, before she came again on her next round. A boyfriend had to be very keen to wait for you by the exits. Sometimes we would have to crawl under a couple of buildings in our good clothes to sneak back in. But despite all the rules and restrictions, and the long work hours, I enjoyed every minute of hospital life. Caring for patients who became very dear to me was what I loved most about nursing. You were plunged into some great sadness at times, and as I was the type who took my patients' sickness very much to heart I think the sneaking in and out of the dormitories was really very good for us. I felt so proud when I finished my training and study and was finally called 'Sister', and had my photo taken wearing the sisters' veil.

In my Sisters' veil at the Mater Hospital in Brisbane.

Having grown up in small country towns, I began searching for work in outback hospitals. My first posting was in Blackall, the town of the original 'Black Stump'. Unlike the larger city hospitals, the sisters in these bush hospitals were expected to do practically everything, but it hardly ever bothered me because I loved the country hospital atmosphere and the people. After successfully completing another certificate and my maternity training, I left with a fellow nursing sister to tour Australia on a working holiday. After several months spent in busy city hospitals in Sydney and Adelaide, we slowly worked our way inland taking jobs wherever we could find them, mostly at smaller hospitals and clinics. I can remember arriving at one bush hospital only to be told that the domestics had taken the weekend off. Double-certificated or not, the other two sisters and myself had to light the coppers and do all the washing, following the rotary clothes line on the edge of Spencer Gulf like Olympic runners!

The country hospitals welcomed new sisters with open arms because they were often understaffed. In one small mining community in Western Australia, the matron was beside herself with happiness to see us. We stayed long enough for her to have a holiday, looking after her pet duck during her absence. After almost a year away, I finally returned to Queensland. I spent the final five years of my nursing career back at the Mater Hospital in Brisbane. This is where I met my future husband, Alan, a grazier from the central west. He was a patient in one of my wards. We were married in Brisbane in 1968 and he brought me out here to Belmore, to begin my real life in the bush.

The rural industry with all its ups and downs became—and still is—the focus of my life. Rare were the times when I could put my feet up and rest. Even though the work was hard, especially during drought, I

always tried to make the best of things. I painted our lovely three-bedroom weatherboard cottage inside and out, laid new carpets and planted a garden—all in an effort to make Belmore as pleasant a home as possible for the two of us. It was such a happy time for Alan and me and there was a real sense of achievement as we worked together.

Whenever I could, I helped Alan around the property and at the same time I continued to organise the household. The days when we dressed for dinner, had a sherry and a chat before tucking into our tea were fast coming to an end. Previously, privately managed properties like ours had been able to employ station hands, but with the sharp downturn in the rural industry, the grazier's wife suddenly found herself the chief cook and bottle washer. More often than not, Alan would holler to me to come outside and give a hand. Along with our few ringers, we worked side by side mustering and drafting in the yards. When the shearing was on, life was even busier than usual and there was hardly any time for rest. After several hours helping to class the wool in the heat and the noise of the shed, I had to rush back to the house to prepare the men's tea. Getting their meals on the table in time was crucial to maintain an orderly routine.

The station hands in those early days of my bush life were an assortment of odd and colourful characters. Once a year Alan and I would leave Belmore to take our holidays. It was lovely to drive away, to leave behind our everyday chores and to enjoy city life once again. We both welcomed the change. The chap whom we had left in charge during our absence almost set our house on fire. Poor Ronnie had put a dish of dripping in the Agar stove to render and went away for the day and forgot about it. The heat of the stove was so strong that it melted the soldering on the thermostat and blew the door right off! There was black smoke from the fat right through the kitchen, hallways, living room and even into our bedroom. It took three trips up the ladder with a bucket of soapy water to remove all the black stains. All Alan could say was, 'Oh well, he has done a great job outside on the property.' Of course I kept reassuring Ronnie that it didn't matter. Men! All was forgotten eventually.

We also had another funny fellow who was so tall that he could hardly fit in the doorway. Sitting down with us at breakfast, his spindly legs took up so much room under the table that we had to shift sideways. He was a heavy smoker, scattering 'dumpers' all over the yard. Once, as I was cleaning the shearers' quarters, I found little empty glue tins in his room. He was a glue sniffer! Suffice it to say that this chap did not remain in our employ long after this discovery.

Some men who came to Belmore were sad sorts because they had not been in touch with their families for years and led fairly lonely lives, while others were 'town alcoholics', drinking only when they went into town. They resisted any temptation of drink in the bush or while working—up to a year or more if necessary—but once they got to town they would always drink themselves into a stupor. They had usually saved their cheques and would have plenty of money to spend. I think it was the loneliness which drove them to drink. But when they were not hitting the bottle, they were caring, helpful men who were loyal to Alan and me.

A good reliable man is hard to find today. Many small properties cannot afford permanent help. Instead they tend to contract men when needed. I have worked Belmore on my own for over a decade since the death of my husband. Occasionally I too have employed contractors—station hands, musterers, fencers and dam sinkers—to lend a hand, especially during the busy shearing season. Although most of the men who have come here have been honest and hardworking, I have had my fair share of shifty ringers. But mind you, they only made life more entertaining!

One ringer was particularly memorable. I had advertised in the *Country Life* for a station hand. A young chap called Darcy answered my advertisement and when he called, I explained that I was an elderly woman managing a sheep property on her own, and that he may have to help with more things than he had bargained for.

'Just the sort of job I'm after,' was his response and so began our working life together.

Darcy talked a lot about rodeos. He had a subscription to *Rough Riders* magazine and was forever boasting about his prowess as a rodeo rider.

What he didn't tell me, however, were the things he couldn't do well, such as being head stockman on cattle properties. I later found out from other stockmen who knew him well that the rodeo riding was just malarkey. After months of good service, poor Darcy went too far—he pinched grog and goods from the property next door. Unusually heavy rains had brought the rivers up and for several days we were stranded at Belmore. The lady from next door was stuck in town because of the floods, so Darcy hopped on his motorbike and raided her house. It didn't take the detectives very long to work out 'who done it'. As it was wet and the ground very soft, Darcy's motorbike had left clear tracks between our two properties! I felt very sad for a long time after that, because in other respects, Darcy was quite a decent chap. During the drought, when I was on my way to pull bogged sheep out of the dams, he would insist on coming with me to help, even if it was his day off. He was also good company and I enjoyed making little cakes and jellies for him.

Several days after the detectives took him away, I decided to clear out his room. A man's quarters were his own on my property, and while he lived here, I would not set foot in them except to clean them. Now, however, I thought I should go and take a look. When I turned his mattress over, I found a bottle of Baileys Irish Cream. I also found a small suitcase full of trinkets and some antiques from my house. I left them there, and when Darcy returned to collect his gear, I said to him, 'You know the importance I place on my belongings in this place, don't you?'

When he departed for good, they were all left behind. Over the next ten months, as new station hands and ringers came and went, I discovered the rest of the goods that Darcy had pinched from next door. He'd hidden them all over Belmore. Records were found in a rusty drinking trough, and an accordion near one of the dams! Darcy was so loyal to me that I still cannot imagine him going away and being trouble elsewhere.

Life wasn't meant to be easy and there was sadness there if I dwelt on it. Really, the main worry is not how to manage the property, but whether you are lucky enough to get rain. The rule of the game seems to be that whenever you have a lovely, classed breed of sheep, with just the right micron wool, then the rains stop coming down. A large sheep property is not really a controlled business. I have had my sheep classed here for ten years before the last drought and the wool was found to be of excellent quality, but then after many years with not a drop of rain, the sheep started to die. I guess others will simply say about folk like us, 'What mugs! Why don't they get out?'

But human beings are all the same. You tell yourself that things will change. You convince yourself that, if you hang in there and wait, in the end you are bound to get some great seasons. My battle with drought always reminds me of Banjo Paterson's words:

> *It's grand to be a squatter,*
> *And sit upon a post,*
> *And watch your little ewes and lambs*
> *A-giving up the ghost.*

When the rains finally come, and everything becomes green and the stock start putting on condition, it seems just like old times and one feels as if the drought could never happen again. But when I had to face the worst, I always tried to stay hopeful. Otherwise the thought of these poor desperate animals trying to dig up a few blades of grass under the parched earth would be simply unbearable. Banjo hit the nail on the head when he said:

> *The hard, resentful look on the faces of all bushmen comes from a long*
> *course of dealing with merino sheep ... his one idea is to ruin the man*
> *who owns him ... he will display a talent for getting into trouble and*
> *a genius for dying that are almost incredible.*

When you are drafting in the heat and still the sheep won't run, you really wish to tear your hair out. I remember helping in the drafting yards and listening to the shrill whistles from the men calling for the dogs to get the sheep moving. Nothing doing. 'Dopey bast---s!' they would loudly curse trying to get the flock through the gates. And yet you get attached to the sheep, so much that it can be soul-destroying to watch them slowly starve to death when there is not enough feed around. How I have loved my little merinos, just like you would love the black sheep in any situation.

This land trains us to be big-hearted. After a long period without rain, watching the black clouds rolling in—waiting for some relief at last, sitting out on the back verandah, just hoping and praying that it will fall—and eventually it does fall, but not on you. This simply breaks your heart. The storm has come and gone, and you have missed out! But after some selfish 'why me's' you start thinking, 'Thank God at least it's fallen somewhere'. After more false hopes like this, you see the dark clouds rising once again in the sky. More sitting out on the back steps, waiting and praying. You watch it coming towards your bogging dams, your sheep that are eating lucerne and lick blocks that you have been buying for so long because there isn't anything left to feed them—but this time the wind changes. It's gone round you once more! This time, it really crushes you down. But just as you feel beaten and utterly defeated—beyond all hope—it doubles back and the triumphant sound of heavy rain drumming down on the galvanised-iron roof lets you know that God has heard your prayers at last. At that moment, you may well be a person with a much stronger heart than mine, but the tears of relief will begin to fall, for you know you are in the hands of a greater power. You keep on praying that this sweet rain will continue to come down until enough has fallen to give your land the relief it needs. Banjo understood it:

It's grand to be a lot of things
in this fair Southern Land,
But if the Lord would send us rain,
That would indeed, be grand!

Recent rains have only just started to bring flourishing pastures. The sweeping Mitchell and Flinders grass plains no longer look as desolate as they once did during the worst of the drought, and the weaners are growing stronger by the day. Still, I will not forget what life was like during those hard times, when all I could do was hope and pray for the big wet to come.

Sister Anne Maree has been such a dear friend to me during these past eight years. She brings companionship and unspoken religion, and is just such a wonderful person to have around. There is never time for chatting in the kitchen over cups of tea because there is too much to do at Belmore. She has been out with me on so many different occasions, helping me burn gidgyeah trees to feed the stock, mending fences and doing water runs. When sheep were carried away in a flash flood, she was there to comfort me. It is always a great joy to see her little plane circling overhead.

With Anne Maree at Belmore.

We met for the first time in 1990, at mass on a nearby property. Since then, she flies out to Belmore once a month. Anne Maree is not what I would call a 'convent' nun. She can get out in a paddock and work hard. I don't think I could take her out with me otherwise. Once, she brought the Bishop of Rockhampton with her to Belmore. I was a little nervous at first. After all, it isn't every day that the bishop comes for tea and stays the night. We had a grand time together and I found him to be a charming gentleman and a most welcome guest.

During the drought, Anne Maree was handier to have around than a ringer. Most of Belmore's dams have very steep banks, and during the drought these banks dried out and collapsed. As the sheep come to drink around the dams, their tracks soften the ground, which in turn becomes a trap for the weaker sheep. They get bogged and need to be rescued. It was too steep for me to drive up the banks and, as Anne Maree had her bus licence, she expertly backed the trusty Toyota close to the dam's edge and helped me get the bogged sheep out. She was also very good at pulling scrub in the paddocks, which we used to help feed the sheep. To do this, we would wrap one end of a very strong chain around a sturdy tree bough and secure the other end to the tow bar of the Toyota. I would lurch forward, accelerating strongly until the bough broke off. The tree always had to be one that the sheep would find edible and we would spend many hours combing different paddocks looking for the right sort that we could use for feed.

Working in the bush has its hidden dangers as Anne Maree unfortunately discovered one day. Water had just been connected to the homestead and I needed to collect extra 'polypipes' down from around the dams. We spent the best part of the morning loading the pipes into the Toyota to transport them back to the homestead. Anne Maree insisted on riding in the back to hold the pipes in place because they had a habit of rolling off. I tried to stop her, telling her, 'I'm the ringer, and you are the nun!', but she would not listen. She is quite stubborn and not one to be easily dissuaded when she has made up her mind.

As I slowed down to pass through a narrow gate, I suddenly heard a scream. The pipes had caught in the gate and swung out and hit poor Anne Maree square in the head. I jumped out of the Toyota and saw that she had been knocked out cold. Blood streamed down her face. My first fear was that she had been hit in the eyes, but after a quick examination I determined a large gash to the side of her forehead. I threw off my shirt and bandaged her head as best I could, then drove her quickly back to the homestead. She came to in the kitchen. Her hairline was cut open to the next layer of skin—about eight inches in length. It was a very nasty wound indeed. I called the doctor on the radio for advice and he told me to drive Anne Maree to the hospital in Longreach. It took about an hour to get everything ready because I had to unload all the pipes from the Toyota as well as refill the fuel tank.

Throughout most of the two-hour trip to town, bouncing and jolting uncomfortably in the truck, I kept talking to Anne Maree in an effort to calm her down. When I think back to the accident, I am glad that, despite the thirty-three stitches she received to her face, Anne Maree does not have any scars—most of the stitches were along her forehead and the rest on her upper lip and inside her nose. She spent nine days in hospital and took a full month to recover. I grounded the flying nun!

But in no time at all, she was back on her feet at Belmore, a little more cautious this time, but the same Anne Maree. She is like family to me now. This all comes as an assortment of memories over a very long time. Now I can look back at it with a smile, and laugh when it will be all over. Sitting out on my back verandah, I can see the grass all lovely and green, and the merinos in distant paddocks seem to have not a care in the world. Thank goodness they know nothing of the days when my tired old eyes looked to the cloudless sky, longing for rain.

These days, when Anne Maree flies in she marvels at how wonderful Belmore looks. I've given the house a fresh coat of paint and the bougain-villea is in full bloom. Driving out to check the water levels in the Gidyea and Duck tank dams, we both sigh with relief—full of water. You would hardly recognise the place. Bit by bit, things are picking up.

Soon it will be time for me to leave Belmore with the hope that whoever follows me will give it the same care and love. I recently learnt that I have cancer. I have been away for the last fourteen months, having to travel to town for treatment. My sister and her husband were kind enough to come here to manage Belmore during my absence. Anne Maree is flying in more often. She boosts my morale. I'm still holding on, and with her love we will see this one to the end.

Please, God, give the country people and their land many good seasons. Even though the merino is almost identical to Banjo's description, I keep my trust and will never lose faith in them.

The candlelight begins to flicker, but the rain is coming in.

BUSH SPIRITUALITY

Doreen Rogers died on 15 October 1997 in Mount Olivett Hospital, Brisbane. She was one of my dearest friends. I was invited to speak at her funeral because I knew and loved her. But in other circumstances where I have to preside at religious ceremonies, it is often because of a shortage of priests.

With fewer men entering the priesthood in the last decade, a whole new religious life has emerged for me. The work of the sisters and priests of the Catholic Church is organised around geographical areas called parishes. Traditionally, a priest was the spiritual leader of each parish. His main role was, and still is, to perform and dispense the sacraments to the congregation, to explain the Word of God according to the Christian scriptures and to gather the people. With the decline in numbers of ordained priests, the need to find substitutes for some of these tasks has become far more pressing and I fill the gap wherever I can.

As a Presentation Sister, I can conduct prayer services in churches or private homes and bring communion (the consecrated Host) to people. I am also able to prepare children for the Holy Sacraments—communion and confirmation. But presently, only an ordained priest can celebrate mass and hear people in confession, and therefore, for the administration of these sacraments, I need to bring a priest with me.

My presence, like that of a priest, also provides them with a link to the wider Church and helps them sustain their faith.

Through force of circumstance, I find myself more involved in practical issues. I have had to meet so many new and unexpected demands—things I wouldn't have thought of doing many years ago.

These days, for instance, it is not uncommon for me to preside over baptisms and funerals, since these ceremonies do not necessarily require the presence of a priest. Religious life is going through uncertain times, but what remains essential for me is to be attuned to the needs of the people of the bush. Jesus was in close touch with people's lives—sharing their pains and their joys, and guiding them into God's love. He went out to meet people where they were and as they were. He had an extraordinary ability to connect with them. I wish to follow in his footsteps and to continue my ministry in an equally direct and practical way.

At any rate, having a priest on board can sometimes generate problems—for them, not me. Father Chris Schick, a parish priest from Barcaldine, was assigned to travel with me back in September 1990. We were leaving Springvale, a property west of Longreach, and I was having problems with the Cessna's battery. Father Chris offered to prop-start the plane for me but on his third attempt I heard him yell as he fell with a heavy thud onto the gravel airstrip. He had dislocated his shoulder and was writhing on the ground in pain. The station manager's wife, Margaret Tulley, radioed the flying doctor who advised her to give Father Chris a needle to ease the pain. The flying doctor was diverted to Springvale and put Father Chris' shoulder back in, there and then on the airstrip. It took several months before Father Chris was game enough to come flying with me again.

Father Jeff Scully from Quilpie has also experienced the occasional flying 'hiccup'. A fortnight after Father Chris' accident, I ran into trouble with my blessed battery again. We had called in at a property where a woman's father had just suffered a stroke. It was already late afternoon when we were ready to leave, which meant I would have to take off into the western sun. I felt I couldn't take such a risk so taxied down instead to the other side of the grassy airstrip. At the end of the runway, just before becoming airborne, I found myself in front of a row of tall gums—quite a menacing sight. With full power on, hurtling down the strip, I had to abort take-off at the last second. We came to a shuddering stop just short of the boundary fence. The incident shook me up somewhat, and it taught me a valuable lesson—never try to fly under stress! Father Jeff was wonderful throughout the whole ordeal. A little rattled and shaken, he was good enough not to panic. He still flies with me from time to time and has been of invaluable support over the years. He rates as one of my favourite passengers.

Both Bishop William Morris from the Toowoomba Diocese and Bishop Brian Heenan, the current Bishop of Rockhampton, have flown with me.

Bishop Brian Heenan

They are strong supporters of the Aerial Ministry and of my work with the women of the west. Once a year, I ferry both Bishop Morris and Bishop Heenan around their respective far-flung dioceses and they thoroughly enjoy the circuit.

The first time Bishop Heenan flew with me was in the autumn of 1992. The Cessna's cramped cockpit was full to bursting with confirmation cakes that I had to deliver to Windorah. Poor Bishop Heenan was strapped in his seat balancing six cake boxes on his lap, holding on for dear life as we bounced our way through the clouds. Although flying may not be his preferred mode of travel, he is a cheerful passenger. Like me, he's a great fan of the State of Origin football series and an avid Queensland supporter, ever willing to share a footy moment or two with the station managers and ringers we visit. Once, he even re-scheduled mass so no-one would miss the game. Bishop Heenan has not only celebrated mass in shire halls, homes and pubs—he has even blessed a bull, Emmanuel, at the request of its owner! (Saint Francis of Assisi would have done the same.) He always comes away from his trips out west with a greater respect for these people who, despite living in isolation, continue to find practical ways for maintaining their faith in their lonely lives.

As I reflect on my last ten years of flying, I can appreciate how my life has been broadened and enriched by my contact with the people of the west. They have taught me much about myself and the experience has changed me forever. The people of the bush have a different form of faith than people in the city. They have developed an earthy spirituality, which I have come to adopt as my own—a spirituality that is quite remote from

Foxtrot Bravo Delta; late afternoon shadow.

the conventional religious approach of my youth. 'Bush spirituality' goes straight to the essential—it doesn't bother too much with formalities.

I take these people as I find them, and they do the same with me. I believe, like the founder of the

Royal Flying Doctor Service, Reverend John Flynn, that 'talk of spiritual matters is empty without some sort of practical gesture'.

At the turn of the century, Flynn travelled to the inland and brought a chain of frontier services to lonely and isolated areas which gave some comfort and security to the people of the outback.

'Never let people say good enough for the bush,' he wrote in 1911. 'The bush must be treated with as much respect as the city, and the people coming from away back need all the love and all the things which speak of love, that we can give them.'

In much the same way, my Aerial Ministry tries to mirror Flynn's practical approach—it is only what we do that gives credence to what we say.

As I fly over this ever-changing land-scape—cattle country, mulga country, desert—I fall under the spell of the outback. Gliding low, the Thomson, Barcoo, Diamantina and Cooper rivers can appear as large waterholes at times, and at others, like streams of molten gold as they thread their way through the cardboard-coloured plains. Sunsets behind fiery red sand dunes, billabong dawns with screeching corellas—the beauty of the bush has become a spiritual food for me.

Aerial view of the Diamantina River from the Cessna.

I'm often asked if I ever tire of flying. I don't. My work gives me energy. I am touched by people's lives—their worries and concerns—but at the same time I must try to maintain an inner peace without which I would have nothing to give to them. I try to be sensitive to each situation. Yes, I've made mistakes, but hopefully these help me learn and grow. I have met the suffering Jesus in the pain of the people I visit. I have also been touched by the living Jesus as I land among them and see the goodness, love and generosity in their lives. The women in particular impress me with their indomitable spirit—the way they accept their loneliness and hardships, their willingness to adapt to a land which at times can be so harsh to them. They have opened their homes and their hearts to me, and for me this is a very humbling experience.

The Windorah Church

Twenty-two years after taking my vows, I continue to honour the commitment I made to God and to my congregation. This does not mean that following this particular way has always been easy. I'm like everyone else. I have had my fair share of 'up and down' days, the 'why am I here' days and sometimes wonder what it would have been like to be married and have children—all fairly normal thoughts and feelings. But I'm dedicated to my ministry. I think I have one of the best jobs in the Church! I sometimes have a little laugh to myself, at the thought that, if Jesus were to return among us today, he would once again go out to meet the people—however, he would probably not travel by foot nor ride a donkey. My guess is that he would fly.